CAPITALISM
AND
UNDERDEVELOPMENT
IN
LATIN AMERICA

Historical Studies
of Chile and Brazil

CAPITALISM
AND
UNDERDEVELOPMENT
IN
LATIN AMERICA

Historical Studies
of Chile and Brazil

ANDRE GUNDER FRANK

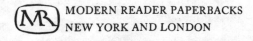 MODERN READER PAPERBACKS
NEW YORK AND LONDON

For

PAULA and THACHER

true friends who had faith

To

PAUL BARAN

pioneer who inspired

PAUL SWEEZY

friend who encouraged

PAUL FRANK

Latin American who must carry on

CONTENTS

PREFACE

I believe, with Paul Baran, that it is capitalism, both world and national, which produced underdevelopment in the past and which still generates underdevelopment in the present.

The following studies were written at different times, in several countries, and for varying purposes and media.* Each of them is in its own way intended to clarify how it is the structure and development of capitalism itself which, by long since fully penetrating and characterizing Latin America and other continents, generated, maintain, and still deepen underdevelopment.

The analysis in these studies centers on and emerges from the metropolis-satellite structure of the capitalist system. Though the characteristics, contradictions, and consequences of capitalism appear throughout, one particular feature of capitalist underdevelopment receives special emphasis in each essay. The historical essay on the underdevelopment of Chile places particular emphasis on the loss and misappropriation of economic surplus in the process of capitalist underdevelopment, to which Paul Baran called attention. The short essay on the "Indian Problem" in Latin America contends that the basis of this problem is the extension of the capitalist expropriation of surplus out to the farthest reaches of society. The contradictions of uneven development and of international as well as national and regional polarization, in turn, receive more detailed analysis in the study on the historical underdevelopment of Brazil. The monopolistic nature of the structure of capitalism, finally, forms the center of the analysis in the last study, on the underdevelopment of contemporary Brazilian agriculture. The persistence of these underdevelopment-generating contradictions of capitalism throughout the history of capitalist development emerges from all the studies.

* It has for this reason not been possible to recheck certain local sources.

The study of Chile provides the historical context of capitalist development and underdevelopment and spells out in greatest detail those essentials of the structure of the capitalist system on the world, national, and local levels which form the theoretical basis of my argument throughout. The concern with history is designed to show how historical capitalist development in Chile generated and explains the underdevelopment of that country. Capitalism began to penetrate, to form, indeed fully to characterize Latin American and Chilean society as early as the sixteenth-century conquest. The study analyzes how, throughout the centuries following, world capitalism imposed its exploitative structure and development on Chile's domestic economy and fully integrated this economy into the world capitalist system by converting it into a colonial satellite of the world capitalist metropolis; the study also suggests how the inevitable consequence of this world, Chilean, and local capitalist structure and evolution has been the development of underdevelopment in Chile.

The second essay, on the so-called "Indian Problem" of Latin America, is part of a larger study prepared as a report to the United Nations Economic Commission for Latin America. As such, its preparation was subject to certain limitations. The essay contends that this same capitalist structure is ubiquitous. Even the indigenous peoples of Latin America, whose supposed non-market subsistence economy is so often said to isolate them from national life, find themselves fully integrated into this same capitalist structure, albeit as super-exploited victims of capitalist internal imperialism. Since they thus are already fully integral parts of the capitalist system, the all-too-common policy of trying to "integrate" the Latin American Indians into national life through one community development project or another is therefore senseless and condemned to failure. The particular condition of the supposed backwardness of the Indians, far from being due to isolation, must be traced to and understood in terms of the same capitalist system and structure and the particular manifestations of underdevelopment to which they give rise under differing circumstances.

The third study, "Capitalist Development of Underdevelopment in Brazil," was prepared in the form of lectures for the Conference on the "Third World" in the *Escuela Nacional de Ciencias Políticas y Sociales* of the National University of Mexico in January, 1965. Similar in intent to the essay on Chile, this essay puts particular emphasis on the inherent limitations which the structure and development of the capitalist system necessarily impose on the industrial and economic development of its satellite member countries. It also emphasizes how these countries, and in particular their former major export regions, like the now extremely poor Brazilian Northeast, are forced into capitalist underdevelopment in the natural course of the development of the capitalist system as a whole.

The essay on "Capitalism and the Myth of Feudalism in Brazilian Agriculture" was written in Brasilia in close touch with the political personages and currents of that capital city in the days before the April 1964 military coup. Being the first of these essays to be written, it reflects the lowest level of maturity in my own analysis and conclusions. Yet this essay complements the others in two important ways. Being more limited in scope and lacking historical depth, this study can examine in greater detail a particular aspect of contemporary underdevelopment, the commercial monopoly structure of agriculture. The essay contends that, contrary to the claim of most bourgeois and Marxist students alike, Brazil—and one could add other parts of Latin America—does not have a "dual economy," and the agricultural sector is not feudal or precapitalist. The analysis then proceeds to show how the universally acknowledged inefficiency and poverty of Brazilian agriculture is produced by capitalism—by the same monopoly and therefore exploitative capitalist structure analyzed elsewhere in this book.

The economic analysis in this essay is clearly and specifically directed at important problems of political analysis and policy. If, as the study suggests, no part of the economy is feudal and all of it is fully integrated into a single capitalist system, then the view that capitalism must still penetrate most of the countryside is scientifically unacceptable and the associated political strategy—of supporting the bourgeoisie in its supposed attempt to extend capitalism and to complete the bourgeois democratic revolution—is politically disastrous. Since this essay was written, its analysis has been borne out by history. The Brazilian "national" bourgeoisie, no less than the "comprador" bourgeoisie, has fully participated in the neo-fascist military dictatorship and the events which have followed. Hopefully, however, the analysis can still serve to strengthen the empirical and theoretical foundation needed for adequate political action to overcome underdevelopment in Brazil, the rest of Latin America, and elsewhere in the future.

These essays make no claim to deal with all the economic and political problems of capitalist development and underdevelopment in Chile, Brazil, or Latin America; and it may be well to take note of the important matters to which I have given little or no attention. My attempt to take the long view and to emphasize the fundamental continuity of the process of capitalistic development and underdevelopment has led me to lend less emphasis to some transformations than they probably deserve *per se*. The most important of these is undoubtedly the rise and consolidation of imperialism. A more detailed analysis of the historical process of capitalist development and the contemporary problems of underdevelopment would have to devote more attention to the specific transformations of the economic and class structure of these underdeveloped countries that were caused by the rise of imperialism in the nineteenth century and its consolidation in the twentieth. Paul Baran suggested that imperialism, far from promoting industrial capitalism, strengthened mercantile capitalism in the underdeveloped countries. The review of Chile and Brazil bears out this insight; but it stops short of examining many of the accompanying changes in the relations between the commercial and industrial sectors of these economies. A more recent transformation, the rise of the socialist countries, receives even less attention, even though it already affects these Latin American countries directly by decisively increasing the range of their political options and indirectly by reducing the scope of the metropolitan countries' capitalist world market and satellites.

The attempt to spell out the metropolis-satellite colonial structure and development of capitalism has led me to devote very little specific attention to its class structure and development. This does not mean that this colonial analysis is intended as a substitute for class analysis. On the contrary, the colonial analysis is meant to complement class analysis and to discover and emphasize aspects of the class structure in these underdeveloped countries which have often remained unclear. This is the case particularly of the place of the bourgeoisie and the role it can or cannot play in economic development and the political process. Nonetheless, since primary attention is given to the colonial structure in these essays, they cannot, nor are they intended to, serve as an adequate instrument to examine the class struggle as a whole and to devise the necessary popular strategy and tactics for its development, for the destruction of the capitalist system, and thereby for the development of the underdeveloped countries.

All the studies come to one conclusion of first importance: National capitalism and the national bourgeoisie do not and cannot offer any way out of underdevelopment in Latin America.

This conclusion and the analysis underlying it have important scientific implications. They point to the need in the underdeveloped and socialist countries for the development of theory and analysis adequate to encompass the structure and development of the capitalist system on an integrated world scale and to explain its contradictory development which generates at once economic development and underdevelopment on international, national, local, and sectoral levels. The specific theoretical categories which were developed on the basis of experience with the classical development of capitalism in the metropolitan countries alone are not adequate to this task. It is fruitless to talk in terms of a national industrial bourgeoisie or class which develops the economy of a supposed "third world" by liberating its national capitalist sector from metropolitan colonialism and imperialism abroad and by expanding the capitalist sector to finally penetrate and eliminate the traditional or feudal sector of the dual society and economy at home. It is fruitless to expect the underdeveloped countries of today to repeat the stages of economic growth passed through by modern developed societies, whose classical capitalist development arose out of pre-capitalist and feudal society. This expectation is entirely contrary to fact and beyond all real and realistically theoretical possibility. It will be necessary instead scientifically to study the real process of world capitalist development and underdevelopment and to develop a realistic political economy of growth in the underdeveloped part of the world.

The analysis and conclusion thus have far-reaching political implications. If the structure and development of the world capitalist system have long since incorporated and underdeveloped even the farthest outpost of "traditional" society and no longer leave any room for classical national or modern state-capitalist development independent of imperialism, then the contemporary structure of capitalism also does not provide for the autonomous development of a national bourgeosie independent enough to lead (or often even to take an active part in) a real national liberation movement or progressive enough to destroy the capitalist structure of underdevelopment at home. If there is to be a "bourgeois" democratic revolution at all and if it is to lead to socialist revolution and the elimination of capitalist underdevelopment, then it can no longer be the bourgeoisie in any of its guises which is capable of making this revolution. The historical mission and role of the bourgeoisie in Latin America—which was to accompany and to promote the underdevelopment of its society and of itself—is finished.

In Latin America as elsewhere, the role of promoting historical progress has now fallen to the masses of the people alone; and those who would honestly and realistically serve the progress of the people must support them in achieving progress for and by themselves. To applaud and in the name of the people even to support the bourgeoisie in its already played-out role on the stage of history is treacherous or treachery.

The analysis and conclusions of these studies also carry implications, again to use Paul Baran's words, for the responsibility of the intellectual; and these may be clarified in the form of a personal note. My own social and intellectual background is that of middle-class North America, and my professional formation that of the most reactionary wing of the American bourgeoisie. (My principal professor and teacher of economic theory became the chief economic adviser to Barry Goldwater in his 1964 presidential campaign.) When I came to Latin America some three years ago, I thought of the problems of development here in terms of largely domestic problems of capital scarcity, feudal and traditional institutions which impede saving and investment, concentration of political power in the hands of rural oligarchies, and many of the other universally known supposed obstacles to the economic development of supposedly traditionally underdeveloped societies. I had read Paul Baran, but I did not really understand him or any part of the world. The development policies, such as investment in human capital and discontinuous strategies of economic development, which my academic research had led me to publish in professional journals, were more or less of a piece with those of my colleagues, even if I did not go to extremes of classical monetary policy and pseudo-Weberian and neo-Freudian attitudinal and motivational analyses and policy.

At the same time, even before coming to the underdeveloped countries, I had always maintained some kind of progressive outlook and political position in my personal life, outside my professional academic work and career. I was, in the words of the title of my father's autobiography, "on the Left, where the heart is." My opinions were always to the Left of most American liberals; for instance, I did not doubt that the Cuban

Revolution was worthy of support—but I did not understand its significance. However, I was fundamentally irresponsible; I was an intellectual schizophrenic: I kept my political opinions and my intellectual or professional work apart, accepting scientific theories more or less as they were handed to me and forming my political opinions largely in response to feeling and isolated facts. Like many of my colleagues, I was a liberal.

To learn to do research in the social sciences worthy of the name, to become socially and politically more responsible, and to dare to tell people in underdeveloped countries what political economy of growth might serve them, I had to abandon my liberal ways and metropolitan environment and go to the underdeveloped countries, there to learn real *political* science and political economy in the classical pre-liberal and the Marxian post-liberal sense. I had to free myself from the liberal maxim, according to which only political neutrality permits scientific objectivity, a maxim widely used to defend social irresponsibility, pseudo-scientific scientism, and political reaction. I had to learn from those who have been persecuted, as Simón Bolívar predicted in 1826 they would be, in the name of liberty and liberalism. I had to learn that *social* science must be *political* science.

Thus, another implication of these studies is that to be both intellectually and socially responsible and, I would add, to become scientifically adequate and politically effective, it is necessary, in this branch of science and policy, to shed the scientific and political stereotypes which most of us, non-Marxists and Marxists alike, in the metropolis and in the colonies, have largely inherited from metropolitan capitalist development in the era of liberalism. Like the role of the bourgeoisie in the satellites of the capitalist system, the place of metropolitan economic, political, social—yes, and cultural—liberalism has passed into history. To free those whom this liberalism and its bourgeoisie have enslaved and underdeveloped, we shall need a new political economy of growth developed along the path Paul Baran pointed out to us. A conscientious effort to develop it, even at the cost of some intellectual security and personal ease, is the least of the sacrifices that history can ask of us.

* * * * * * * *

Part of this book was written and prepared for publication with the financial assistance of the Louis M. Rabinowitz Foundation to which I would like to express my gratitude for the confidence and help extended to me. I should also like to extend my thanks to my friends and colleagues who have read parts or all of the manuscript and made helpful suggestions: Deodato Riveira, Wanderley Guilherme, and Ruy Mauro Marini in Brazil; Enzo Faletto, Clodomiro Almeyda, and Dale Johnson in Chile; and Alonso Aguilar and Fernando Carmona in Mexico. My reader and I must be thankful to the late John Rackliffe, who masterfully edited the manuscript and facilitated communication. My wife, Marta, has had to suffer moving from one country to another and has borne with me throughout my work.

A. C. F.

Mexico
July 26, 1965

PREFACE TO REVISED EDITION

An essay on "Foreign Investment in Latin American Under-development" has been added for this revised (paperback) English language edition and the Spanish, Portuguese, French and Italian language editions. This essay was written at the request of the Bertrand Russell Peace Foundation in May 1966 in Mexico, and was not included in the original edition for technical reasons. Only slight revisions have been made in the essay, to incorporate some new data that have become available in the intervening two years.

The inclusion of the essay, "Foreign Investment in Latin American Underdevelopment," helps to remedy some omissions noted in the preface to the first edition. This essay is an attempt, albeit through the perspective of foreign investment, to deal with the capitalist development of underdevelopment in Latin America as a whole. This essay is also more historical in the sense that it attempts to trace the Latin American economy's transformation through the several stages of the development of its underdevelopment. It is an attempt to do a short economic history of the continent, in which each stage is shown to lead to the next and emerge from the last. Through the instrumental role of foreign investment, each stage is seen to become possible and the next stage necessary.

More than the other essays, this one emphasizes the crucial importance of the first half century following Independence in determining Latin America's subsequent fate. For it was during these early decades of the last century that the battle for Latin American economic independence was fought—and lost. Like North America, Latin America experienced a civil war between the nationalist industrial interests and the anti-nationalist agricultural-export ones. But, while in North America colonial circumstances had permitted the nascent industrial interests to become economically and politically strong enough to win this civil war, in South America the simultaneously much greater foreign investment in underdevelopment had assured that the nationalist interests would lose this war for survival—and therewith their last opportunity to achieve economic development through capitalism. The defeat of the nationalist industrial interests and the victory of the anti-nationalist, primary-commodity export ones in Latin America opened the door to the entrance of classical imperialism when world capitalist development made the time ripe in the metropolis—and in Latin America as well.

This essay, more than the others, also lends greater emphasis to the structural transformation of the Latin American economy and society that this imperialist development generated. And like the other essays, this one suggests how imperialist underdevelopment in Latin America paved the way for contemporary neo-imperialism and still deeper structural underdevelopment, which can now only be eliminated through socialism.

It is important to emphasize that the problem is one of structural underdevelopment at the national and local level, notwithstanding that it was created and is still aggravated by the structure and development of the world capitalist economy. The attention devoted to the contradiction of expropriation/appropriation of the economic surplus of the satellite by the metropolis, and particularly by the world capitalist metropolis, has led some readers to suppose the argument in this book to be one of "external" underdevelopment. It may be well, therefore, to take this opportunity to point out to the reader that the thesis of the book (Section IA) is precisely that in chainlike fashion the contradictions of expropriation/appropriation and metropolis/satellite polarization totally penetrate the underdeveloped world creating an "internal" structure of underdevelopment. Fidel Castro once said that the imperialists would be welcome to the dollars they drain out of Latin America if they would only let the Latin American people use the remaining resources for their own development. Quite so. As is emphasized on page 10, "For the generation of structural underdevelopment, more important still than the drain of economic surplus . . . is the impregnation of the satellite's domestic economy with same capitalistic structure and its fundamental contradictions."

This thesis is confirmed innumerable times by the experience reviewed in this book: by the domestic polarization and generation of the latifundium structure of eighteenth-century Chile (Section IF2-4); by the power structure of nineteenth-century Chile (IG4); in the domestic sector of twentieth-century Chile (IH2); by the economic structure of the "Indian problem" (II); through the generation of the domestic structure of underdevelopment in colonial Brazil, which prohibited development even after the colonial restraints were relaxed (IIIB); through the active involution of the 1930's and 1940's in Brazil (IIIC4); by internal colonialism in Brazil (IIIC6); through the domestic monopoly structure of Brazilian agriculture (IV); through the transformation of the "internal" economic, social, political, cultural structure of Latin America by a century of imperialism and neo-colonialism (V). Furthermore, if underdevelopment were really only an "external" condition imposed from the outside and manifest primarily in a capital drain through trade and aid, as some argue, then the simple "nationalist" solutions criticized in this book might indeed be held to be adequate. But precisely because underdevelopment is integrally internal/external, only the destruction of this structure of capitalist underdevelopment and its replacement by socialist development can possibly constitute an adequate political policy to combat underdevelopment.

Beyond the addition of the aforementioned essay, minor errors have been corrected. The other shortcomings of the book remain. Thus, the book still suffers from the lack—noted in the preface of the first edition—of an adequate analysis of the class structure in Latin America. A related shortcoming has been noted by a reviewer: the use of the colonial or neo-colonial structural approach does not automatically reveal which of the population sectors that are simultaneously satellite and metropolis are potential friends and which are certain or likely enemies of the Revolution. Quite so; we need to know this. But the class structure approach does not immediately and unmistakeably reveal this aspect of socio-political anatomy and physiology either. That requires analysis, not general colonial or class schemas. Another of the author's recent essays, "Who is the Immediate Enemy? Latin America: Capitalist Underdevelopment or Socialist Revolution," attempts to advance another step toward the needed analysis by suggesting how the colonial structure, which forms the core of the present book, has in fact formed and transformed the class structure in Latin America and why therefore, though the principal enemy undoubtedly is imperialism, the immediate enemy is the bourgeoisie in Latin America itself. (This essay is included in a second book of essays on the development of underdevelopment in Latin America, soon to be published, in which the class structure and national politics receive greater emphasis than in the present book).

Another critic has suggested that the present book provides the socio-economic analytic base for the political conclusions of Régis Debray. Would that it were so! But the general approach suggested here is no substitute for analysis. To distinguish between friends and enemies and to find the politico-military means to fight the latter, we must analyze the class and colonial structure at particular times and places—and, of course, we must fight; for revolutionary theory, like the Revolution itself, must be advanced through revolutionary practice among the people.

A.G.F.

Montreal
April 17, 1968

I

CAPITALIST
DEVELOPMENT
OF
UNDERDEVELOPMENT
IN CHILE

The commerce of this kingdom is a paradox of trade and a contradiction of riches not known until its discovery, thriving on what ruins others and being ruined by what makes others thrive, in that its development lies in the management of foreign trade and its decline in the freedom of others, and it is regarded not as commerce that must be kept open but as an inheritance that must be maintained closed.

José Armendaris
Viceroy of Peru, 1736

A. THE THESIS OF CAPITALIST UNDERDEVELOPMENT

This essay contends that underdevelopment in Chile is the necessary product of four centuries of capitalist development and of the internal contradictions of capitalism itself. These contradictions are the expropriation of economic surplus from the many and its appropriation by the few, the polarization of the capitalist system into metropolitan center and peripheral satellites, and the continuity of the fundamental structure of the capitalist system throughout the history of its expansion and transformation, due to the persistence or re-creation of these contradictions everywhere and at all times. My thesis is that these capitalist contradictions and the historical development of the capitalist system have generated underdevelopment in the peripheral satellites whose economic surplus was expropriated, while generating economic development in the metropolitan centers which appropriate that surplus—and, further, that this process still continues.

The Spanish conquest incorporated and fully integrated Chile into the expanding mercantile capitalist system of the sixteenth century. The contradictions of capitalism have generated structural underdevelopment in Chile ever since she began to participate in the development of this world-embracing system. Contrary to widespread opinion, underdevelopment in Chile and elsewhere is not an original or traditional state of affairs; nor is it a historical stage of economic growth which was passed through by the now developed capitalist countries. On the contrary, underdevelopment in Chile and elsewhere, no less than economic development itself, became over the centuries the necessary product of the contradiction-ridden process of capitalist development. This same process continues to generate underdevelopment in Chile, and this underdevelopment cannot and will not be eliminated by still further capitalist development. Accordingly, structural underdevelopment will continue to be generated and deepened in Chile until the Chileans liberate themselves from capitalism itself.

The interpretation offered here differs not only from widely accepted interpretations of the nature and causes of underdevelopment and development in general but also from the views of important commentators on and analysts of past and present Chilean society. Thus, during the 1964 election campaign both the Christian Democrat-Liberal-Conservative presidential candidate and the Socialist-Communist candidate referred to contemporary Chilean society as containing "feudal" elements; and in his post-election commentary, Fidel Castro also referred to "feudal" elements in Chile. G. M. McBride, in his deservedly famous *Chile, Land and Society* written in the 1930's, maintained that all Chile suffered from "the dominance of a small class of landed aristocracy in the old feudal order."

The Marxist Julio César Jobet, in his *Ensayo Crítico del Desarrollo Económico-Social de Chile,* suggested that the nineteenth century witnessed the formation of a bourgeoisie which rose "over the ruins of the exclusively feudal economy of the first part of the nineteenth century" (cited in Pinto 1962:3F).* Anibal Pinto, in his path-breaking *Chile: Un Caso de Desarrollo Frustrado,* which has influenced all historical and economic work on Chile since it appeared in 1957, went somewhat further back to suggest that "independence opened the doors"; but he nonetheless maintained that only subsequently did "foreign trade come to be the driving force of the domestic economic system" and that to the end of the eighteenth century Chile was and remained a "recluse economy" (Pinto 1962:13–15). Max Nolff, elaborating on Pinto's analysis, develops his theory of Chilean industrial development on the basis of the view that during the entire colonial period Chile had a "closed subsistence economy." Even the Marxist Hernán Ramírez (1959), whose *Antecedentes Económicos de la Independencia de Chile* supplies ample proof that the foregoing views of Chile in the eighteenth and later centuries are not well

---

* All sources thus given within parentheses refer to the References Cited, pages 319-333.

based, refers to a supposed "autarchic tendency" in the Chilean economy before that time.

According to my reading of Chilean history, and Latin American history generally, such references to an autarchic, closed, recluse, feudal, subsistence economy misrepresent the reality of Chile and Latin America since the sixteenth-century conquest. Moreover, failure to recognize and understand the nature and significance of the open, dependent, capitalist export economy which has characterized and plagued Chile and her sister countries throughout their post-conquest history bears inevitable consequences in misinterpretation and misunderstanding of the real nature of capitalism today, of the real causes not only of past and present but of the still deepening underdevelopment and of the policies necessary to eliminate that underdevelopment in the future. It is to the clarification of these matters that this essay is devoted.

More specifically, I cannot accept the supposed empirical foundations and therefore the formulations of the problem of, and policy for, development in Chile as set forth by Anibal Pinto and Max Nolff (the latter, chief economic adviser to Allende, 1964 presidential candidate on the Socialist-Communist ticket) and others associated with the principles of analysis of the United Nations Economic Commission for Latin America. These analysts, beginning with the inaccurate view that Chile had a closed, recluse, subsistence economy throughout the centuries before political independence, attribute the subsequent underdevelopment of Chile's economy to Chile's supposed error in choosing development "toward the outside" instead of development "toward the inside," after independence, according to them, opened the door in the nineteenth century. Had Chile only chosen capitalist development toward the inside then, it would be developed now, they suggest; and they argue similarly that Chile could still develop today if it would only hurry up and finally turn to (still capitalist) development toward the inside now.

My reading of Chilean history and my analysis of capitalism

oblige me to reject both this premise and conclusion. Because of capitalism, Chile's economy was already underdeveloping throughout the three centuries before independence. And, if the innate contradictions of capitalism continue to operate in Chile today, as my analysis contends that they must and my observation that they do, then no kind of capitalist development, be it toward the outside or toward the inside, can save Chile from further underdevelopment. Indeed, if dependent and underdeveloped development toward the outside has been ingrained in the Chilean economy since the conquest itself, then the supposed option for independent national capitalist development toward the inside did not even exist in the nineteenth century; much less does it exist in reality today.

1. The Contradiction of Expropriation/ Appropriation of Economic Surplus

The first of the three contradictions to which I trace economic development and underdevelopment is the expropriation/appropriation of economic surplus. It was Marx's analysis of capitalism which identified and emphasized the expropriation of the surplus value created by producers and its appropriation by capitalists. A century later, Paul Baran emphasized the role of economic surplus in the generation of economic development and also of underdevelopment. What Baran called "actual" economic surplus is that part of current production which is saved and in fact invested (and thus is merely one part of surplus value). Baran also distinguished and placed greater emphasis on "potential" or potentially investible economic surplus which is not available to society because its monopoly structure prevents its production or (if it is produced) it is appropriated and wasted through luxury consumption. The income differential between high and low income recipients and much of the failure of the former to channel their income into productive investment may also be traced to monopoly. Therefore, the non-realization and unavailability for investment of "potential" economic surplus is due essentially to the monopoly structure of capitalism. I investigate below how the monopoly structure of world capitalism resulted in the underdevelopment of Chile.

The contradiction of monopolistic expropriation/appropriation of economic surplus in the capitalist system is ubiquitous and its consequences for economic development and underdevelopment manifold. To investigate the development or underdevelopment of a particular part of the world capitalist system, such as Chile (or a part of Chile), we must locate it in the economic structure of the world system as a whole and identify its own economic structure. In this study, we will see that Chile has always been subject to a high degree of external and internal monopoly. However competitive the economic structure of the metropolis may have been in any given stage of its development, the structure of the world capitalist system as a whole, as well as that of its peripheral satellites, has been highly monopolistic throughout the history of capitalist development. Accordingly, external monopoly has always resulted in the expropriation (and consequent unavailability to Chile) of a significant part of the economic surplus produced in Chile and its appropriation by another part of the world capitalist system. Specifically, I review the findings of two students of the Chilean economy who attempt to identify the contemporary potential economic surplus appropriated by others which is not available to Chile.

The monopoly capitalist structure and the surplus expropriation/appropriation contradiction run through the entire Chilean economy, past and present. Indeed, it is this exploitative relation which in chain-like fashion extends the capitalist link between the capitalist world and national metropolises to the regional centers (part of whose surplus they appropriate), and from these to local centers, and so on to large landowners or merchants who expropriate surplus from small peasants or tenants, and sometimes even from these latter to landless laborers exploited by them in turn. At each step along the way, the relatively few capitalists above exercise monopoly power over the many below, expropriating some or all of their economic surplus and, to the extent that they are not expropriated in turn by the still fewer above them, appropriating it for their own use. Thus at each point, the international, national, and local capitalist system generates economic development for the few and underdevelopment for the many.

2. The Contradiction of Metropolis-Satellite Polarization

The second, and for our analysis the most important, capitalist contradiction was introduced by Marx in his analysis of the imminent *centralization* of the capitalist system. This contradiction of capitalism takes the form of polarization into metropolitan center and peripheral satellites; and it was this that Viceroy Armendaris of Peru described in 1736 when he noted that the commerce of the mercantile capitalist empire of Spain, of his own Viceroyalty of Peru within it, and of the General Captaincy of Chile within that in turn, "is a paradox of trade and a contradiction of riches . . . thriving on what ruins others and being ruined by what makes others thrive." Paul Baran observed this same contradiction two centuries later when he noted that "the rule of monopoly capitalism and imperialism in the advanced countries and economic and social backwardness in the underdeveloped countries are intimately related, represent merely different aspects of what is in reality a global problem" (Baran 1957).

The consequences of the metropolitan center-peripheral satellite contradiction of capitalism for economic development and underdevelopment are summarized in the *Fundamentals of Marxism-Leninism:*

It is characteristic of capitalism that the development of some countries takes place at the cost of suffering and disaster for the peoples of other countries. For the soaring development of the economy and culture of the so-called "civilized world," a handful of capitalist powers of Europe and North America, the majority of the world's population, the peoples of Asia, Africa, Latin America, and Australia paid a terrible price. The colonization of these continents made possible the rapid development of capitalism in the West. But to the enslaved peoples, it brought ruin, poverty, and monstrous political oppression. The extremely contradictory character of progress under capitalism applies even to different regions of one and the same country. The comparatively rapid development of the towns and industrial centers is, as a rule, accompanied by lagging and decline in the agricultural districts (Kuusinen N.D.: 247-248).

Thus the metropolis expropriates economic surplus from its satellites and appropriates it for its own economic development. The satellites remain underdeveloped for lack of access to their own surplus and as a consequence of the same polarization and exploitative contradictions which the metropolis introduces and maintains in the satellite's domestic economic structure. The combination of these contradictions, once firmly implanted, reinforces the processes of development in the increasingly dominant metropolis and underdevelopment in the ever more dependent satellites until they are resolved through the abandonment of capitalism by one or both interdependent parts.

Economic development and underdevelopment are the opposite faces of the same coin. Both are the necessary result and contemporary manifestation of internal contradictions in the world capitalist system. Economic development and underdevelopment are not just relative and quantitative, in that one represents more economic development than the other; economic development and underdevelopment are relational and qualitative, in that each is structurally different from, yet caused by its relation with, the other. Yet development and underdevelopment are the same in that they are the product of a single, but dialectically contradictory, economic structure and process of capitalism. Thus they cannot be viewed as the products of supposedly different economic structures or systems, or of supposed differences in stages of economic growth achieved within the same system. One and the same historical process of the expansion and development of capitalism throughout the world has simultaneously generated—and continues to generate—both economic development and structural underdevelopment.

However, as *Fundamentals of Marxism-Leninism* suggests, the metropolis-satellite contradiction exists not only between the world capitalist metropolis and peripheral satellite countries; it is also found within these countries among their regions and between "rapid development of the towns and industrial centers [and] lagging and decline in the agricultural districts." This same metropolis-satellite contradiction extends still deeper and characterizes all levels and parts of the capitalist system. This contradictory metropolitan center-peripheral satellite relationship, like the process of surplus expropriation/appropriation, runs through the entire world capitalist system in chain-like fashion from its uppermost metropolitan world center, through each of the various national, regional, local, and enterprise centers. An obvious consequence of the satellite economy's external relations is the loss of some of its economic surplus to the metropolis. The appropriation by the metropolis of the economic surplus from this (and other satellites) is likely to generate development in the former unless, as happened to Spain and Portugal, the metropolis is in turn converted into a satellite, its surplus being appropriated by others before it can firmly launch its own development. In either event, the metropolis tends increasingly to dominate the satellite and renders it ever more dependent.

For the generation of structural underdevelopment, more important still than the drain of economic surplus from the satellite after its incorporation as such into the world capitalist system, is the impregnation of the satellite's domestic economy with the same capitalist structure and its fundamental contradictions. That is, once a country or a people is converted into the satellite of an external capitalist metropolis, the exploitative metropolis-satellite structure quickly comes to organize and dominate the domestic economic, political and social life of that people. The contradictions of capitalism are recreated on the domestic level and come to generate tendencies toward development in the national metropolis and toward underdevelopment in its domestic satellites just as they do on the world level—but with one important difference: The development of the national metropolis necessarily suffers from limitations, stultification, or underdevelopment unknown in the world capitalist metropolis—because the national metropolis is simultaneously also a satellite itself, while the world metropolis is not. Analogously, the regional, local, or sectoral metropolises of the satellite country find the limitations on their development multiplied by a capitalist structure which renders them dependent on a whole chain of metropolises above them.

Therefore, short of liberation from this capitalist structure or the dissolution of the world capitalist system as a whole, the capitalist satellite countries, regions, localities, and sectors are condemned to underdevelopment. This feature of capitalist development and underdevelopment, the penetration of the entire domestic economic, political and social structure by the contradictions of the world capitalist system, receives special attention in this review of the Chilean experience, because it poses the problem of analyzing underdevelopment and formulating political and economic policy for development in a manner significantly different from—and I believe more realistic than—other approaches to the problem.

The above thesis suggests a subsidiary thesis with some important implications for economic development and underdevelopment: If it is satellite status which generates underdevelopment, then a weaker or lesser degree of metropolis-satellite relations may generate less deep structural underdevelopment and/or allow for more possibility of local development. The example of Chile helps to confirm these hypotheses. Moreover, from the world-wide perspective, no country which has been firmly tied to the metropolis as a satellite through incorporation into the world capitalist system has achieved the rank of an economically developed country, except by finally abandoning the capitalist system. Some countries, notably Spain and Portugal, which were part of the world capitalist metropolis at one time, did, however, become underdeveloped through having become commercial satellites of Great Britain beginning in the seventeenth century.* It is also significant for the confirmation of our thesis that the satellites have typically managed such temporary spurts in development as they have had, during wars or depressions in the metropolis, which momentarily weakened or lessened its domination over the life of the satellites. As we shall see, Chile's greater isolation from the Spanish metropolis relative to other colonies and the lessened degree of inter-dependence with and dependence on the metropolis in times of war or depression, have been of material aid in increasing Chile's development efforts over the centuries.

3. The Contradiction of Continuity in Change

The foregoing two major contradictions suggest a third contradiction in capitalist economic development and underdevelopment: The continuity and ubiquity of the structural essentials of economic development and underdevelopment throughout the expansion and development of the capitalist system at all times and places. As Engels suggested, "there is a contradiction in a thing remaining the same and yet constantly changing." Though structural stability and continuity may or may not have characterized "classical" capitalist development in Europe (the metropolis), the capitalist system, throughout its expansion and development on a world scale, as a whole maintained the essential structure and generated the same fundamental contradictions. And this continuity of the world capitalist system's structure and contradictions is the

* The development of the British ex-colonies in North America and Oceania was rendered possible because the ties between them and the European metropolis at no time matched the dependency of the now underdeveloped countries of Latin America, Africa, and Asia. The industrialization of Japan after 1868 must be traced to the fact that it was at that time the only major country that had not yet been incorporated in the world capitalist system—that had therefore not yet begun to underdevelop. Similarly, the fact that Thailand is today less underdeveloped than other countries of Southeast Asia is due to the fact that it was never a colony like the others, until the recent advent of United States "protection" initiated underdevelopment there as well.

determinant factor to be identified and understood if we are to analyze and effectively combat the underdevelopment of the greater part of the world today.

For this reason, my emphasis is on the continuity of capitalist structure and its generation of underdevelopment rather than on the many undoubtedly important historical changes and transformations that Chile has undergone within this structure. My general purpose is to contribute to the building of a more adequate general theory of capitalist economic development and particularly underdevelopment rather than to undertake the detailed study of past and present Chilean reality.

My emphasis on the contradiction of continuity in change implies that this contradiction in Chile has not been resolved. This does not mean that it will not be resolved. My review of the history of capitalist development in Chile shows that a number of important contradictions have been resolved through the course of time. Though it may have been thought at the time of independence, for example, that events had led or would lead to the resolution of the fundamental contradiction determining the course of Chilean history, this turned out not to be the case. It is important, therefore, to understand the really fundamental contradictions, and not to confuse them with minor contradictions that are resolved more easily and at less cost but which change nothing essential in the end, and in the long run even render the resolution of the fundamental contradictions more costly and/or more distant. I believe that a number of contemporary policies for the "liberation" of the underdeveloped countries and the elimination of underdevelopment, well meaning though their proponents may be, make matters worse in the long run (and often in the short run as well). Understanding the realities of capitalism and underdevelopment is of course not sufficient, but it is certainly essential; there can be no successful revolution without adequate revolutionary theory. Herein lies my purpose.

Related to continuity also is discontinuity. My review of Chilean experience suggests that there may have been times in which even certain structural changes within Chile's capitalist structure *might* have materially changed the course of the country's remaining history. When these changes were not made, or the attempts to make them were not carried out as the circumstances of the times required, these opportunities—such as investment of the economic surplus produced in Chile's nitrate mines—were lost forever. The experiences of Chile suggest that the history of the development of underdevelopment in many parts of the world probably was—and still is—punctuated by such failures to take advantage of opportunities to eliminate or shorten the suffering created by underdevelopment.

B. THE CAPITALIST CONTRADICTIONS IN LATIN AMERICA AND CHILE

The historical process of capitalist expansion and development over the face of the globe created a whole series of metropolis-satellite relationships interlinked as in the surplus appropriation chain noted above, but also in more complicated constellating arrangements indicated below. This is not the place to inquire into the historical origins in medieval Europe of the capitalist system which in recent centuries has spread from there to all corners of the earth—though such inquiry is undoubtedly an important task for the understanding of the essential nature of the contemporary imperialist capitalist system in the world and the problems of economic development and underdevelopment it generated and still generates. It may be enough to note that a commercial network spread out from Italian cities such as Venice and later Iberian and Northwestern European towns to incorporate the Mediterranean world and parts of sub-Saharan Africa and the adjacent Atlantic islands in the fifteenth century; the West Indies and Americas and parts of the East Indies and Asia in the sixteenth century; the other African suppliers of the West European—and later also North American—centered slave trade and economy in the sixteenth to eighteenth centuries; and the remainder of Africa, Asia, Oceania, and Eastern Europe in succeeding centuries until the entire face of the globe had been incorporated into a *single organic* mercantilist or mercantile capitalist and later also industrial and financial capitalist system whose metropolitan center developed in Western Europe and then North America and whose peripheral satellites underdeveloped on all the remaining continents. (Indians and Negroes in North America evidently suffer from the same satellite relationship there; while immigrant whites, but not of course the native population, in Oceania and to some extent in South Africa can be said to be in some measure included in the world capitalist metropolis.)

Latin America became a peripheral satellite, or set of satellites, of the Iberian and European metropolis. In league with its waxing crowns, Spanish and Portuguese merchant capital (and also Italian and Dutch merchant capital) based on the Iberian Peninsula and in search of trade routes to the Indies and gold, conquered some West Indian and coastal continental outposts and converted these into their mercantile satellites through war, slave raids, pillage, the creation of slave-fed mining and plantation export enterprises, and gradually through trade relations as well. These military, productive, and trading satellites of the Iberian metropolis were then used as springboards for the conquest and establishment of new satellite outposts on the American mainland and these in turn for the conquest and incorporation of what were to become still more distant inland satellites (in part, of the above satellites which became *their* metropolises and, in part, of the European metropolis directly). Thus, like other peoples and continents, the whole American continent and its peoples were converted into a series of minor economic constellations, each with its own minor metropolis and satellites, these in turn being composed of still more metropolises with their satellites, all of them directly or indirectly dependent on the European metropolitan center—which had shifted to the Low Countries and then to Britain (which appropriated Luso-Hispanic American and other economic surplus for its own capital accumulation and subsequent industrialization) and thus converted Spain and Portugal themselves into satellites of the British metropolitan center.

In the beginning, the ultimate metropolis of Chile was Spain.

The fact that before long Spain itself became a satellite of Northwestern Europe, particularly of Britain, bears on my analysis; but in an essay devoted specifically to Chile I need take account of this and other transformations in the world capitalist system only insofar as they bear directly on the process in Chile. Chile's domestic as well as international economic structure has been profoundly influenced, even determined, by the structure and transformations of the capitalist system in the world as a whole. But within the confines of this essay we must take these latter changes largely as "data." The same considerations must hold, unfortunately, for the appearance and renewed decline of Lima as the metropolitan center (itself a dependent satellite of the European metropolis) on which Chile was most directly dependent.

Chile came to have its own metropolis in Santiago and the port of Valparaíso. Spreading out from this center, mining, agriculture, mercantile, state and other interests incorporated the remainder of Chile's territory and people into the expanding capitalist economy, converting them into peripheral satellites of Santiago. In relation to the national metropolitan center, we may consider as peripheral satellites mining centers, commercial centers, agricultural centers, and sometimes military centers on the frontier. But these in their turn became (and sometimes remained) metropolises or micrometropolises, in relation to *their* respective hinterlands, such as still smaller towns, mines, agricultural valleys or latifundia, which in turn are micrometropolises to their peripheries.

It is a major thesis of this essay that this same structure extends from the macrometropolitan center of the world capitalist system "down" to the most supposedly isolated agricultural workers, who, through this chain of interlinked metropolitan-satellite relationships, are tied to the central world metropolis and thereby incorporated into the world capitalist system as a whole. The nature and degree of these ties differ in time and place; and these differences produce important differences in the economic and political consequences to which they give rise. Such differences must ultimately be studied case by case. But these differences among relationships and their consequences do not obviate their essential similarity in that all of them, to one degree or another, rest on the exploitation of the satellite by the metropolis or on the tendency of the metropolis to expropriate and appropriate the economic surplus of the satellite.

There are a variety of these metropolis-satellite relationships. There is, for instance, the relationship between the fertile or irrigated flat bottom land of an agricultural valley and its adjoining agriculturally less productive or commercially less valuable hillsides; between the upriver lands and landowners favored by a gravity-flow irrigation system and the less favored downriver lands; between the latifundia and the minifundia surrounding it; between the owner- or administrator-operated part of the latifundia enterprise and its dependent sharecropper or other tenant-run enterprises; even between a tenant farmer (or enterprise) and the permanent or occasional hired labor he may use; and, of course, between each set of metropolises or each set of satellites up and down this chain. Essentially the same relations characterize the relationship between the large industrial firm (often "modern" or "efficient") and smaller suppliers of components for the former's productive process or products for its sales outlets; between the large merchants and financiers and the small traders and moneylenders; between the city merchants and the merchant landowners and/or small rural producers and consumers who depend on them to buy their product and/or to provide their production, consumption, credit, and other needs.

We may briefly note some of the conditions of monopoly control, associated with the appropriation of the economic surplus of the many by the few, which we find again and again in our review of Chilean history. The sources of monopoly power over Chilean-produced economic surplus which is transferred abroad are perhaps more evident than their domestic analogues. Though Chile's principal export product has changed several times during the country's history, each time it has been this export sector which has been the principal source of potentially investible economic surplus, and each time this export sector has been controlled by a few foreign interests. Foreigners have owned the mines from which the surplus came. If they did not own the mines or the land which produced the export commodity, foreigners appropriated much of the surplus by exercising monopolistic buying power over the product in question and then monopoly power over its resale elsewhere. Additionally, foreigners owned or controlled a large share of storage, transport, insurance, and other facilities associated with the export of the principal economic surplus-producing good. Sometimes foreigners exercised monopoly power or control in the provision of productive factors necessary for the export good. Foreigners have often benefited from greater financial strength, from greater world-wide and/or horizontal integration of the industry of which Chile's export good formed a part. Similar monopoly ownership or control has existed over some Chilean industries other than the primary export one.

Through colonial monopoly or through "free trade" based on technological and/or financial superiority, foreigners also have often enjoyed monopoly positions in the export of goods to Chile. These economic relationships of foreign commercial enterprises with their Chilean partners, resulting in the exploitation of the latter by the former, afforded the foreign interests economic and political control over the various Chilean interests. When this economic relationship was insufficient to afford foreigners the desired degree of control, they often supplemented it by exercising political and military force.

Analogous and other forms of monopoly control exist domestically and result in the appropriation of the economic surplus produced by the many at the various lower levels by the few at the respective higher levels in the Chilean national economy. There has always been a greater or lesser degree of monopoly concentration of ownership and control of the major productive facilities in industry and agriculture, of the means of transport and storage, of the channels of trade, and probably most important of all, of the banking and other financial institutions, as well as of the major economic, political, civil, religious, and military posts of the Chilean national economy and society. Indeed the degree of monopoly concentration throughout the history of Chile and other underdeveloped countries has probably always been greater than it has been in the developed countries in recent times.

In our review of Chilean history, we repeatedly find that foreign or national exporters and importers, as well as other large merchants and financiers, exercise control over, and appropriate capital from, relatively smaller merchants in the national and regional capitals. These latter in turn stand above the merchants, producers, and consumers whom they in turn exploit directly or indirectly through still further series of relationships in which one capitalist kills many. Beyond the more obvious expropriation of producers by owners of capital, we may also distinguish another type of appropriation of capital and surplus by one or a few capitalists from the many. This contradiction exists also between a relatively large industrial or agricultural enterprise and its agricultural producers who depend on the supply of some of the inputs they use or the demand for some of the output they produce and/or for capital, credit, merchandising, political intervention, and other services in general. All of these economic relationships within the international, national, local, and sectoral capitalist system and subsystems are typically characterized by the contradiction of expropriation/appropriation associated with the elements of monopoly in the relationships themselves and the economic structure or network they form as a whole.

Each of these metropolis-satellite relationships or constellations, whatever other sentiments or relations it may contain, rests on a strong and in the long run determinant commercial economic base. The whole network of metropolis-satellite relationships, or the whole universe of economic constellations, came into being on essentially economic and commercial grounds. Whatever we may wish to say about its mercantilist, then industrial, then financial capitalist metropolis, in the peripheries of the world capitalist system the essential nature of the metropolis-satellite relations remains commercial, however "feudal" or personal seeming these relations may appear. Moreover, it is through these economic, though of course also political, social, cultural, and other ties, that in principle and mostly also in fact the occasional hired worker is connected to the tenant farmer who employs him (or more usually to the landowner directly), the tenant to the landowner and merchant (or merchant/landowner), who is connected to the provincial metropolis wholesaler (or sometimes to a large national or international merchant), who is connected to the national industrial/financial/commercial/import metropolis which is connected to the world metropolitan center, and so the most "isolated" toe bone is connected to the world capitalist head bone.

Each of these connections between satellite and metropolis is in general a channel through which the center appropriates part of the economic surplus of the satellites. And thus, although some of the surplus gets appropriated at each step of the way up, the economic surplus from each of the minor and major satellites gravitates up or into the capitalist world's metropolitan center.

C. COLONIAL CAPITALIST LATIN AMERICA

The three capitalist contradictions of surplus expropriation/appropriation, metropolitan center-peripheral satellite structure, and continuity in change made their appearance in Latin America in the sixteenth century and have characterized that continent ever since.

Latin America was conquered and its people colonized by the European metropolis so as to expropriate the economic surplus of the satellite's labor and to appropriate it for the capital accumulation of the metropolis—initiating thereby the present underdevelopment of the satellite and the economic development of the metropolis. The capitalist metropolis-satellite relationship between Europe and Latin America was established by force of arms. And it is by this same force as well as by the force of ever-growing economic and other ties that this relationship has been maintained to this day. The major transformations within Latin America have throughout the past four centuries all been the product of its responses to economic, political, and other influences that either came from the metropolis or arose out of this metropolis-satellite structure itself. Excepting post-revolutionary Cuba, all these changes have not altered the essentials of that structure.

Marx noted that "the modern history of capital dates from the creation in the sixteenth century of a world-embracing commerce and world-embracing market" (Marx, I: 146). After Marx, the capitalist contradiction of surplus expropriation/appropriation was emphasized among others by Werner Sombart and Henri Sée. The latter writes in his *Origins of Modern Capitalism:*

International relations are the principal phenomenon one encounters in trying to understand the first cause of capital accumulation. . . . The most fecund source of modern capitalism is found—undoubtedly—in the great maritime discoveries. . . . The origins of colonial commerce consisted, above all, as Sombart says, in the expropriation of the primitive peoples, who were incapable of defending themselves against the invading armies. Through veritable acts of piracy, the European traders obtained enormous profits. . . . No less lucrative were the forced labor practices which the Europeans demanded from the aborigines in the colonies . . . and from the Negroes whom the slave traders imported from Africa: a criminal commerce but one which, nonetheless, created enormous earnings. . . . We must agree that this was one of the sources . . . of capitalism (Sée 1961: 26, 40).

Conquest and incorporation into the metropolis-satellite structure of capitalism went faster and farther in Latin America than elsewhere. The reason was gold and sugar, and their expropriation from the Latin American satellites and their appropriation by the European and later also North American metropolis. Thus, Sergio Bagú writes in his classic *Economía de la Sociedad Colonial:*

By multiplying mercantile capital and stimulating international trade, the commercial revolution, which had begun in the fifteenth century, linked the fate of one nation to others, intensifying economic interdependence. The type of economy which the Iberian metropolises organized was of a definite colonial nature, oriented to the central and western European markets. This same purpose motivated the Luso-Spanish producers in the new continent. Colonial capitalism, rather than feudalism, was the type of economic structure which appeared in America in the period we are studying. . . . Iberian America was born to integrate the cycle of incipient capitalism, not to prolong the languishing feudal cycle . . . if there is a well defined and unquestionable feature of the colonial economy, it is production for the market. From the first to the last days of the colonial regime, this characteristic conditions all productive activities. . . . This is how the trends which then predominated in the European international markets formed the principal elements shaping the colonial economic structure. It might be added that this phenomenon is characteristic of all colonial economies whose subordination to foreign markets has been, and still is, the principal cause of their deformation and lethargy (Bagú 1949: 39, 68, 117, 260).

Capitalist penetration, as well as converting Latin America into a satellite of Europe, rapidly introduced *within* the continent essentially the same metropolis-satellite structure which characterized Latin America's relationship with Europe. The mining and mineral export sector was the nerve and substance of the colonial economy; and, though always a satellite to the European metropolis, it became everywhere a domestic metropolitan center with respect to the remainder of the economy and the society. A series of satellite sectors and regions grew up or were created to supply the mines with timber and fuel, the miners with food and clothing, and the non-working mine owners, merchants, officials, clergy, military personnel, and hangers-on with those means to sustain their parasitic life which they did not import from the metropolis with the fruits of the indigenous and imported forced labor they commanded. Thus there grew up a domestic livestock, wheat, and textile economy, which was no less commercial, and even more of a satellite, than the mining economy itself.

Livestock, then a much more important supplier of consumer and producer goods than it is now, and wheat, the Spanish staple, were from the beginning produced on large *haciendas* owned and administered by Spaniards or Creoles. The work was performed perforce first by slaves, then by *encomendados* and/or those subject to the *mita*, later by hired labor as well, which was forced into debt-bondage and/or various share-cropping arrangements to assure its continued supply. The land, initially largely worthless to the Spaniards but later increasingly desired and valuable as the commercial value of its products grew, was acquired by *merced* (grant), conquest, expulsion of Indians from their communal lands and, later, also of mestizo and even white homesteaders from their private lands, claims being staked out and later legalized through bribery and/or falsification of documents, often through purchase or in default of debt payment by the previous owner, and through a variety of outright fraudulent means, but never, let it be noted, through *encomiendas*, which granted rights only to labor and not to land.

Royal grants of land were made only to those who merited them by living in the colonial or provincial capital city. There the owners of land often became indistinguishable from the owners of monopoly rights in international or domestic commerce, mining licenses, means of transport, loan capital, civil and religious office, and other sources of privilege.

The system of proprietorship was bred in circumstances favoring the exchange of titles; property titles were inherited, transacted, and transferred by purchase and sale; buyers were found among the officials (whose handsome salaries put much monetary purchasing power, which was scarce at the time, at their disposal) and among those who had been able to enrich themselves rapidly through commerce and especially mining. It is thus logical that *encomenderos* and officials were the first rural property owners, and that they began the slow process of land accumulation which reached its apogee in the seventeenth century (Céspedes 1957: III, 414).

It is the cash nexus and the hard economic reality behind it, and not principally aristocratic or feudal traditions, principles, or social relations, which ruled in Latin America from the very beginning. And it was the structurally produced concentration of ownership, control, and accumulation of capital which also concentrated land, *encomienda* labor, commerce, finance, and civil, religious, and military office into few hands.* Capitalist

* Eduardo Arcila Farías (1957: 307) writes in his *El Régimen de la Encomienda en Venezuela:* "The *encomienda* and property in land in [Latin] America are institutions which have nothing to do with each other. Among the students of these institutions there is no confusion at all about the matter, and the historians specializing herein have put each thing in its proper place. Really, there is no justification for making this clarification here about so clear a matter—except for the ignorance which exists in Venezuela about the *encomienda* as well as about the origins of property in land which have not yet been studied. Often, many people who write about history in our country confuse the two terms and attribute the origins of property to the *encomienda.*"

Silvio Zavala (1943: 80, 84) writes in his *New Viewpoints on the Spanish Colonization of America:* "The most generally accepted idea regarding the *encomienda* is that lands and Indians were partitioned among the Spaniards from the first days of the Conquest. . . . But this notion that the *encomiendas* were the true origin of the hacienda is open to serious question, both in the light of the history of the land and of the history of the people. . . . In summary we may state that in New Spain property in the soil was not conveyed by granting of an *encomienda*. Within the boundaries of a single *encomienda* could be found lands held individually by the Indians; lands held collectively by the villages; Crown lands; lands acquired by the *encomendero* through a grant distinct from his title as *encomendero* or affected by his right to the payment of tribute in agricultural products; and lastly, lands granted to Spaniards other than the *encomendero*. The foregoing demonstrates that the *encomienda* cannot have been the direct precursor of the modern hacienda because the former did not involve true ownership. . . . In Chile, in one instance, the *encomendero* of a depopulated village, instead of claiming that the vacated lands belonged to him by virtue of his original title of *encomienda*, petitioned the royal authorities to give him title thereto by a new and distinct grant."

The capitalist functions of the *encomienda* are discussed on pages 125–130 of the essay on the "Indian Problem," and the capitalist origins of the property in land are discussed below in the present essay.

monopoly power reigned supreme from the very beginning just as it continues to reign today. The geographical, economic, political and social site of this monopolistic appropriation and accumulation of capital was of course the city, and not the countryside, however much the latter may have been the productive source of the riches.

The colonial city became the dominant domestic metropolitan center and the countryside the dependent peripheral satellite. At the same time, the domination and capacity for economic development of the Latin American city was limited from the very beginning—not by its hinterland or any supposedly feudal structure of the same (which on the contrary was and remains the principal source of such urban economic development as there has been) but rather by its own satellite status in relation to the world metropolis overseas. Nor in some four hundred years has any Latin American metropolis overcome this structural limitation to its economic development. A student of Middle America observes: "The privileged position of the city has its origin in the colonial period. The city was established by the conquistador in order to fulfill the same purpose it fulfills today: to incorporate the Indian into the economy brought over and developed by the conquistador and his descendants. The regional city was an instrument of colonization and it is still today an instrument of domination" (Stavenhagen 1963:81). Of domination, however, not only by its own ruling group, but of domination over the Latin American countryside also by the imperialist metropolis, whose instrument is the Latin American city with its overblown tertiary "service sector."

Once the capitalist contradictions of polarization and surplus expropriation/appropriation were introduced in Latin America on the international and domestic levels, their necessary consequences, that is, limited or underdeveloped development in the continent's metropolises and the development of structural underdevelopment, far from delaying their appearance several centuries, until after the industrial revolution in England, as is so often suggested, began to be generated and to emerge immediately. Under the subtitle "Dinámica de las Economías Coloniales," Aldo Ferrer confirms our thesis in his *La Economía Argentina, Las Etapas de su Desarrollo y Problemas Actuales:*

If one wishes to determine which were the dynamic economic activities of the colonial economy one would conclude that these activities were those intimately connected with foreign commerce. Mining, tropical agriculture, fishing, hunting, and lumbering (all of which were basically connected with export trade) were the developing industries in the colonial economies and, as such, attracted available capital and labor resources in these instances, production being generally based on large-scale productive units using slave labor. The groups with interests in exporting activities were merchants and property owners with high incomes and high crown and church officials. These sectors of the population . . . constituted both the internal colonial market and the source of capital accumulation. . . . Thus . . . the export sector failed to diversify, and, at the same time, the composition of demand did not favor the diversification of the internal market. The greater the concentration of wealth in the hands of a small group of property owners, merchants, and influential politicians, the greater the propensity to obtain durable and manufactured consumer goods from abroad (most of which consisted of luxury products, difficult or impossible to manufacture internally). . . .

Thus the export sector by its very nature would not allow the transformation of the system as a whole. Once the export sector disappeared, as happened in the Brazilian Northeast with the decline of sugar production due to the competition from the West Indies, the system as a whole would disintegrate and labor would return to subsistence activities. There can hardly be any doubt that, aside from the restrictions which the authorities imposed on colonial activities competing with those of the metropolis, the structure of the export sector, as well as the concentration of wealth, were the basic obstacles to the diversification of the internal productive structure and, therefore, to the consequent elevation of the technical and cultural levels of the population, the development of social groups connected with the evolution of the internal market, and the search for new lines of exportation free from the metropolitan authority. This narrow horizon of economic and social development explains for the most part the experience of the colonial American world and, notoriously, of the Spanish-Portuguese possessions" (Ferrer 1963: 31–32).

Putting Ferrer's observations and analysis in my terms, we

may note how the original establishment of the capitalist metropolis-satellite structure both between Europe and the Latin American colonies and within these colonies themselves served immediately to begin the development of limited or underdeveloped development in the colonial (later national) metropolises and structural underdevelopment in the satellite peripheries of these colonial metropolises. Bagú and Ferrer observe that export of the economic surplus of the colonies was the cause and driving force that brought them into being as integral parts of the expanding world capitalist system. As Ferrer explicitly notes, the dynamic sector of the colonies or satellites was their export sector, that is, their domestic metropolis. From the very beginning, this domestic and later national metropolis expropriated the economic surplus of its peripheral satellites; and it was in using this domestic metropolis as its instrument of expropriation that the world metropolis in turn appropriated much of this same economic surplus. Some of this economic surplus from the provincial peripheries of course remained in the various Latin American metropolises. That is, as Ferrer points out, domestic income was concentrated there, and so was therefore domestic capacity for consumption and investment or accumulation. But the same world capitalist metropolis-satellite structure, whose development brought the Latin America we know into being in the first place, created and still creates (perhaps even more so now) interests in these Latin American metropolises which induced their ruling groups to satisfy a large part of their concentrated consumption demand by imports.

This structure also militated against their investing the economic surplus they appropriated from their countrymen in manufacturing for their own consumption or export—and still less of course for the consumption of those whose income they expropriated. The effects of the international capitalist metropolis-satellite structure on the domestic capitalist structure and process, therefore, are not only that the world metropolis appropriates surplus from the national centers, which are at once satellite to the former and metropolis to their respective domestic peripheral satellites whose actual economic surplus they appropriate in turn. The effects of world and national capitalism go further and result in the misdirection and misuse even of the surplus that does remain available to the satellite.

This then has been the pattern of the development of economic development and simultaneously of underdevelopment throughout the centuries-long history of capitalism. If the ruling groups of the satellite countries have now and then found it in their interest to undertake a relatively greater degree of autonomous industrialization and development, as occurred in the seventeenth century and several times since, it was not because the essential structure of the world capitalist system had changed but only because the degree of their satellite dependence on the world metropolises had temporarily declined due to the uneven and war-torn historical development of the world capitalist system. During depressions and wars, industrial and economic development in the Latin American satellites did indeed spurt ahead—only to be again cut off or rechanneled into underdevelopment by the subsequent recuperation and expansion of the metropolis or by the restoration of its active integration with its satellites.

In Latin America as a whole, therefore, from the very beginning the three capitalist contradictions made their appearance and began to have their inevitable effects. Despite all the economic, political, social and cultural transformations Latin America and Chile have undergone since the immediate post-conquest period, they have retained the essentials of the capitalist structure implanted in them by the conquest. Latin America, far from having only recently, or even not yet, overcome feudalism (which it never really knew) or having only recently emerged as an actor on the stage of world events, began its post-conquest life and history as an integral, exploited partner in the world's capitalist development: and this is why it is underdeveloped today.

D. SIXTEENTH CENTURY CAPITALISM IN CHILE:
SATELLITE COLONIZATION

The same capitalist contradictions began to determine the fate of Chile in the sixteenth century. From the very beginning of its colonial existence, Chile has had an export economy. The domestic economic, political and social structure of Chile always was and still remains determined first and foremost by the fact and specific nature of its participation in the world capitalist system and by the influence of the latter on all aspects of Chilean life. My thesis is of course inconsistent with the widely accepted picture of past and even present Chile as an "autarchic" or "feudal," "closed," and "recluse" economy and society; but it is consistent with Chilean historical and contemporary reality.

Quite typically, Chile began her colonial existence as an exporter of gold. But the mines (in Chile, the surface washings) were not very rich and did not last very long. They began serious production about 1550, and their output declined rapidly after 1580. Yet, untypically among Spanish mainland colonies, though perhaps not unlike Guatemala, even at that time Chile exported a product of her land: tallow from her livestock. In fact, the most careful student of that era in Chile believes that at no time did the value of Chile's gold export exceed that of her tallow export (personal communication by Mario Góngora). The bulk of Chile's tallow export even then went to Lima, the closest large commercial center of the colonial empire, and not to the European metropolis itself. At the same time livestock for domestic sale and consumption and wool for textiles to clothe miners, soldiers, and others formed the basis of a nascent domestic satellite commercial economy.

A few years after the death of Valdivia, a small trade with the Viceroyalty already existed. Ross tells us: It is known that in 1575 a cargo of 400 *fanegas* [bushels] of wheat was exported to Lima via El Maule! This trade was continued by sea and was, on more than one occasion, stimulated by official measures: in 1592, for example, Hurtado de Mendoza abolished export taxes from Chile to Peru. This trade was interrupted temporarily on occasion by the corsairs who followed Drake after 1568, and it was later altered artificially in the interest of the monopolists. As the sixteenth century ended, the influence of the *encomenderos* over the land laid the basis for the large property holdings which were to impress a special physiognomy on agricultural life. The aboriginal *encomienda* has a similar effect on rural labor. At this time the pastoral economy becomes preponderant as the importance of gold washings diminishes; however, the transformation which now begins, in the judgment of Professor Jean Borde, culminates in the eighteenth century. . . . "It is in relation to the boom of wheat cultivation that such a development converges slowly toward the delineation of a new type of labor and agrarian structure—tenancy—which constitutes to this day the characteristic element in the rural life of Central Chile."

When referring to this transitional period in the colonial economy, historians such as Vicuña Mackenna and Barros Ararra have perhaps insisted too much on its subsistence features and on the slight boom reached by the local produce trade. We believe that this trade began early and was of some significance. . . . Chile, taking advantage of its climatological conditions, shifted from gold to agricultural goods and tallow as a means of payment for Spanish merchandise coming from Peru. There is no other explanation for the fact that the ships which the corsairs captured sailing to Peru were full of merchandise, or for the fact that enterprising Spaniards like Juan Jofre and Antonio Núñez owned ships engaged in the permanent commercial navigation between Chile and the Viceroyalty. . . .

More than one reason leads us to believe that agricultural production at the end of the first year of colonial rule exceeded internal consumption. This is evidenced by a communication of García Ramón which, with perhaps some exaggeration, says that agricultural production of the kingdom [Chile] is sufficient to supply fifty cities larger than the capital. . . . There is much evidence of commercial relations with Peru and of a growing population's high income. Thus, for example, the Dutch corsair, Oliverio de Noort, who was in Valparaíso in 1600, enumerates the merchandise found in one of the ships engaged in this pioneering trade; and we find that livestock products predominate over agricultural goods. This is characteristic in the century of tallow. An identical observation is found in the information supplied by Father Ovalle when he says that apart from the 20,000 quintals [hundred weights] of tallow which remained in the country, the rest was distributed through

Peru. However, agricultural production as such occupied a secondary place (Sepúlveda 1959: 13–15).

Contemporary documents confirm Sepúlveda's recent judgment and throw some additional light on the monopoly structure of sixteenth-century foreign and domestic trade and on the use made of the economic surplus generated and concentrated by that structure. In 1583 the City Council (*Cabildo*) *of* Santiago resolved "that since there is a great shortage of candles, and tallow for them, in this City, and if it were to occur that these be taken away and sent to Pirú [Peru], as some people are now said to send them, this city would suffer great shortages; and to remedy the aforesaid, we decree that it be publicly proclaimed, that no one shall take for shipment any tallow or candles without license from this Council, under penalty that he shall forfeit them for the use of this City" (Alemparte 1924:21). A century later in 1693 the Santiago City Council ordered "that no person of whatever standing he may be, take out of this city for shipment through the Port of Valparaíso or others on these coasts . . . wheat, flour, biscuits, under penalty of one hundred pesos and the loss of the goods referred to as well as of the mules on which they are carried" (Alemparte 1924:22). Throughout this time, in the words of another ordinance of the city of Santiago, "we are informed, and experience has shown, that when there is a shortage of goods, some people try to amass all of the ones there are of that kind, only in order to have them in their possession, and then to sell them at whatever price they wish, wherefrom there follows great harm to the Republic" (Alemparte 1924:12). Alemparte speaks of hundreds of examples in the municipal documents of such artificially created shortages, domestic speculation, and export, when to the detriment of the local population this proved still more profitable, and of municipal ordinances designed to bring these practices under control. Alemparte adds that "it is true that a complete review of these documents shows how these regulations were frequently violated; we should not be surprised since the city counsellors and the hacendados—as we already noted—were the same people." Though Alemparte suggests that these regulations were consonant with the economic and moral standards of the epoch, the Council minutes of May 1695 supply a much more revealing reason for them: Without them, "our Republic would perish from greed; or there would be a rebellion, which would be worse" (Alemparte 1924: 17, 21, 24).

The city ordinances of the time, particularly through their attempts to impose restrictions and prohibitions, also throw considerable light on the uses to which the economic surplus so monopolistically generated was put. "In the years that follow [1558], luxury increases and the color black—implanted by the somber [King] Philip—also reaches Chile. . . . In 1559 a bill of lading shows "thirty rolls of *damasco* cloth from China, two pounds of silk from China . . . twenty packs of gold braid . . . one lady's dress inlaid with silver . . ." (Alemparte 1924:64). On October 23, 1631, the City Council of Santiago in meeting "with some private individuals of this City, to consider the reform of dress" ordained as follows: "First, that no man or woman, of whatever station or rank, may dress entirely in luxurious cloth, or gold or silver, nor of silk, nor wear [luxurious] leather, nor sleeves of that kind, nor wool of gold or silver, nor more dress ornaments than in the following ordinances shall be permitted, subject to serious penalties. . . . Eighth, that no Indian man or woman, of whatever tribe, Negro man or woman, mulatto man or woman, may dress in anything other than domestic clothes, or at least domestic cloth. . . . Fourteenth, so that the citizens and residents do not ruin themselves with superfluous and inexcusable expenses, we ordain that, in whatever activity they may engage, they keep and maintain very moderate expenses and manners, without exceeding modesty" and that the authorities will punish not only those who fail to comply with these regulations but also "those who invent and introduce new forms of expenditure" (Alemparte 1924:66). Alemparte notes, undoubtedly with reason and with evident significance for the thesis advanced in this essay, "It is useful to add that these ordinances against luxury were dictated, not for moral or religious reasons—as might be thought at first glance—but for economic reasons, as their text shows. Thus the ruin of individuals caused by the 'very expensive dress, which changes from day to day . . . weaken the republics, draining from them the money . . . blood and nerves which preserve them' " (1924:68). In more modern language, the government was concerned about the balance of payments and the drain on the country's foreign exchange and domestic resources or surplus that the imports of this monopoly sector represented then no less than today.

E. SEVENTEENTH CENTURY CAPITALISM IN CHILE: "CLASSICAL" CAPITALIST DEVELOPMENT

The events of the seventeenth century increasingly clarify how Chile's participation in the world capitalist system determined not only the underlying structure of its economy and society but also its economic and social institutions, their transformations, and indeed Chile's economic and social history as a whole. On the one hand, it is the economic cycles and influences generated by the development of capitalism on a world scale which determine much of Chile's relative economic and spatial isolation from the metropolis (it was poor in mines and, except for La Plata, at the very end of the long journey from Spain via the Isthmus of Panama) which weakened the metropolis-satellite bonds and permitted Chile a greater degree of independence and therefore of potential and actual economic development than other colonies were able to enjoy. Still, it is the temporary or cyclical weakening of these same effective metropolis-satellite relations, as a result of war or depression in the metropolis, which then and now permits the satellites an equally temporary opportunity to initiate capitalist institutions and measures which promote economic development as long as they are not again reversed by termination of the temporary respite from the hegemony of the metropolis.

The seventeenth century brought such circumstances to

bear on Chile and other parts of Latin America. Economic influences generated by the development of world capitalism as a whole produced far-reaching changes in the institutions and level of agricultural and manufacturing production in Latin America, which have been documented for Mexico and Chile. Like most other parts of the Spanish colonial empire, including the metropolis itself, during the seventeenth century Chile witnessed a sharp decline in the supply of indigenous labor and the productivity of its mining economy. The results in Chile were analogous to those studied in detail for Mexico by Chevalier, Borah, and Kubler. The decline in the domestic oligarchy's purchasing power for metropolitan goods, which was caused by the decline in gold production caused in turn by lower mine yields and lesser labor supply due to the conquest-induced decline in the indigenous population, and the lower metropolitan demand for colonial goods and supply of metropolitan goods associated with Spain's and Europe's seventeenth-century "depression," combined to somewhat isolate Chile and the other colonies from the metropolis.

There is some disagreement about the precise consequences in Mexico, Chile, and especially Peru, as well as elsewhere. But it is safe to say that, as in the Brazilian Northeast to whose declining sugar economy Ferrer referred, the bulk of the unfavorable impact was borne by the lower indigenous and mestizo strata of colonial society. Because of the decline in the labor supply, new and often more onerous institutional means were devised to force the lower strata to work for the Spanish and Creole oligarchy. Though some Creoles no doubt went under during the century-long crisis, others rode the storm by increasingly branching out from mining into livestock ranching, wheat production (and in Mexico other foodstuffs which had previously been supplied to the white population from numerous small Indian-worked plots), and textile and other consumer goods to replace the relatively lower supply forthcoming from the metropolis. As Chevalier, Borah, Góngora, and Zavala point out, the century thus, if it did not give birth to the hacienda, saw it grow in numbers, size, internal diversification, and general importance. The rise of the hacienda, it should be emphasized, was not due to the *encomienda*, much less to any feudal institutions the Spaniards might have brought with them in the sixteenth century. The hacienda in Chile and throughout Latin America, and the structure of agriculture, must be traced to the spread and development of mercantile capitalism in the world in general and in Chile and Latin America in particular.

Starting with the great rise of the commercial value of livestock products around 1595, the parcelling of lands begins to include all of the valley [of Puange, near Santiago]. . . . There is not as yet a hierarchical aristocracy of families. . . . The composition of the ruling class is still very fluid, the main requirements for membership being wealth and personal position. . . . Aboriginal labor, up to 1580, is employed mainly in mining. . . . The *encomenderos* disregard their military obligations; on the other hand, they compensate for the decrease in mining production by building up cattle resources, which the market has begun to value more. . . . The importers form the most powerful nucleus of the juridical residential class (those with established residence in the cities and with full rights to participate in the life of the community, but who are not endowed with *encomiendas*). The big merchants who receive *mercedes* in Puange acquire larger ones. . . . The economic power of these merchants seems to have been considerable. . . . The principal motive for accumulating lands is obviously the commercial value of livestock and agricultural products. The Chilean cattle industry consists from its start of large-scale operations. . . . The frequency of . . . auctions indicates that they are not isolated incidents in the history of the fortunes of a few families . . . [but] must arise from the frequent ups and downs in the markets for tallow, *cordobanes* [a type of textile], and wheat in Lima and Santiago (Góngora 1960: 43–44, 49–50, 57, 62).

We may close our review of seventeenth-century colonial Chile with the observation of a contemporary:

What human industry achieves in that country is principally cattle and livestock products, tallow, sheepskins, and local textiles. These products are shipped to Lima, which keeps what it needs, which is twenty thousand *quintales* a year and a proportionate amount of *cordobanes* . . . the rest is distributed throughout Peru, the textiles going to Potosí and the mines and cities in that region which depend solely on Chilean supplies of clothing, Panama, Cartagena, and all those parts of Tierra Firme; clothing is also sent to Tucumán and Buenos Aires and from there to Brazil. The second type of commodity consists of rigging [ropes, chains, etc., for ships] to supply the ships of the South Sea and of *cuerda* [match for firing a gun] for firearms, exported from Chile to all of the armies and garrisons situated along the Peruvian and Tierra Firme [today roughly Colombia] coasts. . . . The third class of merchandise is the mules which are shipped by way of the uninhabited region of Atacama to Potosí (Ramírez 1959: 31–32).

This hardly describes a closed or autarchic economy but rather an open economy whose internal structure and the fate of whose people is determined above all by its relationship to other parts of the mercantilist system and by the structure and development of this virtually world-embracing system.

Perhaps the key determinant factor in the seventeenth century was the increased isolation and decreased interdependence between metropolis and periphery. Chile had already been more isolated or more weakly integrated into the world capitalist metropolis-satellite structure than other Spanish colonies. The seventeenth century depression reduced the amount of commercial intercourse between Spain and her colonies, as evidenced by reduced Atlantic shipping, a decline in mineral exports from the Americas, and a lower level of exports of wheat and manufactured goods from Spain. Chile and the other colonies became more isolated than they had been in the sixteenth century; and Chile, it may be presumed, became still more isolated than the rest. Far from being a direct cause of underdevelopment, it is this lessened degree of interdependence with (and, as a satellite, dependence on) the metropolis which undoubtedly caused the increased domestic production of "import substitute" goods and even of export goods for the markets of other Spanish colonies in the Americas. With the renewed strengthening of interdependence and of Chilean dependence in the eighteenth century, this production and, indeed, productive capacity declined again; thus underdevelopment became more firmly implanted in Chile.

The situation which developed in the seventeenth century on the land was also to be transformed by the renewed increase in trade in the eighteenth century. On the one hand, the seventeenth century witnessed the further development of the hacienda as an agricultural, manufacturing, and trading enterprise to serve the urban market and its own population. The hacienda of course was not to become a self-contained subsistence economy—since its primary *raison d'être* was and still is the commercial supply of farm products to the urban or export market and the appropriation by the owner of the maximum of the economic surplus thus produced by the hacienda's workers, which the owner expropriates through the exercise of his monopoly power over them. This does indeed close off virtually all intercourse between the hacienda and the outside world except for that which passes through the toll gate which the owner controls. But the seventeenth-century Chilean hacienda did not yet have all of these monopoly features. It was to acquire them only with the increase in demand for its products. In the seventeenth century, the livestock hacienda owner who needed relatively little labor often maintained mestizo or "poor white" tenants on his property, from whom he exacted little or nothing for their use of the land, and who in turn worked their own small livestock enterprises, apparently maintaining an adequate standard of living through production for themselves and the market. The metropolis-satellite relationship between the owner and his tenants, if not his Indian labor, was not as polarized as it was to become later.

F. EIGHTEENTH CENTURY CAPITALISM IN CHILE:
RESATELLIZATION, POLARIZATION, AND UNDERDEVELOPMENT

In 1736, Viceroy José Armendaris of Peru noted "the well-known dependency of [Lima] on the kingdom [Chile] which is the warehouse of precious species . . . and the deposit of the grains which feeds the city . . . without Chile, there would be no Lima" (Ramírez 1959: 33). Nonetheless an official observer in 1802 reported that "Chile suffers, in effect, all the losses natural to a merely passive trade" (Ramírez 1959: 51). The dependency of Lima on Chile which nonetheless brought Chile "all the losses natural to a merely passive trade" was, of course, the result and reflection of Chile's capitalist satellite status and relation with respect to its primary metropolis in Lima, and in relation to the Spanish and French metropolises as well.

The review of Chile in the eighteenth century will show how deeply the capitalist contradictions had already been ingrained in Chile, both in its relations with the outside world and in its domestic economic, political, and social structure. So deeply and indelibly ingrained, in fact, did the capitalist contradictions become in the eighteenth century that Chile's people found themselves unable to avoid the continued development of Chilean underdevelopment in the nineteenth and twentieth centuries despite various attempts to resolve the capitalist contradictions and to liberate Chile from inevitably underdeveloping still further. All of these attempts at liberation were made within the framework of capitalism itself—and, until recently, necessarily so. After the 1964 elections, we must affirm again that the necessary liberation from the economic structure and process which inevitably produces both limited development and structural underdevelopment has not yet been achieved by the Chilean people.

The expression of the three capitalist contradictions of surplus expropriation/appropriation, metropolis-satellite polarization, and continuity in change in eighteenth-century Chile is perhaps best reflected in Marx's observation "how in all spheres of social life the lion's share falls to the middleman. In the economic domain, e.g., financiers, stock-exchange speculators, merchants, shopkeepers skim the cream, in civil matters . . . in politics . . . in religion" (Marx: I, 744, note 1). The monopoly power of middlemen expropriated/appropriated economic surplus through and within the capitalist structure of chain-linked metropolis-satellite constellations and dominated the trade and production relations between Lima and Chile to the extent of resisting and overcoming all public and official opposition to them in both countries; it characterized domestic Chilean and Peruvian agricultural production and distribution; it totally transformed the land tenure institution of Chile into forms that only later came to be miscalled "feudal"; it determined the renewed extinction of the Chilean manufacturing industries that had grown up under the protection of seventeenth-century relative isolation.

1. International Polarization Through Foreign Trade

A recent student of Chilean history emphasizes that "the nature of the Chilean colonial economy was essentially export oriented and not, as has sometimes been asserted, oriented to the subsistence sector. This characteristic is generic to the colonial economies of various countries with the exception of Paraguay" (Sepúlveda 1959: 31–32).

Nonetheless throughout the eighteenth century Chile had a decidedly unfavorable balance of trade with respect to Lima, Spain, and France (Ramírez 1959: 46–49). This despite the fact that Chilean mining production (now increasingly silver and copper instead of gold) rose again all through this century and that Chile witnessed and supplied a spectacular increase in foreign demand for the fruits of its land, now primarily agricultural rather than livestock products. Chilean exports of wheat to Lima began to grow rapidly between 1687 and 1690. This has often been attributed to the 1687 earthquake which supposedly destroyed the productive capacity of the wheat lands near Lima. In his *El Trigo Chileno en el Mercado Mundial,* Sergio Sepúlveda challenges this explanation and offers instead an economic explanation which is consistent with my thesis concerning the role of mercantile monopoly in a polarized and polarizing metropolis-satellite structured capitalist system.

It has been established that between November 18, 1698, and December 9, 1699, 113 ship arrivals were registered in Callao [Peru], of which 44 entries were for ships coming from Chile (23 from Valparaíso, 13 from Concepción, 3 from Coquimbo, and 5 from Arica, which the author includes as also coming from Chile). The total cargo brought in by these ships amounted to 86,013 *fanegas* of wheat, 18,402 *zurrones* [bags] also of wheat, and 5,561 bags of flour, in addition to 27,038 hundredweight of tallow. Thus Peru imported at that time around 66,000 hundredweight of wheat and flour from Chile. . . .

As we have suggested, it is true that on the occasion of the 1687 earthquake the Peruvian market opened up, initiating greater exportation of our wheat due to the change of Lima's economic life and the natural scarcity of consumer goods during this emergency. However, the flooding of the Peruvian markets with Chilean wheat became permanent, not because of the effects of volcanic dust, but because of the intelligent economic action of a monopoly which did not delay in organizing itself and knew how to impose itself during the least favorable circumstances. Peruvian internal production was wiped out by virtue of a policy of regulating supply through the imposition of fixed prices. This action was facilitated by the congenital weakness of Peruvian versus Chilean wheat. . . .

In conclusion, it may be inferred that Chilean wheat became dominant since then, beginning the conquest of its first market by virtue of a systematic economic will and thanks to having found adequate means to create dependency. In our opinion this dependency would have been established anyway, even if the earthquake had not taken place. After the earthquake, trading becomes more active between the two colonies, animating the Central Valley region, especially the sector between Choapa and Maule, where in 1695 around 80,000 to 90,000 *fanegas* of wheat were harvested—without counting production obtained in Coquimbo and Concepción. The major part of the exports left Chile at first via Valparaíso, where advantage was taken of the old tallow warehouses and newly built facilities. Valparaíso was also the natural outlet for the fertile valley of the Aconcagua. A few institutional groups participated in this export trade and in time serious conflicts arose between them and the Chilean producers and warehouse owners and Peruvian importers. The initiation of a new commercial flow is interesting because of the economic readjustment it presupposes and the psychological effects it has on a population which was not ready to understand the opportunity which it presented (Sepúlveda 1959: 20).

The economic, political, social and cultural effects on Chile were far-reaching and long-lasting; and from the point of view of the underprivileged population of the domestic satellite periphery whose underdevelopment was furthered, the effects were neither beneficial nor welcome. The reason lay not so much in any lack of preparedness to "understand," as Sepúlveda here suggests, as it lay—and still lies—in the sheer inability to respond differently within the political and economic limitations imposed by the capitalist structure itself, as Sepúlveda himself demonstrates in other passages.

If the Peruvian merchant monopoly interests ruined their country's relatively inefficient wheat production to replace it with Chile's geographically and climatically more favored product, this was not because they had the Chilean wheat producers' interests at heart. On the contrary:

Chile, in addition to being a colony of Spain, found itself economically subordinated to the Viceroyalty of Peru. This latter country was the most powerful economic center of South America. . . . A nucleus of powerful merchants was able to establish itself in the Viceroyalty, controlling not only the productive activities in Peru, but also those in the Spanish colonies of South America from Guayaquil to the provinces of La Plata. The commerce of Lima controlled the mining wealth of Upper and Lower Peru, the mineral, agricultural, and fish production of Chile, the tropical agriculture of Peru and the Guayaquil region, and the livestock production of the provinces of La Plata. Due to their community of interests and their aspirations of hegemony based on their superior financial position, these merchants acted with such unity and effectiveness that they seemed to be acting under the inspiration of one or a handful of persons. . . .

The network of business of this long-armed wealthy group was enormous. The influence of these entrepreneurs, who were guided by a "monopolistic spirit infinitely greater than the Crown's," enabled them to subordinate the political authorities in the Viceroyalty to their designs and allowed them to obtain and consolidate a whole system of privileges established in their favor. These privileges were taken advantage of by the mercantile circles of Lima: Based on the rigorous monopolistic system established by the metropolis (whose benefit they enjoyed), these merchants were able to establish a kind of autonomous empire within the Spanish Empire. When they saw the metropolis orienting its commercial policy along more liberal lines, they mobilized themselves and fought "tenaciously against any franchise which had been granted to other regions. They tried in every possible way to retain the markets which had originally been theirs—more for historical than geographical reasons" (Ramírez 1959: 65–66, quoting also from Guillermo Céspedes del Castillo, *Lima y Buenos Aires*, and from Emilio Romero, *Historia Económica del Perú*).

The situation we have just described made itself felt with particular intensity in Chile. Peru was Chile's sole supplier of certain goods of primary necessity; Peru was the indispensable intermediary of European goods. Moreover, Peru was the principal market for Chilean products. For these reasons, the Peruvian merchants, who were the owners of almost all of the ships which tracked the South Pacific, were able to exercise effective control of our Chile's external commerce. These merchants bought wheat at cost in the Valparaíso warehouses and sometimes paid only for the freight—the workers losing their labor and expenses; moreover, the merchants treated the producers of copper like "hard businessmen who take advantage of necessity in order to fix prices" (Ramírez 1959: 68–69 quoting also from "Informe del Gobernador A. O'Higgins al Gobierno de España," September 21, 1789).

In the meantime, these merchants dealt in some goods "on which they earn 100, 200, or 300 percent profit with one sea voyage lasting from 15 to 20 days, without incurring any further expenses" (Ramírez 1959: 69, citing Alonso Ovalle, *Histórica Relación*, I, 19). "The chronicles and archives of the time are full of stories about the shipowners of Callao and the warehouse owners of Valparaíso; about their plans of reciprocal monopoly to injure each other clumsily and inconsiderately; about the endless lawsuits and their occasional understandings; and even about their solemn alliances to place under their rule all the bakers of both kingdoms and through them to include the whole population" (Sepúlveda 1959: 23, citing Benjamín Vicuña Mackenna, *Historia de Valparaíso*).

Satellite producers and consumers both in Peru and Chile and even their respective governments, far from being blind to what was going on, understood only too well and tried to remedy the situation by breaking the power of the import-export merchant monopolists. But (not unlike today) the logic of the capitalist system did not permit such remedy. On the contrary, the monopoly structure of the capitalist system polarized economic and political power between and within both countries in such a way as to render the monopolists ever more powerful and the "public" and its governments correspondingly less able to take the economic and political measures necessary for their protection.

In fact, we know of documents which show the social and official reaction to the alternative of either absorbing the increase of external demand (and sacrificing consumption) or maintaining internal supply. This documentation demonstrates that the community was opposed from the beginning to this type of trade because of its consequences: the community was against the restriction of consumption, against the rise in internal prices; and this led to an extemporaneous and restrictive policy destined to shackle the nascent trade, limiting export licenses and the export quota, without considering or trying other positive solutions. For example, around 1694 it was officially permitted to export only about 12,000 quintals, and in November 1695 this negative attitude reaches its apex when Marín de Poveda prohibits the export of wheat from Santiago and its environs. . . .

However, despite the crisis provoked by the notable increase of external demand, the economic imperative strengthened; and all the measures adopted to prevent this trade totally failed. Persons close to official channels scoffed at the prohibitions, enabling them to obtain lucrative earnings from the sale of licenses and from premiums of a peso charged on each *fanega* exported. In Lima, a *fanega* was sold for 25 pesos and more, while in Chile the price had tripled from 2 pesos and 6 reales to 8 and 10 pesos, without the producer benefiting from the differential. . . .

Around this time, there arose in Chile at the instigation of the landholders or producers an organization to put an end to the anomalies of the export trade by protecting the interests of this economic sector against the dictates of the Callao shipowners; this move arose in the course of a dispute over the warehouses. According to Vicuña Mackenna, the landowners were "easy victims for the monopolists, while the warehouse owners, willingly or not, contented themselves with being accomplices of the monopolists." Such subordination implied an acceptance of the buying prices and annual volume of exports imposed by foreign businessmen. . . .

The shipowners and merchants of Peru reciprocated by forming a similar organization—a more powerful one, however, due to their economic experience and ability and their greater resources. They established a single buyer, selected the wheat which they imported, and placed their ships under single control; in short, they asserted their control in Valparaíso and Lima, where they suppressed an independent move by the bakers' guild to send two ships to Chile. The merchants and shipowners also subordinated the Peruvian farmers by lowering the price of imported wheat at harvest time. Vicuña Mackenna himself explains how this was accomplished: "In order to extend the monopoly's control to the ultimate limit, the shipowners holding Chilean wheat waited until harvest time in the valleys in the vicinity of Lima; when that time came, they dropped the price of this grain suddenly, losing only a few *fanegas* of the supplies which they held."

But the recovery which the Viceroy saw was not real; his policies were condemned to failure due to the opposition of two powerful forces. He was fighting against the more or less circumstantial reaction of the importers, who profited through speculative prices and who were aware that the demand for essential commodities was inelastic and always positive. What is worse, the Viceroy fought against the all powerful limits imposed by the economic geography of the country. The later history of this market for wheat verifies our interpretation (Sepúlveda 1959: 20–21, 25–27).

2. Domestic Polarization

The events of the eighteenth century in the Chilean economy show that the contradictions of capitalism are not limited to the relations between major regions or countries, but penetrate the domestic economic, political and social body to the last cell, integrating all into its contradiction-ridden structure. Sepúlveda finds that the very same monopolist appropriation of surplus within a polar metropolis-satellite capitalist structure characterizes eighteenth-century domestic Chilean agricultural production and distribution.

The lack of commercial honesty also impeded the *normal* development of agricultural life. A communication in 1788 by Governor

O'Higgins to the subdelegates of Aconcagua and Curimón, asking for information concerning the practices of wheat merchants, tells us about the usurious abuses committed by the merchants against the small producers. In general, the merchant made an installment payment to the peasant in merchandise, buying the wheat crop before it was harvested under such conditions that the only party favored in the course of the transaction was the intermediary. These vicious contracts triggered numerous conflicts at harvest time; because sometimes the farmer, also acting shrewdly, committed himself with several creditors, and deserted his farm when he was unable to pay. (Sepúlveda 1959: 29. Emphasis added.)

In terms of my thesis, the only thing in this observation we must take exception to is the all too common notion that this kind of development is not "normal" under capitalism and that some other kind of development might be more normal. Would that it were so.

Yet the increased foreign demand for Chilean wheat and the conditions under which it grew during the eighteenth century produced effects which penetrated very much further still into the Chilean countryside (even if not in equal degree in all of its regions and valleys), and there transformed the very nature of rural institutions, though not the essentially capitalist metropolis-satellite relations already existing in and around the latifundia. These it only served to polarize still further. The dramatic events, and their causes and significances, are chronicled and analyzed by Mario Góngora in his exceptionally important books, *Origen de los "Inquilinos" de Chile Central* and (with Jean Borde) *Evolución de la Propiedad Rural en el Valle del Puange*. Important evidence from another valley is carefully analyzed by Rafael Baraona and associates in their *Valle del Putaendo: Estudio de Estructura Agraria*.

The commercial and other economic influences and pressures on Chilean agriculture during the eighteenth century produced far-reaching changes in the distribution of landownership among owners and in the institutional forms of owner-worker relation within the farm of any one owner. In both cases, the pressures and tendency were toward further polarization of and within the metropolis-satellite structure on the local scene. On the one hand, there was increasing polarization between latifundia and minifundia; and on the other hand the analogous metropolis-satellite relationship between large owners and their tenants also polarized.

3. Latifundia-Minifundia Polarization

The eighteenth century is different and marked by many transformations. Various mechanisms, principally inheritance, prematurely produce two characteristic and opposite forms of property and landholding. These two forms, already clearly delineated in the fourth decade of the century, become more marked later in the century, reaching the atomized property holding, or minifundia, and the large property holding, or latifundia. The tendency toward property concentration at the end of the eighteenth centry is represented objectively by the formation of two large holdings in the north of the valley: the Putaendo and San José de Piguchen estates. In neither case is the owner a proprietor who "rounded off" his *merced* with surrounding parcels of land, but rather an individual who had no land in the valley and who created a large estate exclusively by large-scale purchases. . . .

Although all the property holdings are at first large units, later those which become subdivided are set aside from those which remain large. In all the known cases, the large property holding, once constituted, never lost its essential characteristic. The four present estates, El Tartaro, La Vicuna, San Juan de Piguchen, and Bellavista have continued as large property holdings since the eighteenth century. Although transactions involving these estates enlarged and contracted them, their essential nature was not altered. On the other hand, none of the large property holdings has been divided, nor have any of the attempts to this effect with holdings in excess of 100 *cuadras* [150 hectares] been successful for more than a few years. The *mercedes* allowed not only the formation of large property holdings but also their opposite, the small landholding. The latter came about by the continual redistribution of paternal lands into equal shares. Another cause of the parceling of lands, albeit of much˚ less importance, was property sales. These sales, in effect, only accelerated this process. They appeared after the effects of the laws of inheritance and were based on lands which had already been distributed. The sale of small lots was characteristic of the second half of the eighteenth century and the nineteenth century. . . .

The dominant characteristic of these new proprietors was their meager economic capacity. The fact that they acquired these lands to farm themselves differentiated them from those who obtained the land as just one more asset—as capital. Due to the scarcity of financial resources, the new proprietors began operation with little labor and equipment. Under these conditions, farming was unprofitable, and was transformed into a meager means of subsistence. This type of operation was extremely sensitive to market fluctuations and to irregularities of physical environment. A prolonged drought, a flood which would demolish the crop and exterminate the livestock, a plague, or one of the frequent oscillations of prices, would result in the collapse of these farms. The consequent low economic level (shown by frequent financial indebtedness; land, livestock and crop mortgages; property auctions arising from improper cancellation of debts; the sale of land to finance burials, etc.) was the direct cause of the subdivision of land. . . .

The land constituted the principal, indeed the only, source of production, and therefore of rent. Aside from public positions, which in the seventeenth and eighteenth centuries were auctioned at high prices, the landless son had a very limited economic perspective: He lacked the capital to become a lender, one of the most lucrative activities of the time; nor had he the money to set up a small trade, such as tanning, milling or cloth manufacture. Moreover, even if the father owned slaves, Indians or cattle equivalent in value to the land, he would not have been able to leave the landowning son without the labor and other means to continue operating the farm. And there was tradition weighing in the background: the farmer felt attached to the land. . . .

For a while, the large estates were saved from subdivision by the mere existence of large amounts of undistributed property: land in Putaendo and outside the valley, money, slaves, etc. However, if this were the only important factor, the large estates would have been reduced to the condition of the poor property holdings in two or three generations, and thus the unstoppable process of subdivision would have begun. But reality was another thing; on the one side, assets reproduced themselves and were not static; wealth created wealth; capital, which was available to the larger estates, was converted into added labor power, more and better farming tools, cattle, seeds, proper irrigation, and so on. On the other side, the larger estates could count on optimal physical conditions: long extensive pastures and abundant water for irrigation. In the majority of cases known in the valley, the subdivision of land had its roots in inefficient farming operations, which were due as much to the lack of capital as to the conglomeration of unfavorable physical factors. Therefore, the beginnings of subdivision, in Putaendo as in other places, might have been accidental. The interesting thing is that if local circumstances permit, once the process is begun, it continues. Undoubtedly, there are many frustrated small property areas in Chile, which began to subdivide themselves and then were consolidated (Baraona 1960: 146, 153, 174–176).

Eighteenth-century Chilean agriculture, Baraona tells us, is permeated by the polarization and surplus appropriation contradictions of capitalism. It is the polar metropolis-satellite structure of capitalist agriculture and of the capitalist economy as a whole, he is saying, which itself generates further polarization. We return to Baraona's analysis of this essentially capitalist structure and process when we come to discuss historical periods closer to our own. In this area of our inquiry, the concrete existence of the capitalist contradiction of continuity in change would, however, seem to be established by the evidence presented so far.

4. Owner-Worker Polarization Within Latifundia

The external demand for wheat and the substitution of livestock by this crop on the Central Valley floors raised the value of land and also transformed the institutional arrangements for its use within the latifundia.

The introduction of cereal agriculture brought a considerable change in this respect. Parallel to it, there is a notable increase of small dependent enterprises within the hacienda, not now of tied Indians, but of "tenants" (*arrendatarios*) who arise outside of the Indian statute itself. They are not, like the tenants (*arrendatarios*) of the ranch, men of certain economic standing, but rather poor people who occupy small plots of land within the haciendas as well as in the towns, where they easily achieve better conditions than the Indians. . . . We can assert, therefore, that the institution known in the nineteenth century as *inquilinaje* [tenancy] appeared in the district which we have studied as the result of the process of "cerealization" of the land, and of the increase in the value of the land due to agricultural production. This process did not stem from the activities of the tied Indians who had served as the labor force in the purely pastoral economy of the seventeenth century. . . . The exhaustion of the mines had as much influence on the development of property holding as their discovery. . . . Thus, once the mineral wealth had disappeared, a certain degree of impoverishment followed, which, however, did not sink into absolute misery, and which led eventually to isolation. . . .

But in a more general way, it may be said that grain production infused new power and concentration into the diffuse life of livestock ranching, causing the price of land to rise and increasing the need for labor. Therefore, the number of various types of rural workers rises—slaves, peons, and that mixture of farmer and cowboy called *inquilino*. More than a direct connection that can be shown in each case, there occurs a general rise in the level of the haciendas, which renders tenancy more desirable and on the other hand leads the owner to look for more workers and to demand more labor or higher payments from them for the use of the land. It is this factor which best explains the gradual substitution of loans based on the low value of land and the advantage of permitting its use by others for almost nothing— by renting and by a form of renting which carries with it not only a payment, but also a whole complex of duties which begin to become more and more onerous insofar as Chilean agriculture advances toward greater commercial development. . . .

We have already said that in the previous century the tenants (*arrendatarios*) had to help in the roundups. . . . But now we find that rural practice has broadened this principle where there are important irrigation works, establishing a new norm of doing this work with a peon. . . . The work obligations for the use of property increase. . . . This is an index of the general tendency of the institution to increase the rental obligations toward the hacienda, to make tenancy more costly. . . . But these tendencies also evolve. From free use of land with only a symbolic payment, things pass to tenancy that involves care of pasture and help in the roundups. In the eighteenth century there is a crucial change: The wheat trade with Peru, which brings with it a more intensive organization of the hacienda and a rise in land prices from the Aconcagua to Colchagua export regions. Tenancy becomes renting, the payment of rent becoming significant. . . . The tenants (*arrendatarios*) . . . no longer help only with the rodeos . . . but rather the large hacienda begins to impose its need for labor on the tenant (*arrendatario*). . . . From the point of view of rural history, this transition can, for the most part, be looked at as the outcome of the slow process of rise of land values in the context of a system of large property holdings which had not been put to full use by the owners (Góngora 1960: 101-102, 114-115).

Thus economic influences coming from abroad during the eighteenth century and arising out of the contradictory structure of the capitalist system and the unequal course of its development penetrate into the furthest reaches of Chilean rural life, where they force the institutional arrangements of production and distribution even *within* a particular farm to adapt themselves to the exigencies of the capitalist metropolis-satellite structure. Enterprising small tenant farms and farm owners during the seventeenth century produced for themselves, keeping most of what they produced, and paying over to the larger landowners little or none of the economic surplus of their work as long as the land remained of little value to these owners. Beginning in the eighteenth century, the tenants were forced to pay an ever larger share of their economic surplus to the appropriating landowners as the capitalist market increased both the value of land and the need for labor to work it. To quote Góngora again, "the *inquilino* was transformed into a worker who became more and more dependent . . . within a tendency of proletarianization of the *inquilino* which intensified in the nineteenth century" (Góngora 1960: 98).

Given the widespread impression that the institution of *inquilino* in Chile and similar ones elsewhere in Latin America are "feudal," it is important to emphasize, as Góngora rightly does, the real source and significance of these still surviving institutions:

To summarize, rural tenancy has nothing to do with the *encomienda* nor with the institutions of the conquest. It originates during the second stage of colonial history and when class stratification occurs, putting the landlords on top and the poor Spaniards and various types of mestizos and castes on the bottom. . . . As class stratification becomes more marked in the eighteenth and nineteenth centuries, so do the duties on the *inquilinos* increase proportionately. The transition from pastoral occupations to grain farming coincides with, and in part begins, this process. Thus tenancy institutions reflect the social and agrarian history of a whole region (Góngora 1960: 116–117).

5. Polarization and Industrial Underdevelopment

Led astray possibly by some modern notions about the inevitable economic benefits accruing from increased exports, cyclical upswings, and "good times" generally, one might be tempted to suppose that the renewed eighteenth-century rise in mineral exports and the increase in agricultural exports had beneficial effects on other sectors of the Chilean economy, such as trade and manufacturing. Reality in the eighteenth century, however, was otherwise—as it still is in the twentieth century. As my thesis about the role and effects of the capitalist contradictions in an already dependent peripheral satellite economy foretells, economic good times on the world capitalist or metropolitan level bring bad times to the satellites, at least as far as concerns developments which further their own economic development and underdevelopment. Chile's increased exports were, of course, associated with the capitalist world's eighteenth-century recovery from its seventeenth-century "depression." And the capitalist world's recovery in turn spelled renewed doom for Chile's manufacturing development and forced Chile into still further structural underdevelopment.

The abundance of low-priced European merchandise had favorable effects only at first, for the country did not produce anything which Europe might have found worthwhile to import. Consequently, there ensued a disequilibrium. . . . In the apt phrase of a historian: "The flood of French merchandise had no other effect than the exchange of earnings and savings accumulated in tallow and wheat commerce by the local inhabitants for clothing, furniture, and various other European articles. This influx gave a European varnish to the local life; but it weakened the Chilean economic potential." This same lack of economic rationality in the use of profits stemming from an increase of wheat exports was repeated in the middle of the nineteenth century with the earnings from the California and Australia trade. The difficulties in the Peruvian market worsened when the flow of imports—traditionally composed of

Spanish merchandise which passed through Peru to reach Chile—diminished greatly when it was replaced by articles delivered directly to Chilean ports by the French. Contributing to the worsening of the situation was the admission into the Chilean market of Asian merchandise, together with goods coming from the Rio de la Plata region. The latter were smuggled secretly into Chile up to the last decade of the seventeenth century. The French and Asian ships dared to supply the Viceroyalty even by way of Callao, taking advantage of some of the uninhabited Chilean harbors (Sepúlveda 1959: 24).

Yet the worst was still to come. Spain, itself increasingly subordinate to Britain and France, attempted to adapt her own economic and political relations to the exigencies of her disadvantaged position in the world capitalist market by revamping the whole set of regulations governing the external economic relations of her colonies, instituting "free trade" in 1778, opening the port of Buenos Aires, etc. The effects on manufacturing and general economic development in Spain's colonies, including Chile, were far-reaching.

The unfavorable balance of trade continued throughout the eighteenth century and became exceptionally acute after 1778. . . . It was really after 1783, when the regulations of 1778 began to show their effect, that the Chilean market became virtually saturated with foreign products. . . . With the establishment of the 1778 regulation, Chilean commercial relations with Spain were directly established by way of Cape Horn or Buenos Aires. The regulation also eliminated obstacles to a greater exchange between Chile and the rest of the colonies . . . the prices of European and American goods fell. . . . All of these circumstances favored the penetration of our country by foreign manufacturers. . . . Chilean industry . . . began its well-known decline, experiencing a reduction in the volume of production and the elimination of some of its branches . . . there was a reduction in the sale of Chilean-produced rigging . . . these commercial franchises damaged another industry which had developed in our country—shipbuilding. There was also a considerable decline in textile production; the volume of consumption of nationally produced pottery and metal products was reduced, the hide industry suffered a serious breakdown; etc. In short, there began a gradual reduction of the economic importance of producing activities, those which satisfied the internal market, and even export industries.

Chile began to be a consumer country of foreign manufactures, a phenomenon that became more marked after Independence. . . . It is of first importance to underscore that the phenomenon analyzed here appeared in various American countries (Ramírez 1959: 40-43, 54, 57). It was, in effect, the active trading which started with the 1778 regulations that caused the decadence of the first national industries (*Ibid.*: 44, citing Ricardo Levine, *Investigaciones Acerca de la Historia Económica del Virreinato del Plata,* II, 152).

An observer of those times talks as though he were speaking of today: "Today all those branches which constituted the happiness of the kingdom, insofar as interest is concerned, and others of lesser importance, see themselves extremely depressed, although for different causes. However, the main factor undoubtedly is the effects of having Europe inundate these provinces with luxury and entice the people to value what is superfluous before what is necessary" ("Informe de Domingo Diaz de Salcedo presentado al Gobernador Ambrosio O'Higgins," March 11, 1789, in *Archivo Vicuña Mackenna,* cited in Ramírez 1959: 45).

To conclude, I shall again let others, both contemporaries and eighteenth-century writers, speak for me. What they say and even the words they choose confirm my thesis: Capitalism produces a developing metropolis and an underdeveloping periphery, and its periphery—in turn characterized by metropolis and satellites within it—is condemned to a stultified or underdeveloped economic development in its own metropolis and inevitably to underdevelopment among its domestic peripheral satellite regions and sectors:

The Viceroys of Peru, following an autarchical and mercantilist concept, regarded Chile "as an appendix of the Viceroyalty; as a granary destined to supply the Viceroyalty's needs for wheat and tallow; as a market to feed the prosperity of Lima's merchants; and a colony which was only costly for Spain and which was necessary to maintain, not for her intrinsic worth, but for the security of Peru" (Encina, *Historia de Chile,* V, 264, cited in Sepúlveda 1959: 29).

Nor were Chile's relations with the Spanish metropolis itself much different:

Not in one instance did the metropolis abandon the basis of her mercantilist policy toward America, whose object was the exchange of Spanish manufactures and produce for the gold and silver which were extracted from the local mines. . . . All of these measures have an extraordinary importance in our economic history . . . [and] did not go unnoticed by the rulers or businessmen of the time . . . it became evident, first, that the actions carried out by the metropolitan government to strengthen the Spanish economy were neither adequate nor appropriate for the Chilean economy. In the second place, as a result of these measures, there began the well-known antagonism between the needs and economic interests of Chile and those of the economic system established in America by the metropolis. Finally, . . one fact remains perfectly clear: Chile became an economic unit so defined that for its later development it required a particular policy which took account of its specific interests, determined, as they were, by the singular nature of all the aspects of its economic life. . . . The general economic life of the country suffered the effects of a violent contradiction. On the one hand, there were the productive forces struggling to expand . . . on the other, there were those factors which tried to maintain a rigid framework and impeded or obstructed this normal expansion. This is not an internal contradiction; that is, it did not exist within the economic body of Chile. Instead, it showed itself between the economy of this country and the structure of the Spanish empire. Its effect was to place the entire national economy in crisis, given the nature of Chile as a colonial or dependent nation. This meant that Chile could not maintain commercial relations outside the Spanish orbit and that it was subjected to the dictates of metropolitan economic policy (Ramírez 1959: 40, 98-99).

José Armendaris, as Viceroy of Peru, was qualified to speak in 1736:

The commerce of this Kingdom is a paradox of trade and a contradiction of riches not known until its discovery, thriving on what ruins others and being ruined by what makes others thrive, in that its development lies in the management of foreign trade and its declines in the freedom of others, and it is regarded not as commerce that must be kept open but as an inheritance that must be maintained closed (*Memorias de los Virreyes,* III, 250, cited in Ramírez 1959: 68).

Could there be a better and more poetic statement of the

harsh realities of the three capitalist contradictions, which in the past and still in our day simultaneously and jointly cause both development and underdevelopment?

G. NINETEENTH CENTURY CAPITALISM IN CHILE:
THE CONSOLIDATION OF UNDERDEVELOPMENT

The capitalist contradictions of surplus appropriation within the metropolis-satellite structure of world and national capitalism were also to determine the development and underdevelopment of Chile in the nineteenth century. Indeed, not only the new contradictions of the post-Independence "national" period but also, and perhaps primarily, the continued effects of the capitalist contradictions of the colonial period, both being the concrete nineteenth-century manifestations of the fundamental capitalist contradictions in Chile's entire history, frustrated Chile's attempts at national economic development and condemned its people to the continued development of underdevelopment. The choice of the word "frustrated" I owe to Anibal Pinto's pathbreaking and masterful study, *Chile: Un Caso de Desarrollo Frustrado.* I accept his analysis as far as it goes: Pinto suggests that colonial Chile was a recluse economy and only opened its doors after Independence and attempted a development toward the outside which was frustrated by the adverse interests and combined power of imperialism and domestic reaction. But my explanation of this frustration differs from Pinto's in that I seek to trace the causes and roots of the frustration of Chile's economic development and the stimulation of its underdevelopment to the beginning of its history and to the structure of the capitalist system whose roots were implanted then and whose bitter fruits are reaped now.

In my terms, the nineteenth-century experience of Chile may be characterized as that of a satellite country which attempts to achieve economic development through national capitalism and fails. For a time, indeed repeatedly, Chile tried to resolve some of its capitalist contradictions with the imperialist world metropolis. All too aware of it as it was, Chile tried to escape from its capitalist satellite status. Chile embarked on attempts to achieve economic development through state-sponsored Bismarckian policies of national development long before Bismarck had though of it and while Friedrich List was still trying to persuade Germany to do so. But all these attempts were still made within the framework of capitalism, even if "national" capitalism.

Whether in the nineteenth century national or state capitalism could still have liberated Chile—or any other then satellite and now underdeveloped country—and whether it could have undone the effects of its previous satellite status and thus opened the way for it to economic development in the style of the metropolis is now difficult to say. I would be inclined to believe that such national liberation of a dependent country through national capitalism was probably no longer possible in the nineteenth century, as it certainly is no longer possible in the twentieth century. What can be said with confidence, because the historical evidence is clear, is that neither Chile nor any other country in the world which had already previously been firmly incorporated into the world capitalist system as a satellite has, since the nineteenth century, managed to escape from this status to achieve economic development by relying only on national capitalism. The new countries which have developed since then had, like the United States, Canada and Australia, already achieved substantial internal and external economic independence, or like Germany and most significantly Japan had never been satellites, or like the Soviet Union have broken out of the world capitalist system by socialist revolution. Notably, these now more or less developed countries were not richer when they began their development than was Chile when it made its attempt to do the same. But—and this I believe is the crucial distinction—they were not already underdeveloped.

Chile, on the other hand, already had the structure of underdevelopment from colonial times. We will see now how the economic and political structure of underdevelopment plagued

Chile throughout the nineteenth century and particularly at the times of its two major attempts at national development, around 1850 under Presidents Bulnes and Montt and around 1890 under President Balmaceda. It was the already existing capitalist metropolis-satellite structure of Chile at the international and national levels, which, having already implanted in it the structure of underdevelopment, frustrated these Chilean attempts at economic development.

Two major aspects of this structure of underdevelopment were spared Japan but plagued Chile during its attempts at national development: Integration in the world capitalist market as a satellite, including foreign ownership and control of Chilean resources and commercial institutions; and a domestic metropolis-satellite structure, intimately interlinked with the structure of world capitalism, which allied the most powerful interest groups of Chile to those of imperialism and its interest in maintaining and indeed in furthering Chile's underdevelopment. It was these two consequences of the previous and continued capitalist structure and contradictions in Chile which in the nineteenth century frustrated Chile's attempts at economic development and condemned it to underdevelopment, and which continue to condemn it to still further and deeper underdevelopment now and in the future until Chile extracts itself from its capitalist metropolis-satellite structure—that is, until it resolves the contradictions of its capitalism, international and national alike.

1. Attempts at Economic Independence and Development: Portales, Bulnes and Montt

During the first forty years of independence, Chile made valiant efforts to achieve economic independence and development under the leadership of its Liberator, O'Higgins, Prime Minister Portales, and Presidents Bulnes and Montt, with whose names we may associate successively each decade between 1820 and 1860. After this, publicly sponsored efforts declined, though some private efforts persisted, until the renewed major effort of President Balmaceda in the years 1886–1891.

In 1834 the Minister of the Treasury (Hacienda), Manuel Rengifo, addressed the Congress:

Everywhere cities are expanding and becoming more beautiful; agriculture is prospering; pastures are covered with livestock and the fields with wheat; rich and abundant mines spontaneously offer the gift of treasures hidden in their breast; commerce flourishes, fed by hundreds of ships which dock unceasingly at our ports; new branches of industry take root in the country; population is increasing, favored by the most benign climate; the condition of the farmer and the fate of the artisan improve and the comforts of life penetrate even to the humble abode of the poor (*Memoria de Hacienda* 1834, cited in Sepúlveda 1959: 35).

To take advantage of the apparent opportunities of the times, laws favoring Chilean national development were passed under the inspiration of the same Minister:

The customs reform, conceived by Rengifo and confirmed in the laws of January 8 and of October 22, 1835, destined to promote the growth of the merchant marine and consequently of commerce, established principles such as the following: reduction of import duties equivalent to 10 percent of foreign merchandise introduced by Chilean ships of foreign construction and 20 percent if the ship had been built in Chile. With respect to the wheat trade, grain export required payment of a 6 percent tax, while the [tax on the] export of flour was fixed at 4 percent of its valuation (Sepúlveda 1959: 35).

The policy of stimulating commerce and promoting such independence as Chile could by acquiring its own national merchant marine (though part was composed of foreign-owned ships flying the Chilean flag) met with some success for a time: "In the first place, thanks to the external stimulus, the national merchant marine grew to some 103 ships in the years prior to 1848, 119 in 1849, 157 in 1850, and 257 in the year 1885—a real achievement. In the second place, Valparaíso managed to become a first-class port with warehouses" (Sepúlveda 1959: 37). Sepúlveda suggests that this kind of development "towards the outside" was about the only possible development path open to Chile since it cost less capital than trying to compete with the metropolis industrially and since capital was precisely what Chile lacked. To the extent that this judgment is well taken, we may observe that this lack of capital must be traced, at least in good part, to the expropriation of economic surplus which Chile had already suffered for many decades past, due to the monopolization of its trade by others. Fulfilling the old dream of acquiring its own ships, to escape from at least that source of foreign monopoly power over Chile's economy, was of course an attempt to remedy this situation. But it was not enough.

Still, domestic measures for national economic development were not lacking. On the contrary, they were surely among the most significant and progressive of those times.

During the years 1841-1861, under the governments of Bulnes and of Montt, . . various events stimulated the economy. After about 1845, coal exploitation began in earnest. The economy received a new impulse as a result of the discovery of gold in California, which produced, along with a big Chilean emigration to that region, an appreciable increase in agricultural and industrial production. All this wealth was reinvested in great public works. Roads were opened, railroads built . . . steamships travelled the extensive Pacific coasts. . . . The telegraph shortened communication. . . . Economic and technical progress transformed the standard of living. Mining expanded. . . . The development of railroads and the growth of commerce produced the enrichment of many families (Pinto 1962: 19, citing J. C. Jobet).

The audacity and vision of Montt in the use of the resources and administrative capacity of the state in railroad development can be justly appreciated only by taking into account the deep prejudice which existed against state intervention and which in almost all the rest of the Latin American countries resulted, as an inevitable alternative, in foreign investors taking charge of the task (Pinto 1962: 22).

Nor was there any lack of attempts to promote Chilean manufacturing and other industry. Our review of previous centuries shows that it is an all too common mistake to see manufacturing only in the future and never in the past of today's underdeveloped countries. On the contrary, at various times of their past, Chile, many other now underdeveloped countries of Latin America, and India of course, had industrialized relatively more by their own efforts than many now developed countries. In this connection ex-President Carlos Dávila of Chile suggests: "At the beginning of the seventeenth century, the industrial production of colonial Brazil was greater than that of England, and in the eighteenth century greater than the industrial production of the United States" (Dávila 1950).

In the second half of the last century [in Chile], an important effort was made in the field of metallurgy. Numerous industries of this type were installed in the region of Santiago and Valparaíso, the majority of them directed by foreigners [but resident in the country and economically Chilean]. The projects of these metallurgical industries were ambitious: They manufactured plows, threshing machines, locomotives, railroad freight cars, large bells, etc; they also constructed four steam locomotives. The initiative developed in the metallurgical industry showed its efficiency by being able to provide the necessary arms and equipment for the Chilean army and navy during the War of the Pacific. Nevertheless, this effort, so promisingly begun, was later nullified for the most part by competition from imported products (Nolff 1962: 154).

Despite all these measures, Chile remained (not became, as some would have it) an export economy. Its mining production, now including increasingly copper, and its agricultural output, still based principally on wheat, expanded rapidly in response to foreign demand. Anibal Pinto, who suggests that foreign trade came to be the driving force (*fuerza motriz*) of the Chilean economy only after Independence opened the doors, comments:

The expansion of the export sector cannot be considered less than spectacular. Statistics permit examination of it only from 1844 on, but it is sufficient to note that between that year and 1860 the value of exports quadrupled. . . . From 1844 to 1880, agricultural products constituted on the average 45 percent of the total. Mining activity brought the most significant contribution to the great jump motivated by the demand of expanding markets. . . . The production of silver multiplied six times between 1840 and 1855. That of copper grew some 6,500 tons in the years 1841–1843 to reach about 50,000 tons in the decade of 1861 when Chilean deliveries reached 40 percent of world production, providing around 65 percent of the needs of British industry and consumption (Pinto 1962: 15).

By 1876, we might add, Chile produced 62 percent of the world's copper, all from Chilean-owned mines opened by national investment. In 1913 Chile still owned 80 percent of its copper mines. Today it owns 10 percent. The other 90 percent are American-owned and were acquired and expanded with hardly any investment of American capital. The capital used for expansion was expropriated from Chilean-produced economic surplus and appropriated by the American companies for their own benefit (Vera 1963: 30 and *passim*).

Returning to the nineteenth century, Anibal Pinto continues:

Agricultural growth did not fall behind. Production quintupled in the period 1844–1860. Wheat exports—which reached some 145,000 quintals before independence, with Peru as principal market—in the decade of 1850 were almost invariably above 300,000 quintals. "Chilean agriculture," says a conscientious recent study, "reacted with evident success to the external stimulus which changed its orientation. The livestock ranch became less important while the number of haciendas dedicated exclusively to wheat production increased. The wheat economy was imposed at the expense of the pastoral economy." The country's economic growth and the political stability on which it was based solidly cemented Chile's prestige in the rest of the world. Comparison among South American bond quotations in the London market offers decisive testimony. About 1842–1843, Chilean 6 percent bonds were quoted at between 93 and 105, those of Argentina at 20, those of Brazil at 64, and those of Peru were not in demand (Pinto 1962: 15-16, also citing Sepúlveda).

Until 1865 the principal export markets for Chilean wheat were on the Pacific, with Peru remaining the major buyer just as it had been throughout colonial times. After that, though Peru continued as a major buyer, exports shifted increasingly to Europe, and principally to Britain. In California and Australia, whose gold rushes after 1849 and 1851 produced sudden temporary increases in demand for wheat, Chilean wheat was increasingly displaced by the growing production of the Great Plains of the United States.

This intense integration of Chile into the world market was, to say the least, a mixed blessing. In fact, for a country which participated in that market and in the world capitalist or imperialist system as a satellite of the overseas metropolis, it was necessarily a curse.

Before long, Chile's strong bonds with the imperialist world market again had profound and almost catastrophic consequences, with the renewed closing of the wheat markets of California and Australia between 1858 and 1861 and even more so with the contemporary world crisis of 1857. At the end of August 1857, credit and monetary contraction had become so intense that commercial transactions were completely paralyzed in Valparaíso. The commercial crisis had fatal repercussions for farmers, miners and industrialists. They were obliged to reduce their activities, to abandon or postpone the large installations and improvements. which they had undertaken. There were many noisy bankruptcies. The price of rural property fell 40 percent (Encina, cited in Pinto 1962: 29).

Similarly, with an open economy integrated in the world market as it was, the world-wide depression of 1873, and the War of the Pacific and its aftermath produced violent swings in the Chilean economy including its "domestic" as well as its export sectors.

A general rise of prices occurred which began in 1850 and ended in 1873. The prices of one hundred articles rose 32.9 percent in the period between 1847-1850 and 1875. After that date there was a general decline in prices. The drop in copper prices was the final blow. In 1872 the English ton was quoted at £108. This price sank, bit by bit, falling to £39.5 in 1878. Farm owners found it impossible to cover the interest on their debts . . . there were no buyers with the necessary resources for acquiring farms for the amount of the debt. . . . Many creditors including banks had to accept payment in land (Encina, cited in Pinto 1962: 26-29).

The upshot of this situation was the declaration of inconvertibility in 1878 and the beginning of a regime of paper money (Pinto 1962: 29).

The Chilean wheat economy, large in national terms but supplying only a small percentage of world consumption, was necessarily also subject to the violent swings of the world market and the whole capitalist economy. "Basically, the amount of our exports depended on world production" (Sepúlveda 1959: 62). The only saving grace was the Peruvian market, which, itself relatively isolated from metropolitan fluctuations, showed much less variation in its demand for Chilean wheat and therefore served as a partially stabilizing influence.

During the last century, the foreign trade in wheat was affected from time to time by the export crises or declines, and as the trade was influenced by and sensitive to the fluctuations of the world economy . . . the total export index showed very large fluctuations with really extraordinary increases and also with sudden declines of great magnitude. . . . The acute depressions of 1873, 1878, 1890, and 1895, for instance, which affect the total export curve, are not felt in the exports to the Pacific Coast which remain substantially constant. The same thing happens if we look at the opposite side; the highest exports show up clearly in the index of total trade, but also fail to show up in the exports to the Pacific (Sepúlveda 1959: 60-61).

The War of the Pacific of 1879-1882 [Chile against Peru and Bolivia] produced another upset in the economy. The import of all things that were not necessary to clothe and equip the army was spontaneously restricted. Mining and agriculture paid the excess of what the restrictions on luxury imports did not cover. . . . Industry, for its part, increased 10, 20, and up to a hundred fold its production of clothing, shoes, articles of leather, powder, chemical and pharmaceutical products, wagons, barrels, sacking, blankets, cannons, ship boilers, etc. . . . . Once the war was over, this improvised industry disappeared (Encina, cited in Pinto 1962: 42).

The rise and decline of the number of industrial establishments is suggested by the following (Nolff 1962: 153):

	1868	1878	1888
Flour mills	507	553	360
Textile factories	177	302	281
Tanneries	61	101	70
Noodle factories	7	10	5
Copper smelters	250	127	69

Though shipping traffic in Chilean ports increased threefold between 1860 and 1870, the Chilean merchant fleet, which had numbered 276 vessels in 1860, declined to 21 ships in 1868 and by 1875 increased again to only 75 ships (Sepúlveda 1959: 72). Sepúlveda comments:

Since then, the merchant fleet plays practically no further role in foreign trade. The influence of foreign merchant ships was to be decisive and was to become a strong monopoly for a long time. The Bulletin of the Sociedad Nacional de Agricultura of December 26, 1898, puts it thus: "Chilean agriculture is blocked by a foreign merchant marine which, thanks to the unintentional privileges which we give it, precludes the development of a national merchant marine without which the country will not be able to exist as a unit of autonomous, secure, and independent commercial expansion" (Sepúlveda 1959: 72).

The economically conservative historian Francisco Encina regards Chile's abandonment of its coastwise shipping to foreign interest as "one of the greatest and most transcendental errors made in the history of the Spanish American people and, among those factors subject to human will, the one that has weighed most adversely in the historical evolution of the Chilean people" (Encina, *Historia de Chile,* XIV, 644, cited in Sepúlveda 1959: 72).

The entire period after the immediate post-independence years is reviewed by Encina:

In less than fifty years, the foreign merchant strangled our incipient commercial initiative abroad; and even at home, he eliminated us from foreign trade and replaced us, in large part, in retail trade. . . . Almost all the progress of agriculture between 1870 and the War of the Pacific was due to the direct influence of the mining industry. The mining magnates, just as in mid-century, bought and created large haciendas in the Center [Central Valley], irrigated them, and their spirit, which was more progressive and enterprising than that of the old landowner, moved them to acquire modern machinery and to plant new crops. In the meantime, the old agriculturalist was inhibited not only by his lack of initiative but by lack of capital. . . . Around 1890, almost all the industries of any importance in the country were in the hands of foreigners and their immediate descendants (Encina, cited in Pinto 1962: 58).

How may we interpret and understand both the temporary economic expansions and contractions as well as the underlying trend of growing structural underdevelopment in the half century following Chile's political independence? The general interpretation of development and underdevelopment in terms of metropolis-satellite relations within the structure of the capitalist system can be of aid.

The temporary expansions and contractions of the Chilean economy and its national metropolis may, through its links to the world capitalist metropolis, be traced to the uneven development of the world capitalist system as a whole. Dale Johnson has suggested to me that the initial post-Independence measures of Chilean national investment and development should be traced to the increased amount of economic surplus available to Chile, after its liberation from Spain ended the latter's, and to some extent Lima's, expropriation of that surplus. Part of this additional surplus was channeled into investment at home and part into consumption, as we have seen.

The Chilean historian Enzo Faletto, after reading a draft of this essay, suggested that three other Chilean efforts at economic expansion in the period should probably also be interpreted as national responses to events in the world capitalist system as a whole and to their effects on satellite Chile. Taking advantage of its independence, Chile sought to break the previous monopoly which, thanks in part to the control of shipping, Lima had for so long exercised over the Chilean economy. The measures to stimulate the expansion of a national merchant marine after 1835 should be interpreted in this context. In 1837 these measures led to war with Peru, whose commercial oligarchy was in no mood to give up without a fight.

Mr. Faletto suggests that the ups and downs in the war against the Araucano Indians and the War of the Pacific against Peru and Bolivia can probably also be traced to changing tides in the world economy. The Araucanos inhabited the southern regions of Chile which were destined to become wheat lands. Mr. Faletto suggests that historical research would probably demonstrate that the important military campaigns to rob the Araucanos of their lands took place precisely at those times when the world demand for Chilean wheat was on an upswing, such as after the abolition of the corn laws in England and after the discovery of gold in California and Australia. The War of the Pacific, which was quite openly undertaken to rob Peru and Bolivia of their nitrate-producing areas, was part of the economic expansion of Chile during the 1870's which, Mr. Faletto suggests, in accordance with the thesis of this essay, should in turn be associated with the relaxation of satellite Chile's ties with the world capitalist metropolis brought on by the serious economic depression in the latter after 1873.

The same three events, Mr. Faletto believes, also confirm another part of my thesis about development and underdevelopment and the interpretation of the Chilean experience: it was domestically capitalist. These three Chilean economic expansions not only took place in response to external stimuli which affected Chile as an integral part of the world capitalist system. On the domestic level as well, these three economic expansions took place entirely within the framework of a national metropolis-satellite capitalist structure. Any Chilean economic development, however limited it may be by the world metropolis, necessarily takes place at the expense of domestic satellites. Thus the expansion of metropolitan Chilean wheat production during this period occurred at the expense of the Araucanos who were thereby increasingly satellized and most certainly more underdeveloped than they were before. Similarly, the later economic expansion and the incorporation of the nitrates into the process of Chilean development had to involve the conversion of the nitrate regions into a domestic capitalist satellite of the Chilean metropolis, just as the latter in turn was a satellite of the world capitalist metropolis.

2. Free Trade and Structural Underdevelopment

Accompanying these ups and downs in the Chilean economy, and underlying them, was a trend of ever deepening structural underdevelopment which has not ceased to this day. This underdevelopment too must be traced to Chile's participation in the world capitalist system and to the domestic economic and political structure which the latter imposed on and still maintains in Chile. This entire period of Chilean economic expansion, which lasted little more than a generation, occurred at the very time of the world-wide expansion of free trade. Thus, before strong domestic Chilean interests tied to independent national development could emerge, restricted as they were by the domestic social, economic and political structure inherited from colonial times, free trade fully re-integrated the Chilean metropolis and its most powerful interest groups into the world capitalist system, this time as a satellite of Great Britain.

In the nineteenth century, free trade signified industrial monopoly and development for Great Britain and continuation of the exploitative capitalist metropolis-satellite structure and inevitably ever deeper structural underdevelopment for the satellites. Once Britain itself had industrialized behind its protective tariff, its Navigation Acts and other monopolistic measures, its major export product became the doctrine of free trade and its twin, political liberalism. The debate over liberalism and free trade raged throughout the world. In Chile, the debate took forms which might be summarized by the following arguments of the mid-nineteenth century. The British argument in favor of free trade was expressed in an official note of the Foreign Office in 1853:

The Chilean Government may be assured that a liberal commercial policy will produce the same results in Chile as in England, that is, the increase of government income and the increase of the comforts and morality of the people. This system, which in the United Kingdom has been accepted after much consideration and which after having been tested by experience has been successful beyond the most optimistic expectations, can be—well considered—worthy of a try on the part of the Government of Chile (Instructions of the Chargé d'Affaires of Great Britain in Chile, September 23, 1853, cited in Ramírez 1959: 68).

Her Majesty's Government, like that of all metropolitan powers, did not confine itself to mere advice:

On February 7, 1853, the Foreign Minister of Great Britain instructed his representative in Santiago to register a complaint before the Government of Chile against the new export tax on copper. . . . "I have to inform you that the Government of Her Majesty cannot look upon this measure other than as prejudicial to the return shipping from the West Coast of America which now obtains freight in the transportation of minerals from the Region for metallurgical processing in this Country. The trade is of considerable value and will surely increase since Great Britain currently imports copper ores to be smelted. . . . Mills to reduce and work these products have been built, and the business tends to grow; but the Chilean law of the past October 21 cannot but restrain these enterprises in this Country and deprive Chile of the advantage of extracting and exporting its own mineral products. . . . I express the hope of the Government of Her Majesty that the law in question shall be annulled, as it is calculated to restrict the commercial interchange between the two countries and to limit the benefits which Chile now derives from the extraction and shipping of minerals" (Ramírez 1960: 64-67).

The contrary argument was advanced, on May 4, 1868, by *El Mercurio*, today Chile's leading newspaper, which then had not yet seen the light that was to transform it, beginning twenty odd years later, into imperialism's staunchest Chilean ally to this day.

Chile can be industrial, for it has capital, arms and activity; but the decided will to be is missing. There is strong foreign capital represented in the importation of manufactures. This capital is and will always be disposed to place as many obstacles as it can before the establishment of industry in the country. . . . Protectionism should be the mother's milk of all infant arts or industries, [it should be] the soul that lends it real positive spirit; because without it any nascent progress is exposed from the beginning to the ferocious and well combined attack of the foreign imports represented by free trade (Ramírez 1960: 89).

There can be little doubt today which side had the better of the argument; it is also clear which side won: free trade—that is, the metropolis-satellite relationship which had become most advantageous to the surplus appropriators in the world and national metropolises.

The tendency towards free trade increased exactly at the time when the big wheat export begins. In the end, the consequences of this orientation were: the internationalization of our economy, the annihilation of our merchant marine (customs ordinance of 1864), and the failure to capitalize on the increased receipts from wheat and later from nitrates in the construction of works in the national interest. . . . The new customs ordinance of 1864 which declared absolute free trade in coastwide shipping . . . in the train of liberalism caused the destruction of the national merchant marine, which was unable to resist the foreign competition. . . . The commercial treaties which Chile made at that time all included the "most favored nation clause." By this clause the contracting states obligate themselves to grant to the other contracting party whatever privileges they may grant to a third country. This happened with the European countries, especially England, which thanks to this clause made a veritable commercial colony out of [Latin] America and prevented the progress of manufacturing and of the national merchant marine in Chile (Sepúlveda 1959: 36, 71-72).

These free trade measures, such as the abolition of the corn laws in Britain in 1846 and of restrictions on foreign shipping by Chile in 1864, did increase exports of wheat from Chile to Britain, in part because the more liberal opening of Chilean ports to foreign bottoms reduced the cost of shipping Chilean wheat to Britain. But these same free trade measures, instituted after the Presidency of Manuel Montt who had sponsored national investment in railroads, etc., also served quickly to depress Chilean coal industry and brought competition from British coal cross-shipped with wheat. It was not long before free trade strangled Chilean manufacturing as well. The tide of satellization of Chile by metropolitan Britain, or the tide of colonization of Chile by Britain once Chile had gained its independence from Spain, was inevitable. It did not go unnoticed in Chile. With respect to copper, for instance, *El Ferrocarril* of Valparaíso (which also was yet to change its editorial policy) wrote on January 19, 1868:

Turning to examine the reasons to which Chile owes the riches which have raised it above the other countries that were Spanish colonies, we have found that it is all due to its mines and principally to copper which has supplied the world with more than half of what it consumes. . . . Nonetheless, this product of our industry has been subject to a monopoly which has considerably reduced our gains, taxing them moreover with transportation charges, commissions, and other charges invented by the English smelters. . . . For lack of other markets, the [Latin] American miners of necessity have to send their products to Great Britain and to rest content with the price that the smelters of that country offer them. For twenty years these have been abusing the dependence in which the sellers find themselves, and during the last two years and at the beginning of the present one the foundries have obtained profits out of all proportion. . . . Is this bearable in a country which has the means to free us from so hateful a monopoly? . . . . Ever since the monopoly of the English foundries made them into arbiters of the price of this product and ever since they limit or extend our mining by means of their capital, the real wealth of our society remains subject to the interests of foreign speculators who, looking out for themselves, place us in the sad situation in which we are. . . .

Is it bearable that a country which has all the means to smelt its ores, and to refine them to their purest form so that they may be sent to India, China, Europe and the whole world, be chained to such a monopoly and that it submit its main wealth to the capricious desires of a few individuals? As experience has shown, it is not demand and supply that make the price of our copper fall; it is only our carelessness and abandon on the one hand; it is the power of the capital which by our ignorance we have formed abroad at our expense. The trick of the English smelters is well known: upon the notice of the departure of rich shipments of our products, they lower the price in order to buy them upon their arrival and then raise it again once they are in their hands, thereby creating a permanent fluctuation in the price of our minerals which they arrange at their convenience. It could not be otherwise ever since they have made themselves arbiters of our wealth so that only their wish may prevail (Ramírez 1960: 82-84).

And all this thanks to the truly monopolistic arrangement liberally called "free trade."

But of course the metropolis did not rely only on the effects of its free trade policy through the world market. Wherever convenient and possible, the metropolis, now represented by Great Britain as it was by others before and still others afterward, penetrated into the very heart of the periphery's domestic mercantile, industrial and often agricultural structure (insofar as the satellite country had any "national" economy), to make it its own. In this connection, Hernán Ramírez observes in his *Historia del Imperialismo en Chile:* "After 1850, British predominance in the mining industry grew, thanks to the English railroads which criss-crossed the zone. . . . Along with controlling international trade and monopolizing the production of copper, the English were constantly on the alert to prevent Chile from ceasing to be an exporter of raw materials and food and a consumer of manufactures" (Ramírez 1960: 63–64). And Ramírez continues:

A large part of the internal commercial activity was under the direct and immediate control of British businessmen. One of the vehicles for the creation and maintenance of this situation was the great dependence in which domestic trade found itself with respect to English wholesale houses, which . . . had the international trade in their hands. . . . These houses extended the range of their business and entered various branches of national production. . . . Another vehicle was the participation that the British had in the Chilean merchant marine. . . . "A large part of the ships . . . though sailing under the Chilean flag and under the cover of Chilean owners, because foreign ships are excluded from coastwise shipping, are really of English construction and the property of British subjects."
. . . The big foreign, that is to say, English, commercial houses, played an important role in the financial life of the country: They granted credit, issued vouchers and even currency, traded in money, etc., in a word, virtually operated like banking institutions. . . . This means that no sooner did we cease being a colony of Spain than we became a dependency exploited by English capitalism (Ramírez 1960: 73-75).

It should not be thought, however, that the economic colonization of the Chilean periphery by the British metropolis, and
its conversion into a satellite, occurred only because the capitalist world's metropolis is by definition strong and its periphery
weak or because the metropolitan British free trade doctrine
convinced everybody in the periphery (or in other parts of the
metropolis) by the power of its logic. No, the capitalist world
metropolis undoubtedly had allies in the peripheral metropolises; and the British free trade doctrine fell on interested ears
in the capitalist peripheral satellites like Chile, if less so in
other metropolitan or independent countries such as Germany
and Japan. The polar metropolis-satellite contradiction of capitalism runs through the entire world capitalist system, from its
macrometropolitan center to its most microperipheral satellite.
Under differing circumstances, economic and other interests
which this central contradiction brings into being, the countless minor concrete contradictions of course take a wide variety
of forms.

Unfortunately, the circumstances of this period of Chilean
history have not yet been as well studied as those of a later
period. Nonetheless, one may make some suggestions about the
conflict and alliance of interests created by the capitalist contradictions in Chile at mid-nineteenth century. A clue is available from Courcelle-Seneuil, world-renowned free trader of his
time who was imported (or exported) to Chile as official government adviser and whom many Chilean historians have identified with Chile's adoption of free trade after 1860. He observed that "A large part of the new earnings have been used
to give vent to the tastes of the landowners; the majority of
these have set themselves to building pompous houses and to
buying sumptuous furniture, and the luxury of the ladies' dresses
has made incredible progress in only a few years. . . . It may
be said that while the farm workers spent their increased income on a few pleasures, the owners spent theirs in increasing
more durable tastes; but the ones like the others have built up
very little capital" (Sepúlveda 1959: 51). These landowners
doubtless looked askance at trade restrictions that impeded such

progress for their ladies. The Minister of the Treasury of the administration following that of Montt explained to the Congress that the restraint on foreign shipping still in force, that is, the privileged position of Chilean shipping, should disappear, and should disappear to benefit "those interests for whom it [the privilege] was designed," (Véliz 1962: 240)—that is, no doubt, landowners and even more so exporters and importers. Congressman Matta argued that tariffs are only a sign of the weakness and cowardliness of the government, and that all of them should be abolished.

We may surmise, therefore, that the metropolis-satellite structure of the world capitalist system and of Chile within it produced definite interest groups within the metropolis of the Chilean satellite which, whatever their conflicts with imperialism may have been, found themselves drawn to support, above and beyond any other policy, one that served to render Chile a still more dependent satellite of the world capitalist metropolis. It is not surprising, therefore, to find these groups taking advantage of the weakness of the government caused by the 1857 world depression to revolt against President Montt and his national development policies. One may therefore agree with Claudio Veliz:

> Manuel Montt faced two revolutions . . . the second one in 1859 was closer to the political and economic interests of the mining and agricultural pressure groups of the country. . . . A large part of the opposition to the centralist, strong, statist attitude in economic matters of Montt came from the liberal—and, of course, free trade— groups that were close to the exportation of minerals and of agricultural products of the North and South of the country. Of course, it is more than a trivial coincidence that the centers of resistance against the government of Montt were in [the mining and wheat areas respectively of] Copiapó and Concepción (Veliz 1962: 242).

3. The Industrial Revolution Frustrated: Balmaceda and Nitrates

The following period was decisive in welding this trend toward underdevelopment firmly into the Chilean social, economic, and political structure. Decisive only in a manner of speaking, of course. For the seeds of structural underdevelopment had been sown by the very conquest and by the international, national, and local economic structure into which the people of this otherwise potentially rich land were thereby incorporated. Decisive only in that the events following marked what has been perhaps the most spectacular attempt to uproot the plant of underdevelopment and put in its place a plant of development instead. On the other hand, this attempt, associated with the name of President Balmaceda, was less decisive than writers like Pinto, Nolff, Ramírez and others suggest. If it failed after all, as it did in spectacular fashion, it was only because its chances for success had been prejudiced by the very same circumstances that had already produced similar if perhaps less publicized failures in the past three centuries; the roots of underdevelopment had been too deeply and firmly struck in the structure, organization and functioning of the economic system in which Chile participated from its inception to this day.

The explanation of the frustration of development in the era of the nitrates and Balmaceda by students like Jobet, Pinto, Ramírez, Nolf, and Vera is, sometimes explicitly and sometimes more implicitly, to account for Chile's failure to "take off" at the end of the nineteenth century by the unhappy concatenation of a series of more or less special circumstances. This explanation might be acceptable if, as these same authors maintain, Chile had been closed, "recluse," autarchic, or feudal until the second half of the nineteenth century (Jobet), or the first half of the nineteenth century (Pinto and Nolff), or at least until the eighteenth century (Ramírez), and had only later belatedly tried to jump from autarchy to "development toward the outside" instead of "toward the inside." The hard fact of Chile's history and economic structure is that Chile has had an open, capitalist, and dependent satellite economy since the very beginning; in other words, the roots of its underdevelopment go much deeper, lie in the structure of capitalism and not in feudalism or development "toward the outside" or a combination of the latter two. Consequently, if Chile is to change from underdevelopment to development, its structural transformation will have to go much deeper than just switching from capitalist development toward the outside to capitalist development toward the inside.

Some people living in Chile in the second half of the nineteened century did, after all, see the trend toward ever deeper underdevelopment; and some of them sought to reverse that trend. The newly formed *Sociedad de Fomento Fabril* (Society for Industrial Development) set its and Chile's sights high in 1883—though not unreasonably so, one might think—in its inaugural Prospectus:

Chile can and should be industrial. . . . It should be industrial because of its agriculture; because the fertility of the lands of the Central Valley demand richer crops . . . and at a much larger scale than at present; and because our country, small in size compared to others that are already wheat producers, will in a few more years perforce find it necessary to stop exporting this product. . . . It should be industrial because of its mining; because its real wealth does not lie in its richest veins of silver or copper, but in its mountains of poorer ores which offer sure incomes over long years to the intelligent industrialist. . . . It should be industrial because of its people, intelligent and strong, and able to understand and run any machinery after little instruction and able to do any sort of work if it only calls upon their proverbial enthusiasm and good will. . . .
It should be industrial because it has the means to be so: it has the minerals of greatest importance in extraordinary abundance: copper, iron, hard coal, nitrates, sulphur and with these sulphuric acid and all the chemical products that industry needs for its creation and development; it has the vegetable matter, woods of all kinds, linen, first-class hemp . . . and it has the animal products, leather, wool, and silk from which the most delicate clothing and cloth can be made. It is unjustifiable that such rich and varied products leave our soil to receive their final processing elsewhere, only to return to our country to be sold at prices which cost us much more than the income from the sale of the primary product. It should be industrial because geographically it has a working force of immense value which can be used in all industries to produce more cheaply than any other country. This force is the current of its

rivers, which in their course from the Andes to the sea form thousands of waterfalls which are so many motors and sources of wealth for the country.

And in conclusion, Chile should be industrial because it is the condition to which its natural evolution as a democratic country conduces and because only by dedicating its forces to industry will it come to have the stable base of social and political equilibrium which the most advanced nations enjoy; only thus will it come to have a middle class and an educated working people and therewith a future of peace and greatness for many generations (*Prospecto de la Sociedad de Fomento Fabril*, 1883, cited in Ramírez 1958: 149).

The truth is that in the period 1830-1930 Chilean agriculture had everything in its favor: foreign markets, foreign exchange to mechanize itself with, abundant credit, "social peace," total liberalism in public policy, protection of the government . . . even monetary devaluation to lighten its debts. And, nonetheless, instead of progressing, it retrogressed (Pinto 1962: 84).

What bitter irony, that word for word the same can be and still is said with equal justification today! What happened?

The War of the Pacific brought enormous riches to Chile in the form of the previously Peruvian and Bolivian northern provinces which contained the world's only known major deposits of nitrates. These, before the later development of a synthetic substitute, constituted along with Peruvian and Chilean guano the world's major commercial fertilizer. The nitrate mines had been opened with Peruvian and Chilean capital and in large part by Chilean workers, and it was essentially for the control of these mines that the war was fought. Chile won the war and the mines—but the aftermath of its victory was disastrous. It attracted a still greater measure of interest in Chile on the part of a metropolitan power, whose participation in Chilean economic and political affairs further sealed the doom of Chile's underdevelopment.

The nitrate industry had begun to develop before the War of the Pacific, thanks to the energy of Peruvian and Chilean entrepreneurs; in addition, a few citizens of British and other nationalities also participated. The capital used came in its entirety from Peruvian and Chilean financial centers and reached the nitrate region through credits or investments. This is significant and should be emphasized: Tarapacá did not receive the investment of English capital; the English played no significant part in the birth, promotion, and initial development of the nitrate industry (Ramírez 1960: 114).

English-American capital represented 13 percent of the industry and Peruvian-Chilean 67 percent; the remaining 20 percent belonged to foreigners who were economically Chilean (Encina, cited in Pinto 1962: 55).

The bonds and certificates issued by the Peruvian government, which had lost almost all of their value [because of the War of the Pacific], all of a sudden began to be bought by mysterious buyers ... who paid between 10 percent and 20 percent of their nominal value for them in devalued *soles* [Peruvian currency]. ... Once the Chilean Government decided [to honor the Peruvian bonds]; the new bond-holders came to be owners of the most valuable part of the industry. The central figure in this drama, as absurd as it was suspicious, was the almost legendary Mr. John T. North, who as the height of irony managed this fantastic speculation, which made him into the "nitrate king," with Chilean capital provided by the Bank of Valparaíso. This institution and other Chilean lenders lent $6,000,000 to North and his associates to enable him to corner the nitrate bonds and the railroads of Tarapacá. The process of de-Chilenization was rapid and curiously went so far as to reduce the part of the industry which the Chileans controlled before the war. According to Encina, ... "by August 10, 1884, Peruvian capital had disappeared; Chilean capital had been reduced to 36 percent; English capital reached 34 percent; and unnationalized European capital accounted for 30 percent (Pinto 1962: 55, also citing Encina).

Soon the British eliminated still more of the Chilean capital:

Ex-Minister Aldunate, who played an important part in the government decision that opened the way to the give-away of the nitrates, later reflected melancholically in 1893: "Unfortunately and thanks to a combination of circumstances that would take too long to recall, the nitrate industry is entirely and exclusively exploited and monopolized by foreigners. There is not a single Chilean who owns shares in the succulent firms of the Tarapacá Railroads. ... The ships which carry the wealth of our shores from our ports to the centers of consumption are all of foreign flag. The fuel used to run the machines is all English; and to render the alien monopoly of these industries complete, all the intermediaries between producers and consumers are also foreigners; and in their hands also remains the entire commercial profit of the industry" (Pinto 1962: 55-56).

Nonetheless, *El Ferrocarril,* whose economic policy was no longer exactly the same as it had been in 1868 (see quotation on page 70) held on March 28, 1889:

The riches accumulated by the foreigners should not inspire jealousies because they are the legitimate fruits of their activity, work and intelligence; and they also serve the country in that they provide new industries which develop greater consumption of national products and benefit our working efforts. . . . There is universal conviction that the future basis of our national prosperity should be sought in the industrial development for which our country is admirably suited, thanks to the abundance and variety of its natural products; and no one can deny that therefore we need foreign cooperation, be it with their capital, or be it with their experience and knowledge. Whoever really loves his country should not therefore oppose the factors of its greatness (Ramírez 1958: 102).

For any objective reader from an underdeveloped country today, be it in Latin America or elsewhere, such experience with the "contribution" of foreign "investment" and its domestic and foreign apologists will come as no surprise. The same fact and fable are still an integral part of his daily experience. The same experience visited the railroads of Argentina and Guatemala, the public utilities of Chile and Brazil, the mines, lands, and factories in underdeveloped countries everywhere. What steady fraud and robbery have been perpetrated under the noble phrase of "foreign investment and aid"! (See for instance Frank, 1963a and 1964b.)

Though *El Ferrocarril* claimed that there was "universal agreement" that Chile would prosper through its foreign economic relations and that "nobody could deny that therefore foreign cooperation is indispensable," such disagreement and denial existed, as the newspaper was all too aware (that is why they wrote as they did), above all in the person of the recently elected President Balmaceda. His speech in acceptance of the nomination for the Presidency on January 17, 1886, proclaimed his economic philosophy and program:

The tax system demands revision and an administration which is in harmony with the equal distribution of the public burden prescribed by the Constitution. . . . The economic situation of recent years proves that within the proper equilibrium between expenditures and revenues, it is possible and necessary to undertake productive public works of special help to the national economy and national industry. . . .

If, following the example of Washington and the great Republic of the North, we prefer to consume our domestic production, though it may not be as perfect and polished as the foreign one; if the farmer, miner, and manufacturer use goods or machinery that can be produced in Chile; if we broaden and vary the production of raw materials, and work and transform them into useful goods for our life or personal comfort; if we ennoble industrial work by raising wages in proportion to the increased intelligent devotion of the working class; if the state, maintaining the level of its revenues and its expenditures, dedicates a part of its wealth to the protection of national industry and sustains and provides for it in its first trials; if we have the state with its capital and its economic laws cooperate; if all of us individually and collectively cooperate in producing more and better and consuming what we produce; then richer blood would circulate through the industrial body of the republic and more wealth and welfare would give us the possession of the supreme good of a diligent and honest people: to live and clothe ourselves, by ourselves. The idea of national industry is associated with the idea of industrial immigration and with building, through special and better paid work, a home for a large class of our people—not the man of the city, nor the tenant farmer, but the working class which roams the countryside and lends a hand in the big construction sites, but which in times of possible social agitation can intensely disturb the peace of mind (Ramírez 1958: 111-112).

Ramírez summarizes Balmaceda's nitrate and other economic policies as follows:

(1) To break the monopoly which the English excercise in Tarapacá in order to prevent this region's becoming a simple foreign factory.

(2) To stimulate the formation of national nitrate companies whose stocks would not be transferable to foreign citizens or companies.

This way, while at the same time neutralizing British preponderance, it would be possible to keep at least a part of the large benefits of the nitrate industry in Chile.

(3) To prevent the further growth of foreign firms, though without interfering with the activities they already had.

(4) To develop the production of nitrates through recourse to better technology, the opening of new markets, and the cheapening of maritime and overland transportation charges. These wise and forward-looking proposals never were to be acted upon (Ramírez 1958: 98).

Ramírez further discusses Balmaceda's active economic policies under the categories of public works, railroads, highways, public health works, financial policy, treasury policy, agricultural policy, mining policy, industrial policy, educational policy, public administration, economic planning and decentralization (Ramírez 1958: 114-160).

The conservatives and the Church seem to have recognized some of Balmaceda's merits, but this did not mean they had to like them. Their mouthpiece, *Estandarte Católico*, wrote on June 4, 1889, under the engaging title, "Antes lo Necesario que lo Conveniente" (The Necessary Before the Useful)—or, in plain English, first things first:

> Mr. Balmaceda is trying to have his name glorified for having crossed the length and breadth of the country with roads of steel, for having raised palaces of education, for having increased the means of the navy and the army, for having opened ports and constructed docks: in sum, for having given a strong push to industrial and material progress. But in this resplendent prodigality for all that glitters, in this lavish expenditure of millions in works of mere usefulness and doubtful value, he has not reserved a penny for improving the economic situation of the country, for lightening the people's heavy load of taxes, for speeding up metallic conversion of the currency, for seeking the general welfare with the reduction of misery (Ramírez 1958: 117).

The precise difference between "necessary" and "useful"— that is, necessary for "the general good" of whom, and the lightening of taxes on what part of "the people"—is clarified by two other editorials that appeared in other papers that same spring of 1889:

Thanks to the innumerable public works that at the present time are being built in the whole republic, wages have risen during the past year to an extent worthy of the note of our economists. The workers who previously were paid seventy cents a day without meals now receive ninety cents on the construction sites and they get food worth twenty-six cents a day (Ramírez 1958: 115, from *La Tribuna*, April 20, 1889).

The evil increases. To the general shortage of workers and the already high wages, the terrible state of the vineyards and the bad quality of goods in general, there are now added the higher wages with which the Clark Railroad Company is attracting the majority of the workers. Today, the winegrowers find themselves in the pressing need to pay the same wages as the Company in order to be able to complete the harvest in good time. It would be very useful if the Company would do its best to attract the rest of the labor supply it needs from other regions (Ramírez 1958: 116, from *Ecos de los Andes*, April 18, 1889).

This leaves little doubt about what was deemed "necessary" for whom and immediately "useful" for which part of the population and in the long run for the development of the economy as a whole as well.

President Balmaceda similarly was quite clear about who was who and which institutions represented what interest groups and forces: "The Congress is a hive of corruption. There is a group which works with foreign gold and which has corrupted many people. There is a rich man who has trapped the press and who has trapped the men. The Congressional forces have vacillated between vices and personal ambitions. The people have remained quiet and happy, but the oligarchy has corrupted everything" (Ramírez 1958: 201). The *Times* of London was no less informed or informative. "The Congressional Party is composed primarily of friends of England who represent the conservative and wealthy elements, as well as of the intelligentsia of the country" (*Times*, June 22, 1891, cited in Ramírez 1958: 197). A few months later after the opposition to him had mobilized, Balmaceda observed: "We are suffering an anti-democratic revolution begun by a centralized and small class which, because of its personal relations, believes itself called upon to be the governing and favorite group in the government" (Ramírez 1958: 201).

The ever ready imperialist and domestic alliance of commercial, financial, mining and agricultural interests was not long in mobilizing its forces against President Balmaceda. "When at the end of 1890 and at the beginning of 1891 some people made preparations for the war that had to come, Messrs. Augustin Edwards and Eduardo Matte remitted to Mr. Joaquín Edwards in Valparaíso the orders for payment of the sums which they contributed to the financing of the events to come" (*El Ferrocarril*, January 17, 1892, cited in Ramírez 1958: 193). "The expenses which were incurred in Europe during the early months of the revolution in the service of the cause of the Congress were covered by us with funds from the Bank of A. Edwards & Compañía" (Augusto Matte and Augustín Ross, *Memoria Presentada a la Junta de Gobierno*, cited in Ramírez 1958: 194). The Bank of A. Edwards y Compañía is still today the most powerful bank in Chile, owned by the family of that name, together with numerous commercial enterprises including Chile's most important newspaper, *El Mercurio*, through whose pages, as through its numerous other activities, the Edwards family now declares its utmost loyalty to American imperialism. They and their bank were still financing the most reactionary political interests and coalition in the epoch-making 1964 election.

In the last century, it was British (appropriated though not contributed) capital which was then predominant in Chile. The American Minister in Chile was not in doubt about this when he informed the State Department on March 17, 1891: "As a matter of special interest, I might mention the fact that the Revolution enjoys the total sympathy and in many cases active support of the English residents in Chile. . . . It is well known that many English firms have made generous contributions to the revolutionary fund. It is openly admitted by the leaders of the civil war that, among others, Mr. John T. North has contributed the sum of 100,000 pounds sterling" (Ramírez 1958: 195). This was undoubtedly a drop in the bucket to what the Nitrate King had already drained out of Chile. Is there any reason to doubt that his American descendants, who lend their names to copper mines and other firms which are rightfully Chile's, are today "investing" otherwise in their future?

The London *Times* summed up the situation on April 28, 1891:

It is obvious that already long before December the majority in the Congress and its allies had come to the conclusion that a break with the Executive and an attempt at revolution were inevitable. What with the influence of almost all the landowning families, the wealthy foreigners, and the Church, it is not surprising that they deemed the fall of the President easy. Moreover, they had obtained the support of the navy and thought they had that of large parts of the army. Therefore, they did not doubt that once the revolutionary flag were waved, it would be the signal for the rise of a popular movement in their favor all over the country. Part of these expectations have been realized. The major families, the big domestic and foreign capitalists, the mine owners of Tarapacá, the navy, and a small number of deserters from the army are with them. But the large majority of the people has shown no sign of revolt and nine tenths of the army remains loyal to the established government (Ramírez 1958: 191).

President Balmaceda's government was overthrown in a bloody civil war, and the President himself was forced into suicide. The foreign economic interests and the governments, American no less than British, which represented them had not been passive. The British Consul cabled the Foreign Office in 1891: "In exchange for the above mentioned help against the revolutionary forces, the government of the United States expects Chile to denounce its treaties with the European countries and to sign a commercial treaty with the United States" (Ramírez 1958: 229). In the same year, the Chilean correspondent of the London *Times* addressed himself to the Foreign Office (rather than to his newspaper) and expressed the fear that "it would be a shame if Chile, which on this Coast has until now been a bulwark against Blaine's interpretation of the Monroe Doctrine, were to get to be 'Blainian' in spite of us" (Ramírez 1958: 229). The then United States Secretary of State James G. Blaine had only recently, in 1889, convened the First Pan American Congress in Washington in order to set up the Pan American Union, whose building, not to mention policy, is still in the hands of its descendant of our day, the Organization of American States. But luckily for the British, if not necessarily for the Chileans, the British fears that Chile would become " 'Blainian' in spite of us" were still premature. That dream would take on the proportions of a nightmare only later.

The consequences of the foregoing events were summarized in 1912 by Encina in his *Nuestra Inferioriad Económica: Sus Causas, Sus Consequencias:*

The foreign merchant strangled our commercial initiative abroad; and at home he eliminated us from international trade. . . . The same thing has happened in our extractive industries. The foreigner owns two thirds of our nitrate production and continues to acquire our most valuable copper deposits. The merchant marine . . . has fallen into sad straits and continues to cede ground to foreign shipping even in the coastwise trade. The majority of the insurance companies that operate among us have their head offices abroad. The national banks have ceded and keep ceding ground to the branches of foreign banks. An ever growing share of the bonds of saving institutions are passing into the hands of foreigners who live abroad (Ramírez 1960: 257).

Ramírez summarizes the consequences in turn for the Chilean economy, singling out some of the features which in our day are called the marks of "underdevelopment": "(1) Unfavorable balance of payments; (2) difficulty in re-establishing the value of money and in getting off the paper standard; (3) slow capitalization of the country, which interfered with the growth of productive forces. . . . As a result of the foregoing, the economic potential of the Republic weakened and acute socio-economic problems arose which hit the small industrialists, small merchants, and especially the large mass of wage-earners very hard" (Ramírez 1960: 249-250). That is, the domestic metropolis-satellite and class polarization was accentuated. So too was the polarization between Chile and the imperialist metropolis. An index of that polarization is the value of the Chilean peso, which was worth 39⅝ pence in 1878, 16⅘ pence in 1900, and 8³¹⁄₃₂ pence in 1914. Today, of course, the peso is worth a small fraction of the penny (Ramírez 1960: 249).

Whether Chile was developing or underdeveloping was answered by ex-Minister Luis Aldunate writing in 1893-1894: "The country's economic forces have been weakened; the country has become poorer" (Ramírez 1960: 251).

4. The Consolidation of Underdevelopment

When we turn to inquire why Chile was underdeveloping and "getting poorer," the answer is supplied by our thesis on the effects of the polarization and surplus expropriation/appropriation contradictions of capitalism, as well as by the plain facts. The imperialist metropolis was expropriating Chile's economic surplus and appropriating it for its own development. Instead of developing the Chilean economy, Chilean nitrates served to develop European agriculture, which was then in the throes of technical advance thanks in part to Chilean fertilizer. After the First World War, Germany developed a cheaper synthetic substitute; and the already substantially exhausted Chilean nitrate mines were largely abandoned. The potential economic surplus or capital from the nitrates had been wasted and contributed to the development of others, never to be recovered by Chile. At the same time, after 1926 Chile ceased to be an exporter of wheat, which the metropolitan countries themselves and a few others like Argentina increasingly produced for their own consumption and for the world market. In the meantime, it is estimated that thanks to nitrates alone, between 1880 and 1913 Britain appropriated some £16 million of profits from Chilean-produced economic surplus, while Chileans and foreigners living in Chile retained no more than £2 million of the surplus produced by Chilean nitrate mines with what was almost entirely *Chilean* capital and labor (Ramírez 1960: 255-256). The Chilean economic surplus expropriated from Chileans and appropriated by the metropolis was not confined to nitrates. Increasingly, it also included that appropriated by Americans through copper. And we must not forget the surplus appropriated by the metropolis through its advantaged position in the market for Chilean wheat—and, of course, in the market of manufactured goods which Chile imported. Moreover, the metropolis appropriates a goodly part of its satellites' economic surplus through "services rendered." In 1913 alone, it is estimated, £2 million were remitted abroad by foreign companies working in Chile in industry, commerce, banking, insurance, telegraph, streetcars, etc. (Ramírez 1960: 256). (For an account of Latin American surplus expropriated through such services rendered in our day, see Frank 1965a.)

Some Chileans living at the turn of the century were well aware of much that was going on, how the metropolis was appropriating Chile's economic surplus. The National Party of Chile observed at its convention of 1910 that "the accumulation of capital, which forms the essential basis of all economic prosperity, is insignificant among us . . . [of the profits from the nitrates] almost two thirds leave the country without leaving the least trace here" (Ramírez 1960: 266). On January 24, 1899, the Chilean Senate heard one of its members declare: "For my part, I do not dream so much about that foreign capital which makes many dizzy; and although I am not ignorant of its importance, it leaves me in doubt. Does it come here for our benefit or for that of its owners? Does it come as a generous contribution to fertilize our lands and shops and to bring us wealth, or does it come as a sponge which absorbs the sweat of our work and leaves us only bread to sustain life?" (Ramírez 1960: 262).

Luis Aldunate, writing in 1894, had no doubts: foreign capital, "far from being useful and productive for us, exhausts us, weakens us, throws us for a loss without giving us anything or teaching us anything. . . . It is not wise but on the contrary very dangerous for us to let the interests of a foreign monopoly grow up into the clouds . . . it could consolidate its industrial domination by a further political domination; and then it would be too late to stop the logical consequences of our shortsightedness. . . . We are letting ourselves be colonized . . . without noticing that we are the victims of stale ideas and false mirages" (Ramírez 1960: 254). The ex-Minister needed no crystal ball to foresee the metropolis's economic, political, ideological and cultural domination of the satellite's life, as Chile has experienced it from his days to ours. The future was already contained in the capitalist metropolis-satellite structure of his day.

Metropolitan appropriation of the economic surplus of its satellites was not limited to Chile's international economic relations; it occurred domestically as well, most notably between the national metropolitan large landowners and merchants and their exploited provincial satellites. Large landowners, who should not be confused with "agriculture," occupied a particularly favored position within the national metropolis-satellite structure. They appropriated economic surplus from the workers of their own land as well as from the adjoining lands of small owners who were forced into an increasing satellite dependency on the larger ones. But the large landowners, who had substantial political control over the Congress, though much less independent political and economic control over the economy as a whole than is often assumed, used their political control as they still do today—to appropriate part of the economic surplus produced by the non-agricultural sectors as well. They paid virtually no taxes, though of course they benefited from public expenditures.

Rengifo, the Minister of the Treasury who initiated measures to protect and develop Chilean trade and industry, had already observed in 1835 that "if Chilean agriculture were to pay only a 10 percent tax on the income that the land produces, it would be enough to cover all the costs of the government" (Pinto 1962: 23). But Chilean landlords, then and now, have at no time paid such a tax. On the other hand, they benefited from irrigation works undertaken in the closing years of the nineteenth century which were financed by what little income Chile retained from its nitrate exports. They benefited from the inflationary consequences of the polarization of the metropolis-satellite structure on the international and national levels, in being owners of landed and other property whose prices and value rose more than did the cost of labor and of the things they bought. Most spectacularly, landowners appropriated economic surplus from the national economy through generous public credits which, thanks to the inflation, they were able to repay with money so devalued that they never paid any interest at all and often repaid only a small part of the principal. Borde and Góngora discuss this mechanism of surplus appropriation in detail:

In the second half of the nineteenth century, credit, which until then had been dependent on the good will of more or less usurious lenders, became organized and was extended. Henceforth, the landowners who wanted credit were able to choose between two alternatives: They could use their personal reputation at the banks . . . to obtain credit without collateral; or they could give their properties as collateral. Curiously, however, the collateral loans were channeled to almost the same recipients. The *Caja de Crédito Hipotecario* [real estate lending institution], which was founded in 1860 and which very rapidly became one of the most powerful lending institutions on the South American continent, was the docile instrument of the landowners for several decades. . . . In many instances, recourse to it impeded or limited the subdivision of properties. . . . But above all the credit allowed the big owners to extend their properties and to form others without handing over any money. . . . If credit was thus used by the landowners and thus came to be one of the main factors in the preservation of the agrarian structure, this was due to the continual devaluation of the Chilean peso which tended to transform the long-term loans into veritable gifts . . . there is nothing which permits us to write, as some authors have, that these landowners, for whom debt had come to be a means of enrichment, were the main instigators of the decline of the peso's value; but they certainly were its principal beneficiaries.

The real estate loans were not always, or more accurately, were not very often, invested in agriculture; thus, they help explain at one and the same time the enrichment of the landowners and the decapitalization of the land. The temptations of an already more diversified local economy, and even more so, the dividends paid by the big foreign capitalist corporations, not to mention luxury expenditure, attracted the money obtained thanks to real estate toward new investments . . . the real estate loans invested in sectors other than that of agriculture resulted in the incorporation of the land in an economy of speculation which could not but threaten stability (Borde 1956: 126-129).

These were hardly feudal landowners sitting on their isolated rural holdings! If we ask, then, with the London *Times*, why "almost all landowning families . . . the rich foreign and ecclesiastical elements . . . the big national and foreign capitalists, the mineowners" lend their political and economic support to the maintenance and further development/underdevelopment of the capitalist metropolis-satellite structure, the answer is not far to seek. Anibal Pinto analyzed it in his book on how Chile's economic development was frustrated; Max Nolff reviews it in his history of Chile's industry—though neither of them tries to place his answer in the context of the inescapable contradictions of capitalism which have determined Chile's fate —and Claudio Véliz discusses the answer in detail:

In the period between independence from Spain and the depression of 1929, the Chilean economy was dominated by three legs of the national economic table. In the first place, there were the mining exporters of the north of the country; then there were the agricultural and livestock exporters of the south; and finally there were the large import firms which were usually located in the center, in Santiago and Valparaíso, but which operated in the whole country. These three pressure groups were in entire agreement about what economic policy the country should follow. There was no other group which was able to challenge their economic, political and social power; and the three totally dominated national life, from the municipal councils to diplomatic representation, economic legislation and the horse races. . . .

The mining exporters of the north of the country were free traders. This policy was not fundamentally due to reasons of doctrine—though they also had these—but rather to the simple reason that these gentlemen were blessed with common sense. They exported copper, silver, nitrates, and other minerals of lesser importance to Europe and the United States, where they were paid in pounds sterling or dollars. With this money they bought equipment, machinery, manufactures, or high quality consumer goods at very low prices. It is hard to conceive of an altruism or a far-sighted or prophetic vision which would lead these exporters to pay export and import duties with a view to the possible industrialization of the country. Tied to the liberal ideas of the era, they would have argued that if it were really worthwhile developing Chilean industry, this should at least be efficient enough to compete with European industry which had to pay high freight charges before getting to our shores. . . .

The agricultural and livestock exporters of the South were also emphatically free traders. They sent their wheat and flour to Europe, California and Australia. They clothed their cowboys with ponchos of English flannel, rode in saddles made by the best harnessmakers of London, drank authentic champagne and lighted their mansions with Florentine lamps. At night they slept in beds made by excellent English cabinet-makers, between sheets of Irish linen and covered by blankets of English wool. Their silk shirts came from Italy and their wives' jewels from London, Paris and Rome. For these *hacendados* who were paid in pounds sterling, the idea of taxing the export of wheat or of imposing protective duties on imports was simply insanity. If Chile wanted its own industry to produce ponchos, very well, let it—as long as it could produce cloth of as good a quality and low a price as the English. Otherwise the proposal was a swindle. For these simple and undoubtedly solid reasons, the mining exporter of the North and the agricultural exporter of the South both put pressure on the government to keep an economic policy of free trade.

The big import houses of Valparaíso and Santiago also were free traders. Could anyone imagine an import firm supporting the establishment of high import duties to protect national industry!

Here, then, is the powerful coalition of strong interests, which dominated the economic policy of Chile during the past century and part of the present century. None of the three had the least interest in Chile and industrialization. They monopolized the three powers at all levels: economic power, political power and social prestige; and only in a few instances did they see the absolute control they exercised over the nation endangered.

The pressure groups which controlled the economic policy of the country were decidedly free traders; they were more free trader than Courcelle-Seneuil, the famous and respected leader of doctrinaire free trade; they were definitely more Catholic than the Pope. There were some theoretical reasons which explain their position in part; but these only supplemented the eloquent overlapping of the theories of the economic school and the economic interests of the pressure groups.

The attitudes of this vast traditional class, which held economic and political power and social prestige in its hands, supported its traditional policy: the free-tradism of the mining and agricultural exporters did not clash with the structure inherited from the colony; on the contrary, it reinforced it. The incentives of this Chilean pseudo-capitalist bourgeoisie were not related to moral motivation —like that stimulated by the Calvinist attitude—nor with political or economic dissatisfactions, like those of the capitalist bourgeoisie in England and the United States, nor even with the demand for a militarist and expansionist foreign policy, as happened in Japan, but exclusively with maintaining high incomes that permitted free access to the highest consumption levels of the civilized world, compatible with the political and social responsibilities which they thought they had (Véliz 1963: 237-242).

Max Nolff presents his quite similar interpretation in summary form as follows:

In conclusion, there begins the spontaneous development of a powerful coalition of interests, based on the export of raw materials and on the import and distribution of foreign manufactured goods. This "export-import coalition" is fundamentally concerned that Chilean development be oriented towards the outside; and, therefore, they were not interested in or benefited by any industrial development. This coalition of forces strengthened its position with the passing of time, and it can be said that it dominated Chilean society without opposition during the second half of the past century and until the crisis of 1930. The doctrine of liberalism, imported from Europe, thus found fertile ground in our country and grew vigorously. It constituted the theoretical basis to reinforce the interests of the controlling forces, inasmuch as it represented and expressed their

desires. But it is possible that the arguments in favor of free trade
and the international division of labor would not have taken such
firm root if the economic development of the first fifty years of our
independent life had not only been "toward the outside." The case
of the development of the United States during the last century,
directed "toward the inside" and based on strong industrial protection and an intelligent distribution of land and income, is decisive in
this respect. It is necessary to add another factor to the foregoing
situation which contributed to the fact that the industrial process
did not bloom before 1930: the high propensity to luxury consumption of the high income classes (Nolf 1962: 162-163).

Nonetheless, in view of similar debates about the role of
differing interest groups in our time, it is noteworthy that the
capitalist metropolis-satellite structure of Chile did not rest exclusively on the foregoing three legs. After noting the obvious
interests of the "commercial bourgeoisie," Ramírez observes,
"sectors of the industrial bourgeoisie had maintained a position
of open opposition to imperialism and had fought for the
industrialization of the country; but with the creation and
development of light industry . . . this sector lost a large part
of its point of view, and many of its members, with some
reservation, joined the pro-imperialist band" (Ramírez 1960:
286).

A more specific analysis of the events surrounding the
counter-revolution against Balmaceda and the sacrifice of his
national development program to foreign and domestic reaction
shows that the Augustín Edwards of the Bank of A. Edwards
y Compañía, who, as we saw, in 1890 financed the counter-
revolution against Balmaceda, was the very same Augustín
Edwards who, in 1883 as first President of the *Sociedad de
Fomento Fabril* (Society for Industrial Development), had
signed that society's inaugural Prospectus which began, "Chile
should and can be industrial." In 1964 the Edwards family, its
Bank of A. Edwards y Compañía, its light industries, and its
newspaper *El Mercurio* were unquestionably Chile's most influential partner with American imperialism in defeating the
popular candidate who still wanted to nationalize "Chilean"

nitrates and now copper too, and who could well have used the *Sociedad's* 1883 inaugural Prospectus as his economic platform for 1964.

The following commentaries place these and more recent events in perspective. In 1891 it was said, "There is in Chile a communist government, a despot or various despots who under the false name of Executive Power have overturned all the peace, all the prosperity and all the education of the preceeding eighty years" (London *Times*, April 28, 1891, cited in *Vistazo* 1964). And in 1964: "Everywhere . . . they have ended systematizing abuse, suppressing the most elementary rights, and imposing hunger, violence, and misery. The parties that support the candidate of the Popular Action Front have dedicated their existence to fighting for Marxism and consequently to promoting the dictatorship of the proletariat, the abolition of property, the persecution of religion and the suppression of the state of right" (*El Mercurio*, July 19, 1964, cited in *Vistazo* 1964).

Returning now to 1892, Eduardo Matte, a member of the banking family whom we already met two years earlier when, with Augustín Edwards, he was financing the beginnings of the counter-revolution against President Balmaceda, was able to say with satisfaction: "The owners of Chile are ourselves, the owners of capital and of the soil: the rest is masses who can be influenced and sold; they do not matter either as opinion or as prestige" (*El Pueblo*, March 19, 1892, cited in Ramírez 1958: 221). For those readers who may have been misled into thinking otherwise about our own day of *Mercurios* and Banco Edwards y Compañía in Latin America, or about Messrs. Eduardo Matte and Augustín Edwards' day in the nineteenth century, or about any times during the eighteenth, seventeenth, or sixteenth centuries, Eduardo Matte, like the insightful Viceroy of Peru in 1736 whose analysis we have adopted as epigraph, appropriately puts the emphasis where it rightfully belongs: capital before land.

I agree with Véliz and the others that the three, or with the industrialists four, Chilean interest groups did indeed hinder Chilean economic development and that they acted as they did for the reasons or interests assigned. But to advance our understanding of economic development and underdevelopment we must go on to ask the following two further questions: Why did the combined interests and actions of landowners, mineowners, merchants and industrialists not produce the same underdevelopment in the English, American and Japanese cases? Secondly, what would have had to exist or to be done so that the interests of these groups in Chile and other underdeveloped countries would induce them to *develop* instead of to underdevelop their countries? To the first question, Véliz, Pinto, and Nolff give no answer; to the second, an inadequate and inaccurate answer. My thesis, I hope, answers both questions more acceptably; or I hope that it at least offers a more fruitful approach to the problem of analysis they pose.

My thesis holds that the group interests which led to the continued underdevelopment of Chile and the economic development of some other countries were themselves created by the same economic structure which encompassed all these groups: the world capitalist system. This system was divided into central metropolis and peripheral satellites. It was in the nature of the structure of this system to produce interests leading to underdevelopment in the countries of the periphery, such as Chile, once they had already been effectively incorporated into the system as satellites. The most powerful interest groups of the Chilean metropolis were interested in policies producing underdevelopment at home because their metropolis was at the same time a satellite. The analogous interest groups of the world metropolis were not interested in policies producing such underdevelopment at home (though they did abroad), because their metropolis was not a satellite. Even the ruling group of Japan, which brought that country from nondevelopment in the Tokugawa period to development after the Meiji Restoration in 1868, did not face such irresistible underdevelopment-producing pressures—because Japan had not previously been a satellite.

The metropolis-satellite structure of world capitalism and the analogous structure it had produced within Chile led the most powerful interest groups of the Chilean metropolis to support an economic structure and policies which maintained the exploitation to which they themselves were subject by the world metropolis. The reason they accepted, and championed, their own exploitation is that they were thereby able to continue their exploitation of the people in the Chilean periphery, of whom the Chilean metropolis itself was an exploiter. Had the groups controlling Chile adopted policies producing national development instead of underdevelopment, as they did, they would, as the British knew, have exported less economic surplus to the world metropolis; but, as the newspapers of the Chilean metropolis noted, they would also have been able to appropriate less of the Chilean people's surplus for themselves. After all, the surplus they had to let the world metropolis appropriate and the surplus that they were able to appropriate through the export of raw materials and the import of manufactured products and the surplus that they were able to appropriate for themselves were economic surplus that the privileged groups of the Chilean and world metropolis were expropriating/appropriating from the vast majority of the Chilean people, who produced the raw materials but did not consume the imported manufactured goods—and who consumed less and less even of the raw materials and food they themselves produced. The same structure and forces are at work elsewhere and are analyzed for the nineteenth and twentieth centuries in the essay on "Capitalist Development and Underdevelopment in Brazil" below.

It was otherwise in the world metropolis. There the ruling groups did not have the opportunity and much less the habit of living well thanks to economic policies, such as the importation of industrial goods, which would serve to underdevelop their country while developing another. Even where, as in

Japan, there was more such opportunity, the power and privilege of the existing ruling group did not rest on a satellite relationship with the metropolis (though after the Second World War this was to come increasingly to pass there as well). On the contrary, in the world metropolis the interests of at least some groups—and in Britain, the United States, etc., of the ultimately decisive ones—lay in economic relationships with the rest of the world, and particularly with the satellites, which served to develop the metropolis and to generate the structural underdevelopment of the satellites.

Whatever role Calvinist or Catholic morality, "true bourgeois," "pseudo-bourgeois" or "feudal" mentality, "expansionist drive" or not, may have played in producing development and underdevelopment, such factors were not determinant or decisive but at best derivative and secondary. Véliz quite rightly rejects the "feudal" mentality or any other as being determinant in producing or maintaining the economic policies of the landed, mining and commercial "pseudo-bourgeoisie" of nineteenth-century Chile. The policies they pursued and imposed on the country were, as Véliz notes, the product rather of the economic circumstances of the times and of the economic structure that produced them. It is curious, therefore, that Veliz does refer to the morality, mentality and drive of the British and American "true bourgeoisie," since these factors played no more determinant a role in the metropolis than the truly secondary or insignificant one he assigns to them in the Chilean satellite. Both in the metropolis and the satellites, the economic policy pursued and the resulting economic development and underdevelopment were produced by the underlying economic structure and must be traced to that structure. Can we maintain that from the point of view of Chile the essentials of that structure, of the capitalist system, have changed since the end of the century? No. My view is that Chile remains part of the same capitalist system with the same fundamental contradictions of polarization and surplus appropriation. What has changed in the twentieth century is that Chile is now *more* underdeveloped, more dependent and becoming still more underdeveloped.

Anibal Pinto, Max Nolff and by inference Claudio Véliz do propose an answer to the second question: What would have to change so that Chile could stop underdeveloping and begin to develop instead? They associate the joint interests of the Chilean bourgeoisie and the metropolis to the fact that, once independent, Chile opted for development "toward the outside." They propose that Chile should now turn to development "toward the inside." Pinto now goes so far as to suggest that, contrary to his book cited above, Chilean underdevelopment is no longer due so much to Chile's relations with the outside world as it is to its domestic structure (Pinto 1964).

It will not be possible to examine this argument here in detail. Let it suffice to point out that both development toward the outside and development toward the inside are, admittedly, capitalist development. Nolff suggests, for instance, that it was development toward the inside which the United States experienced in the nineteenth century. Therefore, both implicitly and explicitly, these authors argue that reforms within the capitalist structure are sufficient to permit Chile to proceed to develop toward the inside and thereby to eliminate underdevelopment—reforms such as those proposed by the defeated 1964 Presidential candidate Salvador Allende and his Popular Action Front, whose economic plan for Chile was prepared under the direction of the same Max Nolff. My thesis maintains that this solution to the problem of development and underdevelopment is inadequate and unacceptable. Evidently, no such reforms can or are intended to eliminate Chile's status as a satellite in the world capitalist system or to transform Chile into a metropolitan member of that system; nor is directing development inward, in fact, calculated to eliminate Chile's satellite status by taking it out of the capitalist system altogether, making it neither metropolis nor satellite. Development toward the inside is directed only toward maintaining Chile's satellite status in the world capitalist system, reducing the amount and proportion of its economic surplus sent abroad, and channeling more of that surplus into internal industrial and economic development in ways not essentially different from those hoped for by Balmaceda. These writers suggest that this can be done through certain governmental reforms under a popularly elected government.

My thesis holds that it is the very satellite status of Chile and of other countries such as Brazil, for which this problem and the contemporary evidence is analyzed in greater detail below, and of course the metropolis-satellite structure of the world capitalist system itself, which do not permit the success or even the adoption of the measures proposed by Pinto, Nolff and Véliz. On the contrary, my thesis suggests—and the experience of Balmaceda and others who followed him in the twentieth century, as well as all available contemporary evidence including that of the 1964 election, confirms—that this is the road to still further satellite dependence on the metropolis and still deeper underdevelopment for the Chilean satellite. As we will see in my brief review of the twentieth century, Chile, underdeveloped at the time of Balmaceda, became more underdeveloped by the second administration of the first President Alessandri in the 1930's and still more underdeveloped and yet poorer in the first administration of the second President Alessandri which ended in 1964. What reason is there to believe that the same international and national capitalist metropolis-satellite structure, if it remains intact, will not make Chile still more underdeveloped and the large majority of its people poorer yet in years hence? If my thesis is well taken, there is no such hope.

H. THE TWENTIETH CENTURY:
BITTER HARVEST OF UNDERDEVELOPMENT

The contradictions of capitalist development/underdevelopment continued to deepen in twentieth-century Chile as they had in the past, generating development in the metropolis and underdevelopment in the periphery. As in the past, the economic surplus of Chile was expropriated/appropriated by the world metropolis, new centered in the United States; and the world capitalist metropolis-satellite structure became more polarized, widening the gap of power and income between the metropolis and Chile and also increasing the degree of structural dependence of Chile on the metropolis. Within Chile itself, polarization also increased; and continued appropriation of economic surplus by the favored groups of the national metropolis and some minor metropolises lowered the *absolute,* not to mention the relative, income of the majority of the people. These twentieth-century tendencies and events are reviewed here briefly, without trying to duplicate the more thorough analysis of recent Chilean experience already made by United Nations, Chilean and other students of contemporary Chile. Many of the same contemporary problems are analyzed in greater detail below for the case of Brazil.

1. The "External" Sector

It has been estimated that in the present century U.S. $9,000 million of economic surplus produced by and in Chile has been expropriated/appropriated by the world capitalist metropolis; this sum is equal to the value of the entire capital stock of Chile in 1964. It should not be supposed, of course, that in the absence of this foreign surplus appropriation Chile's current capital stock would be merely double its present size; had this Chilean-produced economic surplus been available for current investment and reinvestment in the Chilean economy over the course of the twentieth century, Chilean wealth and income would be very much higher today.

Since copper replaced nitrates as Chile's major export product, the copper mines, today 90 percent American-owned, are now the main source of the Chilean economic surplus which is appropriated by the capitalist metropolis. According to OCEPLAN (*Organización Central de Planificación*), the economic planning office of the Allende candidacy in the 1964 elections, the American-owned "Gran Minería" currently earns about 750 million escudos annually and remits about 355 million abroad. This amounts to about U.S. $250 million and $120 million respectively. Of total copper earnings, 47 percent is received by Americans, 35 percent by the Chilean government, 13 percent by the workers who produce the copper, and 5 percent by a few high-income employees. Trying to estimate this and other direct metropolitan appropriation of Chilean economic surplus by measuring Chile's corresponding foreign exchange loss, Novik and Farba, in their *La Potencialidad de Crecimiento de la Economía Chilena: Un Ensayo de Medición del Excedente Económico Potencial*, estimate this loss of foreign exchange surplus in 1960 at about U.S. $108 million or $190 million, depending on the basis of measurement used (Novik 1963: 16-24). These sums represent respectively 20 percent and 34 percent of Chile's total imports of that year. At the time of writing, the press reports that the price differential per pound between the monopolistically controlled copper price on the fictitious New York market, which the American companies use to calculate Chile's copper royalties, and the copper price on the London copper exchange is $0.20. At current rates of production and royalties, each cent of this price difference represents a difference of U.S. $9 million in earnings for Chile.

The magnitude of Chile's loss of economic surplus due to direct foreign appropriation may also be judged in the following terms: Current remittances abroad are U.S. $150 million and payments on foreign debt another $150 million more, totaling $300 million annually; this sum may be compared with the $350 million of Chile's balance of payments deficit or with the $450 million of foreign exchange earnings from its goods exports. Chile's debt in foreign exchange (foreign debt plus that part of domestic debt which must be paid in dollars), which was contracted for reasons noted below, totals $2,430 million. Assuming an interest rate of 4 percent annually, repayment scheduled over twenty years and no incurring of new debt, financing this debt would require payments of $300 million yearly, or double the already impossibly high current payments. Inevitably, however, Chile will have to contract additional foreign debts to implement its current and proposed economic policies within the contemporary capitalist structure (OCEPLAN 1964: 31-33).

The metropolitan appropriation of Chilean economic surplus, which is at once cause and effect of the metropolis-satellite relationship, is but one aspect of metropolitan domination and Chilean dependency. For the generation of structural under-development in Chile, ultimately more important than its loss of actual surplus to the metropolis is Chile's growing inability to produce investible economic surplus up to its potential, due to the capitalist metropolis-satellite structure and its growing dependency within it. Chile's position with respect to the metropolis became increasingly disadvantaged with the dis-appearance, after 1926, of its wheat exports (a sector of its economy in which Chile at least owned the productive facilities, even if it did not control the market or much of the merchan-dising) and the sharp reduction of its nitrate exports (a sector in which, while it did not own much of the productive facilities, Chile at least had a certain degree of monopoly on the world market). In the twentieth century, these export products have been increasingly replaced by copper, a product or sector in which Chile does not own the productive facilities, does not control the marketing, and accounts for a no longer command-ing and ever smaller share of world production. At the same time, except for brief wartime reversals, Chile, like most other underdeveloped countries, has suffered from a continuous and marked decline in its terms of trade.

Chile's economy is increasingly dependent on and vulnerable to the interests and vagaries of the metropolitan economy. Foreign metropolitan interests, through their ownership and control of Chile's copper export sector, now exercise a greater degree of economic, not to speak of political, influence on

Chile than did their predecessors. Chile's economy and its potential for economic development suffer increasingly from the contradictory development of the capitalist economy, interdependent with and dependent on the metropolitan-directed world capitalist economy. Having been a producer of capital equipment in the nineteenth century, Chile now has to import 90 percent of its investment in plant and equipment. Provided by nature with ample coal, petroleum and hydraulic resources, Chile nonetheless has to import fuels. Having been a major exporter of wheat and livestock products in the past, Chile is now highly dependent on food imports from the metropolis. In 1950-1954, Chile had to import an annual average of U.S. $90 million of food products, composed mainly of wheat, meat and milk products, that once were and still could be produced in Chile itself. By 1960-1963 the annual average of food imports had risen to $120 million (OCEPLAN 1964: 54). This sum should be compared with the $450 million of foreign exchange earnings from all Chilean goods exports. At the present rate of increase, Chile's food import needs will reach about $200 million annually in 1970, a rate of increase, which as in the past, is considerably greater than that of Chile's export earnings. This means that an ever greater proportion of Chile's already inadequate foreign exchange earnings would be devoted to the import of foodstuffs.

Chile's twentieth-century experience dramatically shows the development-inhibiting and underdevelopment-generating consequences of its participation in the metropolis-satellite structure of the world capitalist system. Among the countries most heavily hit by the depression of the 1930's, Chile's import capacity declined from an index of 138.5 in 1928 to an index of 26.5 in 1932. Despite its later partial recovery and despite all of Chile's serious efforts at industrial production since then, the per capita availability of goods in 1950 still remained below its 1925 level (Johnson 1964). Since that time, the per capita availability of goods has declined still further; and the real income of the large mass of low income receivers has fallen.

These are not the Chilean consequences of an inadequate recovery of the capitalist economy on a world level. On the contrary, as our review of Chilean economic history shows, it has always been the very recovery of the metropolis which has halted the development of the Chilean and other satellites. Stimulated by the depression, and by war-induced declines of industrial imports, Chilean manufacturing output increased 80 percent between 1940 and 1948, but only 50 percent between 1948 and 1960. That is, in the earlier eight-year period the non-cumulative rate of annual growth of industrial production was 10 percent, and in the twelve-year period after the metropolitan recovery, the growth rate of Chilean manufacturing declined to 4 percent. Since that time, the growth rate has declined to around zero and sometimes less.

There is an increasing inability of both the public and the private sector to generate economic development or even to stem the tide of deepening underdevelopment. The large share of the government's income which depends on revenues from copper exports renders the government budget, and therewith the government's ability to finance capital and current expenditures, highly vulnerable to the metropolitan-controlled production of copper in Chile, the sale of copper abroad, and metropolitan monopolistic manipulation of both. Any cyclical or secular decline in Chile's copper earnings puts a severe strain on the government budget and forces the government to rely on foreign and/or domestic debt financing, both of them inflationary, in a vain attempt to maintain its capital and/or current expenditures. Recourse to such inflationary and especially foreign debt financing makes Chile still more dependent on the metropolis. As the political price of this dependency, the metropolis obliges Chile to keep following and even to initiate new domestic political and economic policies which hinder Chile's development capacity, and deepen its structural underdevelopment and dependence still further. Chile's increasing inability to produce for its own needs, due to the capitalist metropolis-satellite contradictions, has already resulted in total dependence of the Chilean government's capital budget on external financing and is rapidly leading to the dependence of an ever greater proportion of its current expenditures budget on external financing as well. This alarming circumstance and trend of course lends additional significance to Chile's annual loss of U.S. $300 million of economic surplus to the metropolis (half of it on copper account) while the current balance of payments deficit is $350 million.

The private sector—industrial, commercial, and in some respects also agricultural—is also increasingly victimized by Chile's satellite status; at least its dependence and underdevelopment are taking increasingly alarming modern forms. Today, Chile's industry is "being ruined by what makes others thrive" as far as the growth rate of its output is concerned. And 90 percent of Chile's investment in plant and equipment is now composed of imports. Equipment, fuel and foodstuffs account for nearly all of Chile's current imports of goods. This implies that, except for foodstuffs, Chile's consumer goods are almost entirely nationally produced; and this is in fact the case. Superficial observation might deduce that this reflects a healthy development of import substitution in at least the light and medium industry consumer goods sector. The facts are otherwise: the production and in many ways even the financing and merchandising of industrial consumer goods in Chile and other undeveloped countries are also increasingly dominated by and dependent on the metropolis. The mechanics and organization of this trend receive particular attention in my analysis of Brazil below and in my "Brazil: Exploitation or Aid?" *The Nation,* November 16, 1963, and in my "Notes On the Mechanisms of Imperialism; The Case of Brazil," *Monthly Review,* September 1964. Here it must suffice to suggest that through affiliates of metropolitan corporations, through joint metropolitan-Chilean enterprise, through licensing arrangements, through trade marks and patents, through metropolitan owned or controlled advertising agencies, and through a host of other institutional arrangements, much of the Chilean con-sumer goods industry is also coming to have an ever increasing satellite dependency on the metropolis. This direct satellization of the consumer goods industry, in turn, increases the satellite dependency of the Chilean economy as a whole, by rendering it dependent on the metropolis, not only for the supply of its capital goods and other components of its industrial production, but even for the selection of those imports whose specification is already structured into the Chilean economy by metropolitan design of the final product and its productive process. And at the same time, the metropolis appropriates Chilean-produced economic surplus under the title of royalties, services and the like. In Latin America as a whole, the expenditure for these foreign "services" amounts to 61 percent of its entire foreign exchange earnings (Frank 1965a).

OCEPLAN concludes in this respect:

Industry has not grown enough to play a really active part in import substitution. . . . Between 1954 and 1963, for example, in-dustrial imports increased from 226.2 to 477.1 million dollars, that is, they more than doubled (an increase of 110 percent), while domestic industrial production increased less than 50 percent. We cannot, therefore, attribute the slow industrial growth exclusively to limita-tions of the domestic market; since during this period there was an increase in domestic demand which had to be filled by greater im-ports. . . . Furthermore, this lack of response appeared not only in the supply of capital goods—whose imports rose more than 120 percent—but also in the supply of consumer goods, for which the rise of imports was on the order of 85 percent. Given these ten-dencies, the Chilean economy has become not less but rather more vulnerable with respect to the external sector [the original says "in-ternal sector," which must be a typographical error]. Today, not only the supply of a series of essential consumption products depends on imports, but also the supply of raw materials and intermediary prod-ucts which are necessary to maintain the output of industry itself, as well as of the greater part of the capital goods that are necessary to increase our productive capacity in all sectors of the economy (OCEPLAN 1964: 73).

2. The "Domestic" Sector

The contradiction of the capitalist metropolis-satellite structure and surplus expropriation/appropriation has dominated and determined Chile's national or domestic twentieth-century experience as well. Polarization increases; the national metropolis's economic development is ever more structurally limited or underdeveloped; and the domestic periphery is ever more hopelessly structurally underdeveloped. The capitalist appropriation of satellite surplus by the metropolis and the metropolis-satellite structure in general characterize all of Chile's domestic economic relations no less than they do its foreign relations. In consequence, the distribution of income is growing increasingly unequal, and the absolute income of the majority of Chile's people is declining.

The functional, personal and regional distribution of income attests to the growing polarization of the Chilean economy and society. About 400,000 owners, managers and their associates and families, less than 5 percent of the total population, receive these percentages of income in the following sectors of the economy: Large-scale agriculture (about 2,000 families), 66 percent; urban real estate, 66 percent; large-scale monopolized industry (accounting for 25 percent of industrial output), 80 percent; small industry, 67 percent; construction, 75 percent; large commerce and finance, 75 percent; small scale, mostly retail, trade, 33 percent. In proportion to their numbers, the largest part of the remainder goes to employees; and the rest is left for the workers who produce this economic surplus (OCEPLAN 1964: II, 6-9).

As a result of the appropriation of surplus in these and other sectors of the Chilean economy, the personal distribution of income in rounded percentages is as follows: Five percent of the population, composed mainly of urban owners of capital, receives 40 percent of national income. Twenty percent of the population, mainly urban employees, receives 40 percent of national income. Fifty percent of the population, mainly urban workers in industry and trade, receives 20 percent of national income. Thirty percent of the population, mainly rural agricultural workers, receives 5 percent of national income. That is, the one quarter relatively unproductive part of the population receives three quarters of the national income. (The exact, non-rounded, figures are as follows: 4.7 percent of population, 39.3 percent of income; 18.6 percent of population, 37.7 percent of income; 47.7 percent of population, 18.9 percent of income; and 29 percent, 4.1 percent of income; reported in OCEPLAN 1964: II, 10).

Data on the regional (metropolis-satellite) distribution of income are not available for Chile, but OCEPLAN observes:

The enormous inequality of income among socio-economic sectors is supplemented by another aspect which official statistics have so far carefully hushed up: that of the distribution of income among the various regions of the country. Notwithstanding the lack of specific information, there can be no doubt that the disparities in this sense are also very large. One of the determinant factors in this disparity is the excessive concentration of industrial development; but it is not the only one, since at the same time there are operative a number of channels through which the income generated in the provinces by the work of its inhabitants is transferred elsewhere. Of the production generated in the Northern Zone, a large part is transferred abroad in the form of profits of the large foreign firms and another part is transferred to the central government through direct taxation; only a small part remains for the benefit of the region. In the same way, the effort spent in the agricultural provinces is less taken advantage of by the local producer, who receives a fraction of the price at which his products are sold to the final consumer, than it is by the big middleman who operates out of the major urban centers; moreover, the income of the large landowner does not remain in the region, but is spent mostly in the metropolis or abroad. All of the direct and indirect taxation amounts to a flow of income from the provinces to the central government, and only part of it returns to the region in the form of the services of public investment (OCEPLAN 1964: 13).

The expropriation/appropriation of economic surplus by the Chilean national and some provincial metropolises from their peripheral satellites is beyond question. On the basis of an annual Chilean national income in 1960-1961 of about 3,700 million escudos, then equivalent to about U.S. $3,700 million, Novik and Farba estimate the distribution, unemployment, industrial and agricultural production, and foreign exchange surplus loss as follows: The "distributional" appropriation of economic surplus, estimated on the basis of income received in excess of the annual income of middle income receivers, was 1,380 million escudos in 1961; estimated on the basis of the excess over lower income receivers, it was 1,870 million in 1961 escudos. This loss of potentially investible economic surplus represents 37 percent and 50 percent of total national income respectively. The potential economic surplus lost due to unemployment is estimated at 510 million 1961 escudos. Potential economic surplus lost due to industrial production below capacity is estimated at 295 million or 238 million 1960 escudos, depending on the estimating procedure used, or 6 percent and 5 percent of industrial production respectively; this seems to the present writer a very low estimate. Potential economic surplus lost due to agricultural production below potential is 94 million 1960 escudos. The foreign exchange surplus of U.S. $108 or $190 million was already cited above (Novik 1964: 16-24). Since these estimates of potential economic surplus lost to the Chilean economy necessarily overlap somewhat (especially as between the first and the other three), it would not be legitimate merely to add them up in an attempt to estimate the total loss of Chilean investible economic surplus, due to monopoly and expropriation. Nonetheless, to get an idea of the orders of magnitude involved, it is well to note that while the first surplus alone, due to maldistribution of income, ranges between 37 percent and 50 percent of national income, the sum of the unemployment, production and foreign exchange surpluses comes to roughly another 30 percent of Chile's total national income.

Still more serious and telling, perhaps, than this contemporary appropriation and loss of economic surplus through monopoly and excess consumption is the unmistakable trend throughout the twentieth century, which aggravates this concentration of income and polarizes the domestic metropolis-satellite structure still further. Though precise data are, not surprisingly, unavailable, serious Chilean observers have little doubt that food consumption among the rural and urban low income groups has declined since the nineteenth century. Between 1940 and 1952, the income of wage earners appears to have declined, in view of the fact that the 28 percent decline of their share of national income far exceeds the 10 percent decline of their numbers relative to the labor force (Johnson 1964: 55). Between 1953 and 1959, in turn, while employers' share of the national income rose from 43 percent to 49 percent, the middle income receivers' share declined from 26 percent to 25 percent, and the workers' share continued to decline from 30 percent to 25 percent (Pinto 1964: 18). Furthermore, the purchasing power in terms of 1950 pesos of the legal minimum wage (which equals or exceeds the income earned by about half of Chile's income earners) fell from 3,958 pesos in 1954 to 3,098 pesos in 1961. At the same time, the average real salaries of public employees fell from an index of 122 in 1955 to an index of 82 in 1961. (Pinto 1964: 16-17).

There can be little doubt that inflation and other policies, which sacrifice the interests of wage and salary earners to those of property owners who expropriate ever more of the producers' surplus value (not to mention increasingly regressive taxes, whose impact is not even included in the above measures), result in the steady decline in the absolute income of the low income receivers—that is, of the majority of the population. This real decline in the income of the poor should not be confused with the often cited but fictitious increase measured in terms of a statistical average of per capita income. This becomes clear if we note that, while the widely cited per capita income rose from an index of 100 to an index of 118, the ratio of legal minimum wage to per capita income (which reflects the poor majority's income much more accurately, even if it, too, overstates it) declined from an index of 100 to an index of 69 (Pinto 1964: 17).

The truly alarming polarization of income and the expropriation/appropriation of surplus reviewed above is at once effect and cause of the capitalist metropolis-satellite structure and its contradictions in Chile. Beyond the more obvious urban-rural polarization, this metropolis-satellite structure also characterizes through and through the urban and rural sectors taken separately. I confine myself here to some brief observations.

A particularly noteworthy feature of the contemporary Chilean economy, especially its urban sector, is its distribution of employment among sectors. All agricultural, mining and industrial activities (the primary and secondary sectors) together account for only 40 percent of the total employed labor force. The remaining 60 percent of the labor force in the economy as a whole, and probably a greater percentage of its urban sector, must be attributed to the tertiary service sector. Far from being a mark of development, as the reading of Sir William Petty and Colin Clark might once have led us to believe, this structure and distribution are a reflection of Chile's structural underdevelopment: 60 percent of the employed, not to speak of the unemployed and underemployed, "work" in activities that do not produce goods—in a society that obviously in high degree lacks goods.

A large share of employment (though of course not of income) in the non-governmental part of the tertiary sector may be attributed to the occasionally employed and semi-self-employed urban "penny capitalists" (working with even less capital than is available to the Guatemalan peasants to whom Sol Tax first applied this term). It is they, as well as some of the workers of the secondary sector, particularly those in construction, who compose the bulk of the floating urban population of the *callampa* shanty towns and the less notorious but not necessarily less inadequate *conventillo* run-down central slum dwellings. This urban floating population, and its rural counterpart which also supplies its migrants, is often said to be unintegrated in or marginal to the economy or society. Far from being unintegrated, however, it is fully incorporated into, and indeed is the necessary product of, an underdeveloped capitalist metropolis-satellite economy whose extreme monopoly structure characterizes its labor market no less than its product market. The existence of these economic roles in an economy such as that of Chile is the very result of the contradictions and exploitative structure of the capitalist system. These poor are more exploited as consumers than anyone else by the major and minor mercantile metropolises of which they are satellites: thus the low-quality food, housing, and other consumer goods cost more in the places to which they have access than do corresponding high-quality wares bought by middle and high income buyers in other areas. When they do manage to get jobs that permit them to produce something, they are of course also exploited to a higher degree as producers than any other members of the population. Both as consumers and as would-be producers these supposedly "marginal" or "unintegrated" parts of the population thus face a higher degree of exploitative monopoly than anyone else; and having a lower elasticity of demand as buyers and lower elasticity of supply as sellers, they are the most exploited. (This matter is discussed in greater detail in Frank 1966.)

The other face of this same metropolis-satellite capitalist structure is the highly monopolistic organization of trade and manufacturing itself. An inordinately large share of income, expropriated both from the producer and the consumer, is appropriated by the middleman. "For every 1000 pesos spent on food, 400 are paid for merchandising expenditures which do not benefit the producer but go to the intermediaries, of whom the high income merchants receive half. This situation is particularly serious for the people of moderate incomes who live in the big urban areas: The merchandising costs of the food bought by a worker's family absorb 26 percent of its income" (OCEPLAN 1964: II, 17). That is, the metropolis-satellite relationship characterizes the entire trade sector, the many small merchants exploiting the consumer, and being exploited in turn by the fewer medium-sized merchants above them who in turn are exploited by the few largest commercial firms which end up with half of the surplus appropriated throughout the entire exploitative pyramid.

Manufacturing industry suffers from essentially the same structure and contradictions. Production (as well as importation) of industrial commodities is essentially restricted to supplying the high income market. Because of this market restriction, among others, production is limited mainly to consumer goods. Capital equipment accounts for only 2.7 percent of Chilean industrial production. Capacity is typically under-utilized, as was shown in times of war and during the 1930's depression when manufacturing output from existing productive facilities increased sharply and rapidly. Our familiar metropolis-satellite constellation is constantly reproduced in the industrial sector by the existence or establishment of a few large, modern, efficient plants and/or firms surrounded by a whole host of small, antiquated, inefficient shops and/or firms whose dependency on the few large ones for markets, materials, credit, distribution, etc. renders the small ones satellites of the large ones.

It might be thought that this pattern reflects the "natural" growth of large modern firms or plants which are gradually but not yet completely out-competing and replacing the small antiquated shops. The fact is, however, that the growth of manufacturing output over time, when there is any, is accounted for in significantly greater part by *newly* established "antiquated" small shops with uncertain life spans than it is by new "modern" plants and firms. (In this connection see, for instance, United Nations, Economic Commission for Latin America, *Social Development in Latin America in the Post War Years*, 1962, 59-60, Spanish edition.) These large firms, especially foreign ones which enjoy added financial, technological, commercial, political, and other advantages, appropriate the economic surplus produced in the smaller satellite shops and firms no less than do other metropolises from their satellites.

The same structure and contradictions appear throughout the rural agricultural and commercial sector. The well-known failure of agriculture to supply needed food supplies, dramatized in the case of Chile by the switch from exporting to importing basic foodstuffs, is due not so much to the lack of capitalist or market penetration of a supposedly archaic or feudal countryside as it is to agriculture's incorporation in the monopolistic metropolis-satellite structure of the national and world capitalist system. This integration of agriculture into the economy as a whole is—and since the sixteenth century has been—not only one of market integration through sale and purchase. It also takes the form of ties of ownership and control with all the remaining sectors of the economy. In the absence of similar specific data for Chile (though the general picture may be gleaned from Ricardo Lagos's *La Concentración del Poder Económico en Chile*), I refer to some telling data from Peru which is often regarded as even more "feudal" than Chile: Of the 45 family and corporate entities on the Board of Directors of that country's *Sociedad Nacional de Agricultura*, 56 percent are important stockholders in banks and financial companies, 53 percent own stock in insurance companies, 75 percent are owners of companies engaged in urban construction or real estate, 56 percent have investments in commercial firms, and 64 percent are important stockholders in one or more petroleum companies (Malpica 1963: 224).

I believe that detailed examination of the monopolistic metropolis-satellite structure of the economy and of agriculture within it would demonstrate, as I suggest below in my study of Brazilian agriculture, that the scarcity of food in terms of needs, if not in terms of effective demand, can and should be traced in the main to productive and commercial response precisely in this monopolistic market structure. Borde and Góngora's observations in the Puange Valley suggest that expansion and contraction of agricultural production and switches from one crop or livestock product to another over time have indeed been remarkably responsive to market incentives (Borde 1956). If agricultural production does not expand as we should like it to, then this is because those in control of resources potentially usable for greater agricultural production channel them into other uses. They do so not because they live outside the capitalist market and/or don't care much about it, but, on the contrary, because their integration in the market bids them do so. If 40 percent of the economic surplus produced in agriculture is appropriated by monopolized commercialization; if holding land is useful for speculation, for access to credit, for evasion of taxes, for access to supplies of agricultural commodities or to means of limiting their supply in order to profit from their distribution through monopolized trade channels; if capital earns considerably more in urban real estate, commerce, finance and even industry—then there should be little wonder that those in a position to increase or decrease agricultural output do not increase it very rapidly. Instead, the landowners in Chile, like those of the Board of Directors of the Peruvian *Sociedad Nacional de Agricultura*, will shift their capital from where it earns less to where it earns more and/or where they can more readily consume it. As happened throughout the centuries since the sixteenth, when agriculture is relatively bad business, as it is now, these capitalists insofar as possible use their landholdings not to help the hungry by producing more food but to help themselves to do better business in another temporarily more profitable sector of the economy.

Though the evidence is still scanty and inadequately studied, it appears that the small-satellite, enterprising *inquilino*, who existed in the seventeenth century and who was converted into tenant labor and/or hired labor in the eighteenth and nineteenth centuries under the pressure of the expansion of agricultural production, is reappearing in some places in the twentieth century. He reappears today running a small-scale agricultural enterprise in the shadow of the hacienda whose land he uses and fulfills his work obligations to the landowner by means of another man's labor hired by himself as wage labor. (In this connection see Baraona, 1960). My hypothesis is that this phenomenon should be traced to the renewed decline in the relative profitability of agricultural production after its two centuries of relatively better times. This hypothesis seems to be confirmed in part by the appearance of the *inquilino* enterprise more frequently on lands which for geographical, topological or economic reasons are less profitable than other lands over whose use its owners maintain more direct control. The appearance at this level of a micrometropolis squeezed in between the landowners and the agricultural workers, like the proliferation of self-employed ambulatory peddlers and other penny capitalists in the cities, should thus not be taken as a sign of an economic upswing which brings better business prospects. On the contrary, it would seem to be the result of an economic downswing. Moreover, the "rise" of these small entrepreneurs also does not signify that the degree of economic and social polarization in the society is now on the decline. Rather, both the economic opportunity and necessity reflected by the insertion of this micrometropolis-satellite institution in the metropolis-satellite structure of the economy as a whole reflect in turn the still greater poverty of the pool of landless laborers, from which the small entrepreneurs in turn hire labor, and the declining fortunes of the medium-scale landowners and merchant as well as of the rural small town. They reflect the growing polarization of twentieth-century Chilean and world capitalist economy and society.

I. CONCLUSIONS AND IMPLICATIONS

Our review of Chilean history has shown that it was capitalism, with its internal contradictions itself which generated the underdevelopment of Chile and determined its forms; that this remains as true today as it was in the past; that Chile's underdevelopment cannot be attributed to the supposed partial survival of a feudal structure, which never existed there in whole or in part. Domestic power has always been in the hands of a bourgeoisie which was and is intimately tied to foreign interests, was and is primarily commercial, and did and does appropriate economic surplus from all of the important sectors of the economy. Thus power in Chile has never rested directly and primarily on the ownership of land, though the monopoly ownership or control of land and its links with other sectors of the economy of course have made important contributions to the bourgeoisie's appropriation of economic surplus and control of political power. The Chilean state and its institutions, democratic or otherwise, have always been part and parcel of the capitalist system in Chile and in the world and an instrument of the bourgeoisie. We have observed, and this is crucial to the understanding of Chile and all other underdeveloped countries, that both the "national bourgeoisie" and its "national state" have always been and are ever more integral parts of a world-wide capitalist system in which they are a fundamentally satellite or "underdeveloped" bourgeoisie and state. Thus, both "national" satellite bourgeoisie and state became and are dependent on the world capitalist metropolis, whose instrument in the exploitation of the periphery they necessarily have been and remain.

This reality of capitalism—of its contradictions, development and underdevelopment—impose on us important tasks of scientific theory and research, and of political strategy and tactics. We must formulate scientific theory capable of encompassing and explaining the nature, contradictions, historical development and underdevelopment of this world-wide process and system as a whole; and we must pursue research which is designed and adequate for formulating such theory. It has been my intention in this and the accompanying essays to make whatever contribution I can to the pursuit of this goal. Important institutional and other changes and transformations through the course of history have all been *within* this capitalist structure of Chile and most of the world, and they have served to exaggerate and fortify the capitalist structural contradictions. If I have de-emphasized these institutional changes in this essay, it has been to call attention to the essential structural continuity of capitalism and its effects throughout Chile's history. The historical transformations of the institutions and reality of Chile and of other underdeveloped countries, as well as their failure to change in hoped-for forms and directions, can be adequately understood only against the background of this continuity, in the context of this capitalist contradiction of continuity in change. (Without denying this continuity, I have given greater attention to the transformation of the capitalist system in the accompanying essay on Brazil.)

The course of history in Chile and the world has been marked by a secular trend of polarization, both internationally and nationally; and the degree of interdependence—the extent of satellite dependence—has concomitantly increased. The gap between the metropolis and Chile in power, wealth and income, and perhaps most important in the political, economic and technological capacity for economic development, has markedly increased over time and continues to do so. At the same time, Chile, its metropolis and its bourgeoisie have become politically, economically and technologically ever more dependent on the metropolis. Not only its commerce, agriculture and mining, as in the past, but now also Chile's industry is being economically, technologically and institutionally integrated in the world capitalist metropolis, of which all become ever more dependent satellite sectors. If a relatively independent "national" industrial bourgeoisie with Chilean nationalist interests might have arisen in the past (though it is difficult to maintain that it ever did), such an eventuality is ever more unlikely and impossible as long as Chilean industry and industrialists continue to become increasingly dependent on the world capitalist metropolis for finance, commercialization, capital goods, technology, design, patents, trade marks, licenses —in short, practically everything connected with light and/or foreign-assembly "industrial" production.

The domestic underdevelopment and polarization in Chile might seem to be mitigated or even reversed by the rise of the middle classes. On the contrary, the "new" middle classes and the tertiary service sector on which they mostly subsist are an expression and further cause of Chilean structural underdevelopment and polarization. The urbanization and structural transformation of the Chilean economy, society and polity that the middle classes or social mobility or "democratization" represent, are associated with increasing polarization between the Santiago-Valparaíso-Concepción urban metropolises and their rural and small town peripheral satellites, as well as with economic and income polarization both in the city and in the country. The relative and absolute number of Chileans who are essentially unproductive is increasing; and the relative and absolute income of the poorest members of the society, both productive and unproductive, is decreasing over time. With the rise of the middle classes, the *number* of those appropriating economic surplus may be increasing; but the residual income of the expropriated producers is decreasing; and the capitalist economic structure's capacity and potential for generating industrial and economic development in Chile is declining: Chile is becoming ever more structurally underdeveloped.

The political tasks faced by those who would free Chile and her sister countries from their underdevelopment are no less urgent and profound than are the scientific ones; nor are they unrelated to each other. In Chile and structurally similar countries there can be no hope of a bourgeoisie leading the economy and people out of underdevelopment. There should be no talk of a "progressive national bourgeoisie" wresting the state from a backward, primarily landed, feudal obligarchy. The progressive potential and capacity of the Chilean bourgeoisie and its state are strictly limited, not by any "non-capitalist" or "pre-capitalist" institutions or structure in their provincial hinterland, but by the very capitalist structure imposed on it by its own world capitalist metropolis and by its own thus created and vested interest in maintaining this capitalist structure on the world, national, provincial and local level in alliance with other bourgeois vested interest groups. The expropriation of its economic surplus and the other limitations to its development, which the imperialist metropolis imposes on the Chilean bourgeoisie, creates contradictions between it and that metropolis, just as the Chilean metropolitan bourgeoisie creates contradictions between itself and the provisional bourgeois groups which it exploits in turn. These contradictions may lead the most exploited and weakest interest groups of the Chilean bourgeoisie to pursue policies which at one time or another and to some extent confront the interests of those who exploit both them and the people. But these minor contradictions reflect each party's need and desire to keep a greater share of the expropriated spoils generated by the major contradictions of the exploitative capitalist under-development-generating system. The resolution of these minor contradictions and the action of these bourgeois groups cannot therefore constitute either an economically or a politically decisive step toward the elimination of underdevelopment and the structure that produces it. The bourgeoisie and all its parts are "thriving on what ruins others" and must strive to maintain this "paradox of trade and contradiction of riches."

The contradictory development of capitalism and the consequent underdevelopment of Chile impose on the people themselves both the necessity and the possibility of liberating its economy from underdevelopment and of providing for the development of its people. The necessity arises out of the structure and development of the world and national capitalist system which increasingly deepens the underdevelopment of Chile, sinks the majority of its people into ever greater poverty, and at the same time renders its bourgeoisie less and less capable of reversing the centuries-long development of underdevelopment. The process transcends Chile and is world-wide. The contradictions deepen. The possibility emerges from the same structure and process.

Suffering from the same necessity and enjoying the same possibility created by the same world capitalist development in other underdeveloped countries, the people of Chile in alliance with these other peoples must and will take the initiative and leadership in destroying the system whose development has caused and still generates their underdevelopment. In a third of the world the initiative has already been taken. The withdrawal of the socialist countries from the capitalist system and its exploitative market further deepened the contradictions within that system and made itself felt in Chile as everywhere else. Abandonment of bourgeois ideology and theory, of reformist and revisionist policy and opportunism, and adoption of revolutionary Marxist strategy and tactics in the popular leadership of Chile, the underdeveloped countries, the socialist countries, and among the colonialized and exploited people in the heart of the imperialist metropolis itself, will continue to deepen the contradictions of the capitalist system and, through their resolution, to liberate the people of Chile and the world. At the cost of their underdevelopment the capitalist system has developed, and as the price of their development the capitalist system will be destroyed.

The process of capitalist development is discontinuous but permanent, as is the process of its revolutionary decay. In our times, the contradictions deepen, the process accelerates, the discontinuity destroys the system, the opportunity of liberating its people and developing their civilization is at hand; and the people grasp it. Let their leaders follow.

II

ON THE
"INDIAN PROBLEM"
IN
LATIN AMERICA

A. THE PROBLEM

The "Indian problem" in Latin America is in its essence a problem of the economic structure of the national and international capitalist system as a whole. Contrary to frequent claims, the problem is not one of the Indian's cultural isolation, still less one of economic isolation or insufficient integration. The problem of the Indians, like that of underdevelopment as a whole, has its roots in the class and metropolis-satellite structure of capitalism, discussed throughout this book; and its manifestations are part and parcel of that structure. Without going back to the well-known statements of the economic basis of the problem of the Indians made in centuries past by Bartolomé de las Casas in his *Historia de las Indias* and by Jorge Juan and Antonio Ulloa in their *Noticias Secretas de América*, we may consider the judgment of our century's most renowned student of Peru, José Carlos Mariátegui:

All theses about the Indian problem which do not see it as an economic-social problem, or which avoid it as such, are nothing but further sterile theoretical . . . and sometimes merely verbal . . . exercises which are condemned to absolute discredit. They are in no way redeemed by their good intentions. . . . The Indian question grows out of our economy. It has its roots in the system of land ownership. Any attempt to solve it by administrative or police measures, through education or road building, is superficial and beside the point (Mariátegui 1934: 27).

This judgment is seconded by the American anthropologist, Eric Wolf, when he says that the ethnicism and the corporate community of the Latin American Indian have structural rather than cultural roots; and also by his Mexican colleague, Rodolfo Stavenhagen, who says that "the basis of ethnic relations is colonial relations and class relations" and "the regional city was an instrument of conquest and is still today an instrument of domination" (Wolf 1955: 456-457; Stavenhagen 1963: 91, 81).

B. THE HISTORY

The problem of the Indian lies in his economic relationship to the other members of the society; and this relationship has been in turn determined by the metropolis-satellite structure and development of capitalist society as a whole since the Indian's incorporation into it by the conquest. Stavenhagen suggests that "the colonial system operated, in fact, on two levels. The economic restrictions and prohibitions that Spain imposed on its colonies (and which would generate the independence movements) were repeated, only many times worse, in the relations between the colonial society and the Indian communities. The same commercial monopolies, the same restrictions of production, the same political controls that Spain exercised over the colony, the latter imposed on the Indian communities. What Spain was for the colony, the latter was for the Indian communities: a colonial metropolis. From then on, mercantilism penetrated the most isolated villages of New Spain" (Stavenhagen 1963: 91).

Thus the supposedly isolated "folk" society or rather community popularized by Redfield (1941, 1960) and the corporate Indian community, far from being original in Latin America or traditional to it, in fact developed or, better, underdeveloped as a product of the development of capitalism in Latin America in the colonial period and also in the national period. Eric Wolf summarizes how the dependent and apparent isolation, but actual satellite status, of the Indian community was historically generated by the process of capitalist development which began with the conquest. As Cortés noted to a Mexican upon his arrival: "The Spaniards are troubled with a disease of the heart for which gold is the specific remedy." Beginning with this observation, Wolf continues:

[The] conquering Spaniard became a mining entrepreneur, a producer of commercial crops, a rancher, a merchant. . . . He wanted to convert wealth and labor into salable goods—into gold and silver, hides and wool, wheat and sugar cane. . . . The motor of this capitalism was mining. . . . All the claims to utopia—economic, religious, and political—rested ultimately upon the management and control of but one resource: the indigenous population of the colony. The conquerors wanted Indian labor. . . . In the eyes of the colonist it was not its medieval provenance which lent merit to the institution [of the *encomienda**]; it was rather the opportunity it provided for the organization of a capitalist labor force over which he alone would exercise untrammeled sway (Wolf 1959: 176, 189).

Wolf's judgment is confirmed by the world's three indisputably most authoritative students of the subject, José M. Ots Capdequi, José Miranda, and Silvio Zavala. Ots Capdequi writes:

It is not possible to penetrate into the heart of the real historical significance of the social, economic and legal institutions incorporated into the so-called Indian Law [*Derecho Indiano,* which refers not to Indians but to the Indies, as Spanish America was then called] if one does not keep in mind this historical fact, which I have amply dealt with in some of my writings: that the task of the discovery, conquest and colonization of America was not in the strict sense, in its origins, a state enterprise. . . . If we analyze the whole of the *capitulaciones* [grants] that are preserved in the General Archives of the Indies in Seville we clearly find the evident and absorbing predominance of private interest, of private initiative in the organization and the maintenance of the expeditions of discovery. It was normal that these expeditions were financed by great merchants. . . . The new law that arose in these countries, the strictly Indian [Spanish American] rights, had a fundamentally pact-like character, a contractual character. . . . These *capitulaciones,* these contracts, became truly juridical and negotiable instruments; and before the business venture based on them was undertaken, they were subject to exchange, transfer, purchase and sale, corporate contract (Ots 1946: 8-11).

After simple slavery, the principal institution through which the Spanish entrepreneurs recouped their investment was the *encomienda,* which permitted them to exact tribute and labor from the Indian population. José Miranda summarizes the "economic function" of the *encomenderos*—those to whom the *encomiendas* were granted—as follows:

* The *encomienda* is discussed in the following pages and on pages 23-24.

Although the continental *encomendero* has much of the feudal lord, European style . . . he seems to have no real interest in his feudal-style position or function. No; the *encomendero* is above all a man of his time, moved by desire for profit and pursuing the goal of wealth. Among his contemporaries, the *encomendero* is the man of action in whom the ideas and anxieties of a new world take strongest root. . . . For this reason, he does not, like the feudal lord, limit himself to the mere enjoyment of tribute and service; but he converts the one like the other into the principal base of several business enterprises. . . . He will do the same as any entrepreneur from that time till now: use his own and others' resources and the work of others in the pursuit of his own wealth and well-being. Thus the *encomendero* gives place of pride to the capitalist grant element of the *encomienda*, which is the only one which can bring him what he pursues with vigor: riches. . . .

The businesses which the *encomendero* establishes to take economic advantage of the *encomienda* are, therefore, of three kinds: mining (for the extraction of gold, at first), livestock, and agricultural (the agricultural ones, at first, being limited almost exclusively to the production of wheat). . . . With respect to the first one, he would extract from his *encomienda* for his businesses, gold, means of subsistence, slaves, clothing, etc. These goods would be used by him: the gold, in the most necessary investments, like the purchase of tools, and where necessary, in the payment of Spanish workers (miners and helpers) and the purchase of food; the means of subsistence in the maintenance of his slaves, *encomienda* Indians, and other workers, and livestock raising; the slaves, in the mining work, where they were the main source of labor, and in agriculture and livestock raising. . . . We often see the *encomendero* caught up in a complicated net of economic and legal relationships: he participates in various mining companies, established before a notary public; he is owner of a herd of swine or sheep, which he grazes on the range of another *encomendero*—with whom he has entered into an economic contract for the purpose—and which are under the care of a Spaniard whose services he has obtained through some contract or payment; and all this after having conferred general powers to some relative, friend, or employee to administer his *encomiendas* and after having conferred special powers to other people so they might administer his haciendas or livestock ranches, his shops or sugar mills, or to take care of his interest wherever it may be necessary (Miranda 1947: 423–424, 427, 446).

Thus the expansion and development of capitalism incorporated the Indian population into its exploitative monopoly structure immediately upon conquest, and the capitalist and his fast-growing cattle and sheep herds appropriated the Indian's land. The new capitalism penetrated the Indian economic organization so quickly and profoundly that ten years after the conquest of Mexico "due, undoubtedly, to the increase in money and the large demand for consumer goods, some Indian villages, especially those near the capital and important cities, came to prefer paying their tribute in money and asked that their payments in goods or labor be commuted to gold or silver. Ramírez de Fuenleal informed the King of this turn of events and asked him to remove the legal obstacles to the payment of tribute in money . . . 'it seems that now some villages prefer to keep their corn and blankets for trading, and would rather give gold; because through their trading they earn enough to pay their tribute and to provide for their subsistence'" (Miranda 1952: 204). Like all those in a capitalist economy who must pay, in times of inflation the Indians preferred to pay in devalued money.

The immediate consequences of capitalist penetration of the Indian society were the decimation of the Indian population and the transformation of his society and culture. In Mexico, the Indian population dropped from 11 million at the time of conquest in 1519 to a low of 1.5 million in 1650 (Borah 1951: 3). At the same time, as Miranda notes, "the heavy load of tribute caused important changes in the distribution of the population: on the one hand, the population decline due to death or absence; and on the other hand, the spread of many Indians to the less populated areas, the settlement of uninviting or inaccessible places, and the change of residence or transfer of home from one village to another. Some villages died out or declined; new settlements were born, some of which became small towns with the passing of time; and some places grew. Many of the Indians who did not wish to pay the excessive tributes adopted the only way to evade them, that is, abandoned their place of residence, either to go to live where the Spaniards could not bother them or to go to live somewhere else where the weight of tribute was lighter" (Miranda 1952: 216-217).

The Indian settlements of later times, and least of all their structure and relation to the larger society, are not then survivals of pre-conquest times. They are, on the contrary, the underdeveloped product of capitalist development. Since then and still in our day, insofar as the corporate Indian community has been isolated at all, this reflects the self-chosen retreat which is the Indians' only available means of protection from the ravages and exploitation of the capitalist system.

In Mexico, the *encomienda* based on the payment of tribute in labor and the legal use of *encomienda* Indians lasted until 1549. Silvio Zavala writes:

> On February 22 of that year, the Crown issued an important cedula addressed to the president and judges of the Audiencia of New Spain . . . directed the cancellation of all commutations to personal service of tribute in kind and money. The enforcement of this prohibition marked the end of the *encomienda* as a labor institution, for from this time forth all tributes had to be paid in money, produce, or native wares. Proof exists that the law was enforced. . . .
>
> Through what channel would the labor necessary for carrying on the work of the colony now be obtained? . . . The aim, therefore, was to establish a system of voluntary wage labor with moderate tasks; but in anticipation that the Indians might not offer their services voluntarily . . . New Spain [developed] the *cuatequil* or the system of forced wage labor. This system, combined with the previous indigenous customs, was to develop on a much larger scale in Peru under the name of *mita,* an institution distinct from both slavery and the personal service of the *encomienda,* both of which were displaced in the process we are describing. . . . The Indian . . . received a daily wage. . . . The main differences between the *cuatequil* of New Spain and the *mita* of Peru lay in the fact that the former usually affected the Indians in districts near the place of work, while in Peru the laborers had to travel much greater distances. In New Spain the work period was almost always one week and each Indian presented himself for work three or four weeks a year. The Peruvian periods of labor lasted for months. The quota of workers raised by the villages of New Spain was commonly 4 percent, in Peru one-seventh, or about 14 percent. In Tucumán one Indian was taken out of every twelve. . . . The system of compulsory wage labor . . . in the end became the chief source of labor in the colony. Not even the *encomenderos* succeeded in remaining independent of the institution

of the *cuatequil*. If they needed laborers, they could no longer take them directly from their villages as they had formerly done as a form of tribute. Like other private colonists, they were forced to apply to a justice or *juez repartidor* for the number of Indians they needed, and the workers thus provided no longer worked gratuitously but were entitled to customary wages from the *encomendero*. . . . In the preceding chapter we noted that the *encomienda* carried with it no title to the soil, and we now see that the *encomendero* lost control over the labor of his Indians since this was regulated independently by the royal authorities. . . . In 1601 and 1609 new cedulas were issued for the purpose of establishing voluntary, and of putting an end to compulsory, labor for wages. . . .

For years past the Spanish farmers had begun to attract to their farms the Indians of the neighboring villages who were known as *gañanes* or *laborios*. Thus instead of waiting for the periodic assignment of Indians by the public authorities, they had Indian families continuously in residence on their own lands as laborers. . . . Moreover, the landowners had begun to do everything in their power to strengthen their hold on their *gañanes* by depriving them of freedom to leave their farm at will. The legal means of accomplishing this purpose was found in advances of money and goods, which bound the *gañan* to the land by placing him in debt. This method, and not the old *encomienda* of the sixteenth century, constitutes the true precursor of the Mexican hacienda of more recent times. Under the latter system the master is the owner of the land through grant, purchase, or other legal title, or perhaps only as a squatter, and he attracts the *gañanes* to his lands and then keeps them there by means of debts. Liberal thought in the period of colonization did not fail to look with mistrust upon this system of agrarian servitude through debt, and it denounced the system as formerly it had denounced slavery, the *encomienda*, and *cuatequil*. The Spanish government made significant provisions for limiting the amount of legal indebtedness. . . . In spite of these legal restrictions . . . the farmers had succeeded in extending the system of *gañanía* and had secured it by means of debt. . . . The growing number of peons and the isolation of the estates gave rise gradually to the custom of punishment of the peons by the master or his representatives, but this does not mean that the latter possessed judicial authority, for the king's justice intervened where a serious crime was committed. The system of peonage thus had colonial roots, but in that period the vigilance of public authorities afforded a measure of protection to the laborers. When, subsequently, laissez faire and other abstentionist theories of public law left the peons alone and defenseless against the economic power of their masters, the harshness of the hacienda regime increased, and the population and importance of the Indian villages steadily diminished in comparison with the estates employing peons. We have already said that the compulsory labor of mines persisted beyond the year 1633, but that the number of free workers attracted by the relatively high wages of miners increased. . . . The device of juggled indebtedness functioned in the mines as well as on the haciendas (Zavala 1943: 85-101).

In its incorporation of the Indian, then, no less than of anybody else, the development of capitalism generated the institutional forms appropriate to its changing needs at different times and places. This capitalist development and its institutions transformed the entire fabric of Indian society from the very beginning, and it has continued to determine the manner and quality of Indian life ever since. Wolf comments:

The conquest not only destroyed people physically; it also rent asunder the accustomed fabric of their lives and the pattern of motives that animated that life. . . . The society produced by the Spanish conquest . . . sacrificed men to the production of objects intended to serve no end beyond the maximization of profit and glory of the individual conqueror . . . the exploited Indian could perceive no universal meaning in his suffering. . . . Thus the Indians suffered not only exploitation and biological collapse but also deculturation —"cultural loss"—and in the course of such ill use lost also the feeling of belonging to a social order which made such poor use of its human resources. They became strangers in it, divided from its purpose and agents by an abyss of distrust. The new society could command their labor, but it could not command their loyalty. Nor has this gulf been healed in the course of time" (Wolf 1959: 199).

Nonetheless, Indians do not all suffer the same economic, social and cultural fate. The difference between the hacienda Indian as a worker and the communal Indian as a producer in his own right is emphasized by Antonio Quintanilla, among others, as far as its socio-cultural manifestations are concerned:

The Indian of the communities [in Peru] . . . is conscious of being free. What he most values is land, and he owns land. On this ownership of land rest a series of civic virtues which the other Indians [of the haciendas] do not have. Communal organization and legal protection have allowed hundreds of thousands of Indians to lead a relatively acceptable life in that, as was mentioned above, standards of living, civic values, freedom of action and opinion, and in one word the happiness of the Indians in communities are beyond comparison with the infra-human conditions of the Indians of the haciendas or of those who wander around the cities of the Andes in search of work. . . . The Indian employed on the haciendas is shy, sullen, and silent, often servile, a liar, and treacherous. These essentially negative features are the expression of . . . his state of inferiority and of his long experience with exploitation and injustice (Quintanilla N.D.: 12, 18).

Though undoubtedly important, this difference between hacienda and communal Indians—especially when the latter, for lack of enough land of their own, are forced to work like the former—is counterweighed by their common exploitation through the same capitalist system as a whole. We may return, then, to examine the role of the Indians in the structure and development of this system.

As we already noted in our review of Chile, the seventeenth century witnessed the decline of mining production in the colonies, brought depression to the metropolis, and isolated the two from each other more than they had been in the previous century or would again be in the later ones. Urban-rural polarization in the colonies seems to have increased. Urban population, manufacturing and demand for rural products increased in the face of the continued population decline (Borah 1951: 30). In response to this urban development and to the decline of both the output and profitability of mining, agricultural production also grew in importance and was increasingly concentrated in the Spanish hacienda rather than the Indian village. The students of this process in Mexico have interpreted it as the involution of an economy which was turning it upon itself due to an economic depression (Chevalier 1956, Borah 1951, Wolf 1959). I have argued elsewhere that this is a misinterpretation of these events (Frank 1965a). The growth and consolidation of the monopolistic hacienda and the associated decline of small-scale, in this case Indian, agricultural production in Mexico was then and has always been due to the increase of demand for and price of agricultural products, just as in the cases of Chile and Brazil which are reviewed in this book and in the clear cases elsewhere in Latin America of Argentina and the West Indies (Frank 1965b). The seventeenth century, then, witnessed the development of the principal rural institutional forms which, in the hacienda and the Indian community, have persisted in most of Indian Latin America to this day; but these institutions themselves have been flexible enough to adapt to the world and national economic fluctuations and transformations since that time.

Latin America has been involved in major shifts and fluctuations of the market since the period of initial European conquest. It would appear for example that the rapid expansion of commercial development in New Spain during the sixteenth century was followed by a "century of depression" in the seventeenth century. The slack was taken up again in the eighteenth century, with renewed shrinkage and disintegration of the market in the early part of the nineteenth century. During the second part of the nineteenth century and the beginning of the twentieth, many Latin American countries were repeatedly caught up in speculative booms of cash production for foreign markets, often with disastrous results in the case of market failure. Entire communities might find their market gone overnight, and revert to the production of subsistence crops for their own use.[*] . . . Redfield has recognized aspects of this problem in his category of the "remade folk" . . . which were once in the mainstream of commercial development, only to be left behind in its poverty-stricken margins. . . .

In this cycle of subsistence crops and cash crops, subsistence crops guarantee a stable minimum livelihood, where cash crops promise higher money returns but involve the family in the hazards of the fluctuating market. The peasant is always concerned with the problem of striking some sort of balance between subsistence production and cash production. Preceding cycles of cash crop production have enabled him to buy goods and services which he cannot afford if he produces only for his own subsistence. Yet an all-out effort to increase his ability to buy more goods and services of this kind may spell his end as an independent agricultural producer. His tendency

[*] For particularly important examples and their analysis see "Capitalist Development of Underdevelopment in Brazil," pp. 143–218.

is thus to rely on a basic minimum of subsistence production to expand his cash purchases only slowly (Wolf 1955: 462–464).[*]

Being the integral part of uneven capitalist development that it is, this process still continues. When the world and monopolistically manipulated local price of coffee drops so far that the Indians of southern Mexico receive one pound of corn for one pound of coffee which they produce for the national and world market, they stop producing coffee, increase their production of corn, and *become* "isolated subsistence farmers."

Two things seem to be clear from this discussion. First, in dealing with present-day Latin America it would seem advisable to beware of treating production for subsistence and production for the market as two progressive stages of development. Rather, we must allow for the cyclical alternation of the two kinds of production within the same community and realize that from the point of view of the community both kinds may be alternative responses to change in conditions of the outside market. This means that a synchronic study of the market is insufficient. . . . Second, we must look for the mechanisms which make such changes possible (Wolf 1955: 464).

C. THE STRUCTURE

For our day, the structure and mechanisms are summarized by the *Instituto Nacional Indigenista* (National Indian Institute) of Mexico, whose choice of terms is even the same as my own:

The Indians, in reality, rarely live isolated from the *mestizo* or national population; there exists a symbiosis between the two groups which we must take into account. Between the *mestizos* who live in the nucleus city of the region and the Indians who live in the agricultural hinterland there is in reality a closer economic and social interdependence than appears at first glance. . . . The *mestizo* population, in fact, almost always lives in a city which is the center of an intercultural region, which acts as a metropolis of an Indian zone, and which maintains an intimate connection with the underdeveloped communities which link the center with the satellite commu-

[*] For non-Indian peasants this pattern is analyzed in detail on pp. 233–238 and 257–266.

nities. [Our study found] the Indian or folk community was an interdependent part of a whole which functioned as a unit, so that the measures taken in one part inevitably had repercussions in the others and, in consequence, on the whole. It was not possible to consider the community separately; it was necessary to take account in its totality of the intercultural system of which it was part. . . . That the large Indian mass should remain in its ancestral status of subordination, with a strongly stabilized folk culture, was not only desired but even coercively imposed by the city. . . . [It is in] Ciudad de las Casas that . . . one sees with greater emphasis the dominion which the *ladinos** exercise over economic and political resources and over property in general (*Instituto Nacional* 1962: 33-34, 27, 60).

This then is the contemporary situation in Mexico after the "fifty years of Revolution" of which this country is so proud because it freed the rural population from the domination of the supposedly feudal hacienda. In his *La Democracia en México*, the Director of the National University's School of Political and Social Science calls this state of affairs "internal colonialism" and notes that it affects an absolutely *increasing* number of 10 to 25 percent of Mexico's population (González Casanova 1965: 52-89). It may be left to the reader's imagination how things are in Peru and Ecuador where half the population is Indian and where no revolution has occurred, or in Guatemala and Bolivia where the counter-revolution has already taken over.

As Wolf notes, "Robbed of land and water by the conquest and subsequent encroachment [particularly the nineteenth-century liberal reforms which substituted private for communal property], the Indian community can rarely be self-sufficient. It must not only export people; it must also export craft produce and labor. . . . Without the outside world, moreover, the Indian

* *Ladinos* are ex-Indians and sometimes also descendants of *criollos* (Creoles) who differ economically and ethnically from the Indians and who occupy the intermediate strata of society in the Latin American countries which have significant Indian populations. Elsewhere in Mexico they are called *mestizos,* in the Andean countries *cholos* or, in somewhat higher strata, *mistis.* For a classification of social stratification in Latin America in cultural terms see, for instance, Wagley, 1955.

can never close the ever opening gap between his production and his needs" (Wolf 1959: 230). Stavenhagen continues:

> The Indian economic world is not a closed world. The Indian communities are only apparently isolated. On the contrary, they participate in regional systems and in the national economy. Markets and commercial relations are the principal link between the Indians and the world of the *ladinos,* between the subsistence economy and the national economy. It is true that the largest part of the Indians' agricultural production is consumed by themselves. It is also true that the income produced by the Indians represents only a very small share of the national product (even in Guatemala, where the Indian population is more than half of the total population). But the importance of these relations does not lie in the amount of the product sold or in the value of the goods bought; it lies rather in the quality of the commercial relations. It is these relations which have transformed the Indians into a "minority" and which have put them in the state of dependence in which they now find themselves (Stavenhagen 1963: 78).

The relations between Indians and others then are many; but, as all the writers cited here agree, they are never relations of equality. The Indian is always exploited.

Alejandro Marroquín notes that "traditionally, the Indian in the Tzeltal-Tzotzil region is exploited in two ways: he is exploited as a worker at the service of the landowners and *hacendados* who use Indian labor and pay low wages for each day of work; and he is exploited in his capacity as a small producer; the Indian produces goods which are sometimes very much in demand in the national market" (Marroquín 1956: 200).

D. THE LABORER

It is hard to find many Indians, even in Mexico after its land reform, who own enough land to permit them to lead a life worthy of their integral membership in human society. It is a generally acknowledged fact that the Indians have been robbed of their lands by legal and illegal means over the course of history, often not so much because others wanted the land in itself as because they sought to render the Indians dependent by denying them ownership of the resources necessary for their independent survival.

Contemporary land tenure studies in various countries of Latin America show that the Indians are still losing their lands, not to speak of the lands' fertility. This shortage of land is undoubtedly the key to their status of inferiority, exploitation, poverty, lack of culture, in a word the status of underdevelopment of the Indians and of many others who participate all too fully in the social process of capitalist development. It is for this reason that Stavenhagen can claim that "from the point of view of the global economic structure, the self-subsistence community plays the role of a labor reserve; . . . private land-ownership benefits the *ladinos* and is prejudicial to the Indians . . . the accumulation of land on the part of the *ladinos* serves them to obtain and control a cheap labor force . . . the Indian is always the employee and the *ladino* always the employer" (Stavenhagen 1963: 71, 75, 77). Little wonder that Indians value the corporativeness of their community which affords them some protection against outside encroachment on their land through its communal ownership and through strong social sanctions against the sale of individually owned land to outsiders.

Obviously it is their lack of land which forces the landless Indians and ex-Indians to contribute their labor for very low wages and sometimes for none at all to landowners and others in order to obtain a little piece of land of low fertility, a leaky roof over their heads, a little corn or wheat or beer, a few pesos. But it is also the shortage of land among those who have a little of it which forces the communal Indians and other small owners, in order to obtain bread for their children and grass for their animals, to submit to the exploitation of the *ladinos* and others who are fortunate enough to have stolen, extorted or inherited enough land and capital from the Indians and others to enable them now to live off their exploitation. Thus Melvin Tumin reports that in Jilotepeque "a *ladino* laborer earns 50 percent more than an Indian laborer, but the cost of maintaining a mule is still higher than the wages of a *ladino*" (quoted in Stavenhagen 1963: 71).

The organization of this exploitation takes all sorts of forms, like being born, working as an ordinary laborer, and dying on the same hacienda; or working as a half-share cropper on such a hacienda—if you are fortunate enough to obtain even half of what you produce for yourself; or leaving your own small plot in the hands of your family while you go to work on the neighboring hacienda; or coming down hundreds of miles from the mountains every year to harvest other people's coffee—especially if it is these others who own "your" land in the mountains; or migrating as a *bracero* thousands of miles to California to serve as a supply of cheap labor; or combining these activities with some minor trading and any kind of occasional labor if you can find it in the provincial small towns; or emigrating to the provincial or national capital, there to become an occasionally employed slum dweller; in any case, becoming wholly integrated in a capitalist metropolis-satellite economic, social, and political structure which takes all possible advantage of your short, sad life without ever also integrating you into the benefits which this same social structure generates.

E. THE MARKET

The Indians and others, besides being exploited as laborers, as Alejandro Marroquín notes, are also exploited as small producers, both as sellers and buyers in the local, regional, and national market. The Indian's "limited familiarity with the laws of supply and demand inhibit him from placing the proper value on the goods he brings to the urban market; it is thus that the Indian becomes an instrument in the hands of monopolists who take his products away from him and pay ridiculous prices only to sell the same goods later at relatively high prices" (Marroquín 1956: 200). Stavenhagen maintains that "among the various kinds of relations between Indians and *ladinos,* it is their commercial relations that are the most important. The Indian participates in these relations as producer and consumer; the *ladino* always as the merchant, the middle-man, the monopolist. . . . It is precisely the commercial relations which link the Indian world with the socio-economic region, the national society as well as the world economy into which it is integrated. . . . It is obvious that the commercial relations between Indians and *ladinos* are not relations of equality" (Stavenhagen 1963: 80).

These commercial relations take on a multitude of forms. Marroquín summarizes some of these in his study of *La Ciudad Mercado* (*Tlaxiaco*) [The Market Town (Tlaxiaco)]:

The function of distribution consists in the job which the weekly market of Tlaxiaco does in distributing the multitude of goods brought from Puebla, Oaxaca, Atlixco, or from Mexico. . . . The function of concentration is the inverse: the weekly market concentrates a series of regional goods in Tlaxiaco so that they may then be sent to the major centers of consumption; on the other hand, the two foregoing functions are accomplished mainly through the function of commercial exchange, that is, through the growing activity of buyers and sellers, which leaves an excess of profit for the professional merchants. The function of monopolization is a higher stage of the function of concentration and consists in the monopolizing work of the buying agents of the big merchants principally from Puebla and Mexico, who try to control the production of those Indian goods which are in great demand in the most important centers of consumption of the country. . . .

The Indians who produce straw hats belong to the economically most backward villages. . . . Parents as well as children are engaged in the production of hats in very long workdays which exceed 18 hours daily. The cultural backwardness of these Indians leaves them completely at the mercy of the buyers who, relying on their economic power, fix the prices of their hats entirely at their own will and with no other limit than that which they fix among themselves through competition. Even in the Indian villages there are one or two monopolists who buy many hats in order to take and sell them in Tlaxiaco on Saturday. They assure themselves of profit buying the hats produced by the Indians at very low prices which these sell in their village, forced perhaps by some economic need. . . .

The buying agents try to get a corner on particular Indian goods in order to send them to the urban centers where there is a big demand for these goods. The buying agents depend on important commercial centers like Mexico, Puebla, or Oaxaca, etc. and keep in perfect touch with the market fluctuation in these places. In accord with these fluctuations, they determine the prices of the Indian products. The Indian products in greatest demand by the buying agents are eggs, chickens and turkeys, avocados and coffee. . . . The work of the buying agencies is eased through a typical network of middlemen to gather up the Indian products through small purchases and then deliver them to their respective agents in large quantities. These middlemen are all native to Tlaxiaco. . . . Seven pairs of hands have introduced themselves between the producer and the consumer and have caused the price [of eggs] to rise from 16 cents to 50 cents, more than 300 percent. The Indian products reach Tlaxiaco in order then to spread out to the major urban centers of the country; but in their brief passage through Tlaxiaco they have contributed to strengthening the commercial sector of the city. This profit, parasitically extracted from the hunger and misery of the Indian, consolidates the power and the concentric force of Tlaxiaco as the fundamental nucleus of the Mixtecan economy.

Summarizing, we may note the following as the general characteristics of the urban market of Tlaxiaco: (1) the total predominance of the mercantile capitalist system, (2) intense competitive fighting, as in any capitalist economic system, (3) powerful influence of the distributive monopolies, (4) a dense network of middlemen which weighs heavily on the Indian economy, (5) the parasitic aspect of the economy of Tlaxiaco which is based on the exploitation of the devalued work of the Indian. . . . All of which shows that Tlaxiaco is not a producing center but a distributive center which depends mainly on outside production. Tlaxiaco is the base around which take place the weekly markets of the villages which are subordinated to the orbit of the head city (Marroquín 1957: 156-163).

It should be especially emphasized that the shortage of resources and low bargaining power which puts the Indians in a very disadvantageous position in the market is heightened by the frequent and large fluctuations in demand, supply, and price which for speculative ends are often monopolistically generated by the merchants themselves. Eric Wolf has described the situation:

[The] buyers of peasant produce have an interest in the continued "backwardness" of the peasant. Reorganization of his productive apparatus would absorb capital and credit which can be spent better in expanding the market by buying means of transportation, engaging middlemen, etc. Moreover, by leaving the productive apparatus unchanged, the buyer can reduce the risk of having his capital tied up in the means of production of the peasant holding, if and when the bottom drops out of the market. The buyers of peasant produce thus trade increasing productivity per man hour for lessened risk of investment. We may say that the marginality of land and the poor technology are a function of the speculative market. In the case of need, the investor merely withdraws credit, while the peasant returns to subsistence production by means of his traditional technology (Wolf 1955: 464).

F. CAPITALISM

The structure and development of the monopoly capitalist system thus manifest themselves in the "Indian problem" in particular and in the generation of underdevelopment at the provincial level in general, as Marroquín outlines it in his conclusions from his study of Tlaxiaco:

First: The economic concentration and centralization observed in Tlaxiaco has brought forth a notable contrast in the life of the relatively opulent city and the poor and stingy life of the villages of the region. This contrast also manifests itself in the city itself, between the scattered suburbs of the rural periphery and the urban nucleus of the center.

Second: The city takes advantage of its privileged position with respect to the means of communication in order to exploit the Indian villages and suburbs. This produces a deep contradiction between the urban nucleus of the center and the rest of the region.

Third: The land reform of the Revolution broke up the socioeconomic equilibrium of the villages. With the disappearance of the hacienda, which was the center of gravity of the earlier social system, the Indian perforce looked for a new support which would lend him order and stability within the social upheaval produced by that Revolution. The store of the big merchant became the center of gravity of the region. The big merchant became the substitute for the hacendado in his patriarchal role. The big merchant, while he exploits and takes advantage of the Indians' production, presents himself to them as their great supplier of favors.

Fourth: The economic structure of Tlaxiaco gives rise to the following characteristics: (1) Extreme individualism. The competitive fighting is intense and produces strong rivalries among persons of the same standing and among the various sectors of the economy in general. (2) The only source of capital accumulation is commerce (mining activities have declined and the profits they generate, on the other hand, are accumulated beyond Tlaxiaco). Neither agriculture nor artisanry can permit the formation of large fortunes. Hence the idealization of the merchant profession. The big merchant is the model whom all imitate, respect, and admire. (3) Without any productive basis of its own, the economy of Tlaxiaco is a parasitic economy which rests on the exploitation of Indian labor.

Fifth: Given its own economic structure, Tlaxiaco is not a homogeneous whole; it is divided into sectors and social classes with mutually and increasingly antagonistic interests.

Sixth: The new means of transportation which were built during the past ten years have changed the economy of Tlaxiaco profoundly. Their most important effects are: (1) ruination or decadence of the majority of the artisanry or trades like the manufacture of candles and soap, hardware, the textile industry, etc. (2) Strong stimulus to the production and consumption of alcohol. (3) The growth of an important new economic center: Chalcatongo. (4) The development of an artificial economy in Tlaxiaco in that this city, not producing what it consumes, promotes the functions of exchange, distribution, and concentration of goods. (5) Finally, the new means of communication gave access to the Tlaxiaco market to the representatives of the big monopolies and speculators of Mexico City, who ruined the local monopolists, caused the cost of living to rise, and at the same time undertake large scale speculative manipulations to the disadvantage of the Indian population (Marroquín 1957: 239-241).

The development of capitalism, then, generates ever more underdevelopment in the Indian community just as it does in most others. Thus the "problem" of the Indian and his community, from his point of view, is one of constant struggle for bare survival in a system in which he, like the vast majority of other people, is the victim of uneven capitalist development within a fully capitalist metropolis-satellite structure. It is a losing battle the Indian has fought for over four centuries. He is still losing. And, like millions of others, he will continue to lose until he can overthrow the system, a task which no one is prepared to do for him. For abandoning his community offers no way out to the Indian either. Writing for the Commission on Land Reform and Housing of Peru, Antonio Quintanilla describes the ongoing process of transformation of the Indian community and of its abandonment by the Indian:

From the economic point of view, the Indian who leaves his community, obliged by circumstances and also by his own desire, adopts an individualist economic attitude instead of a collective attitude. What we mean is that the Indian outside his community and as an individual enters into an attitude of competition with respect to every other Indian in circumstances analogous to his own. This competition appears under all conditions, but it is particularly serious in the labor market, given the large supply of labor and the conditions of great inferiority of the Indian groups as a whole in that market. For the Indians who continue as farmers, the disappearance of communal organization would bring with it not only their easy exploitation by unscrupulous people—whom experience has shown to be in the majority; but also the Indian farmers themselves would enter into competition which would be ruinous for them, given their limited financial capacity, their poor agricultural techniques, and the uneconomic size of their plots. To have the Indians, with their limited resources, incorporate themselves to compete actively in an individualistic system would mean sinking them into even greater misery. It is therefore necessary to find new organizational forms to replace the community which will inevitably disappear. . . . This process, left to its own, can finally achieve the incorporation of the Indian into Western ways and the disappearance of the subsistence economy, but at a terrible price in misery, massive tuberculosis, terrible infant mortality, unemployment, crime, etc. The problem is thus changing stage but not actors. The same human masses which cease to be the object of the "Indian problem" become the object of the "slum problem" which is the problem of the urban subproletariat which lives in extreme misery and which is ever growing (Quintanilla N.D.: 19-20).

Rodolfo Stavenhagen also believes that "Ladinization . . . only means the proletarianization of the Indian . . . or, in his case, a rural *lumpenproletarianization* (forbid the word)" (Stavenhagen 1963: 99, 103).

The "Indian problem" therefore does not lie in any *lack* of cultural or economic integration of the Indian into society. His problem, like that of the majority of people, lies rather in his very exploitative metropolis-satellite *integration* into the structure and development of the capitalist system which produces underdevelopment in general.

III

CAPITALIST
DEVELOPMENT
OF
UNDERDEVELOPMENT
IN BRAZIL

A. THE MODEL AND HYPOTHESES

Underdevelopment in Brazil, as elsewhere, is the result of capitalist development. The military coup of April 1964 and the political and economic events which followed are the logical consequences of this.* My purpose here is to trace and to explain the capitalist development of underdevelopment in Brazil since its settlement by Portugal in the sixteenth century and to show how and why, within the metropolis-satellite colonialist and imperialist structure of capitalism, even the economic and industrial development that Brazil is capable of is necessarily limited to an underdeveloped development. My intent is not an exhaustive study of Brazil *per se;* it is rather an attempt to use the case of Brazil to study the nature of underdevelopment and the limitations of capitalist development.

To account for the underdevelopment and limited development of Brazil, and similar areas, it is common to resort to a dualist model of society. Thus the French geographer Jaques Lambert says in his book *Os Dois Brasis* (The Two Brazils):

The Brazilians are divided into two systems of economic and social organization. . . . These two societies did not evolve at the same rate. . . . The two Brazils are equally Brazilian, but they are separated by several centuries. . . . In the course of the long period of colonial isolation, an archaic Brazilian culture was formed, a culture which keeps in isolation the same stability which still exists in the indigenous cultures of Asia and the Near East. . . . The dual economy and the dual social structure which accompanies it are neither new nor characteristically Brazilian—they exist in all unequally developed countries (Lambert N.D.: 105–112).

* This essay is the revision of a lecture delivered in a symposium devoted to the "Third World" at the School of Political and Social Sciences of the National University of Mexico, February 26 and 28, 1965. My aim was to interpret the military coup and its economic consequences against the background of history and in terms of a theoretical model capable of accounting for the development of underdevelopment in Brazil as a whole. As the reader will observe, this concern with the events of 1964 colors the treatment of the entire history of Brazil. I cannot, of course, subscribe to the concept of a "third world"; for what it refers to is part and parcel of the capitalist world.

The same view is shared by Arnold Toynbee (1962) and many others. Celso Furtado (1962), Brazil's Minister of Planning until the April 1964 coup, refers to the one Brazil, the modern capitalist and industrially more advanced Brazil, as an open society and to the archaic rural Brazil as a closed society.

The essential argument of all these students is that the modern Brazil is more developed because it is an open capitalist society; and the other archaic Brazil remains underdeveloped because it is not open, particularly to the industrial part and to the world as a whole, and not sufficiently capitalist, but rather pre-capitalist, feudal or semi-feudal. Development is then often viewed as diffusion: "In Brazil, the motor of evolution is everywhere in the cities, from which it radiates change to the countryside" (Lambert N.D.: 108). The underdeveloped Brazil would develop if only it would open up, and the more developed Brazil would develop still more if the other Brazil would stop being a drag on it and would open its market to industrial goods. My analysis of Brazil's historical and contemporary experience contends that this dualist model is factually erroneous and theoretically inadequate and misleading.[*]

An alternative model may be advanced instead. As a photograph of the world taken at a point in time, this model consists of a world metropolis (today the United States) and its governing class, and its national and international satellites and their leaders—national satellites like the Southern states of the United States, and international satellites like São Paulo. Since São Paulo is a national metropolis in its own right, the model consists further of its satellites: the provincial metropolises, like Recife or Belo Horizonte, and their regional and local satellites in turn. That is, taking a photograph of a slice of the world we get a whole chain of metropolises and satellites, which runs from the world metropolis down to the

[*] The dualist model and thesis itself is examined and criticized in greater detail below, in "Capitalism and the Myth of Feudalism in Brazilian Agriculture," beginning on p. 219.

hacienda or rural merchant who are satellites of the local commercial metropolitan center but who in their turn have peasants
as their satellites. If we take a photograph of the world as a
whole, we get a whole series of such constellations of metropolises and satellites.

There are several important characteristics of this model:
(1) Close economic, political, social and cultural ties between
each metropolis and its satellites, which result in the total integration of the farthest outpost and peasant into the system as
a whole. This contrasts with the supposed isolation and non-
incorporation of large parts of the society according to the
dualist model. (2) Monopolistic structure of the whole system,
in which each metropolis holds monopoly power over its satellites; the source or form of this monopoly varies from one
case to another, but the existence of this monopoly is universal
throughout the system. (3) As occurs in any monopolistic
system, misuse and misdirection of available resources throughout the whole system and metropolis-satellite chain. (4) As
part of this misuse, the expropriation and appropriation of a
large part or even all of and more than the economic surplus
or surplus value of the satellite by its local, regional, national
or international metropolis.

Instead of a photograph at a point in time, the model may be
viewed as a moving picture of the course of history. It then
shows the following characteristics: (1) Expansion of the system from Europe until it incorporates the entire planet in
one world system and structure. (If the socialist countries have
managed to escape from this system, then there are now two
worlds—but in no case are there three.) (2) Development of
capitalism, at first commercial and later also industrial, on a
world scale as a single system. (3) Polarizing tendencies generic
to the structure of the system at world, national, provincial,
local and sectoral levels, which generate the development of
the metropolis and the underdevelopment of the satellite. (4)
Fluctuations within the system, like booms and depressions,
which are transmitted from metropolis to satellite, and like the

substitution of one metropolis by another, such as the passing of the metropolis from Venice to the Iberian peninsula to Holland to Britain to the United States. (5) Transformations within the system, such as the so-called Industrial Revolution. Among these transformations we give special emphasis below to important historical changes in the source or mechanism of monopoly which the capitalist world metropolis exercises over its satellites.

From this model in which metropolitan status generates development and satellite status generates underdevelopment, we may derive hypotheses about metropolis-satellite relations and their consequences which differ in important respects from some theses generally accepted, in particular those associated with the dualist model:

(1) A metropolis (for example, a national metropolis) which is at the same time a satellite (of the world metropolis) will find that its development is not autonomous; it does not itself generate or maintain its development; it is a limited or misdirected development; it experiences, in a word, underdeveloped development.

(2) The relaxation, weakening or absence of ties between metropolis and satellite will lead to a turning in upon itself on the part of the satellite, an involution, which may take one of two forms:

(a) Passive capitalist involution toward or into a subsistence economy of apparent isolation and of extreme underdevelopment, such as that of the North and Northeast of Brazil. Here there may arise the apparently feudal or archaic features of the "other" sector of the dualist model. But these features are not original to the region, and they are not due to the region's or country's lack of incorporation into the system, as in the dualist model. On the contrary, they are due to and reflect precisely the region's ultra-incorporation, its strong (usually export) ties, which are followed by the region's temporary or permanent abandonment by the metropolis and by the relaxation of these ties.

(b) Weakening of ties together with active capitalist involution which may lead to more or less autonomous development or industrialization of the satellite, which is based on the metropolis-satellite relations of internal colonialism or imperialism. Examples of such active capitalist involution are the industrialization drives of Brazil, Mexico, Argentina, India and others during the Great Depression and the Second World War, while the metropolis was otherwise occupied. Development of the satellites thus appears not as the result of stronger ties with the metropolis, as the dualist model suggests, but occurs on the contrary because of the weakening of these ties. In the history of Brazil we find many cases of the first type of involution—in Amazonia, the Northeast, Minas Gerais, and Brazil as a whole—and one major instance of the second kind of involution in the case of São Paulo.

(3) The renewal of stronger metropolis-satellite ties may correspondingly produce the following consequences in the satellite:

(a) The renewal of underdeveloped development consequent upon the reopening of the market for the retrenched region's export products, such as has occurred periodically in Brazil's Northeast. This apparent development is just as disadvantageous in the long run as was the satellite's initial metropolis-sponsored export economy: underdevelopment continues to develop.

(b) The strangulation and misdirection of the autonomous development undertaken by the satellite during the period of lesser ties through the renewal of stronger metropolis-satellite ties as the result of the recuperation of the metropolis after a depression, war, or other kinds of ups and downs. The inevitable result is the renewal of the generation of underdevelopment in the satellite, such as that which took place in the above-named countries after the Korean War.

(4) There is a close interconnection of the economy and the socio-political structure of the satellite with those of the metropolis. The closer the satellite's links with and dependence

on the metropolis, the closer is the satellite bourgeoisie, including the so-called "national bourgeoisie," linked and dependent on the metropolis. In the long run, and disregarding short-run ups and downs, an important historical transformation of the system is the ever greater structural interconnection of the system as a whole and of the metropolises and satellites within it due to the rise of imperialism, metropolitan technological monopoly and other transformations. Accordingly, we must expect ever greater ties and interdependence of the bourgeoisies in metropolis and satellite.

(5) These ties, this growing interconnection, is accompanied by—no, produces—increasing polarization between the two ends of the metropolis-satellite chain in the world capitalist system. A symptom of this polarization is the growing international inequality of incomes and the absolute decline of the real income of the lower income recipients. Yet there is even more acute polarization at the lower end of the chain, between the national and/or local metropolises and their poorest rural and urban satellites whose absolute real income is steadily declining. This increasing polarization sharpens political tension, not so much between the international metropolis with its imperialist bourgeoisie and the national metropolises with national bourgeoisies, as between both of these and their rural and city slum satellites. This tension between the poles becomes sharper until the initiative and generation of the transformation of the system passes from the metropolitan pole, where it has been for centuries, to the satellite pole. This model and its hypotheses are further examined in relation to Chile (pp. 1-120).

B. THE DEVELOPMENT OF UNDERDEVELOPMENT

Turning to the experience of Brazil, this model can provide for the study and understanding of the discovery and settlement of Brazil by the Portuguese, while the dualist model cannot. In the fifteenth century and earlier, Europe was already in the throes of mercantilist expansion emanating from several metropolises and incorporating other areas and people into the expanding mercantilist system as satellites. The instruments were then, as they have been since, conquest, pillage, plantations, slavery, investment, unequal trade, and the use of armed force and political pressure. Portugal's fifteenth-century rise to metropolitan status was based on its breaking the Venetian monopoly of the Oriental trade by discovering the circum-African route to the East and by developing its own satellites along the way.

The discovery of America and the settlement of Brazil were the result of this same intra-European competition to become monopolistically exclusive metropolises. Upon discovery, Brazil, unlike Mexico and Peru, did not have a settled high civilization whose descendants might today be (erroneously) said to constitute an isolated, archaic "other" part of the society. It was the European settlement and capitalist development of the land which itself formed the society and economy we find there today. If today there were indeed an archaic survival in Brazil, separated from us by several centuries, it would have to be a remnant of something the European metropolis itself implanted there in the course of its capitalist expansion. But what the capitalist metropolis did implant in Brazil was not any archaic economic and social structure but rather the still live and developing metropolis-satellite structure of capitalism itself.

In Brazil, unlike New Spain and Peru, no gold or silver was found. But the competition between the European centers in expansion forced Portugal to occupy as much of the Brazilian territory as possible on threat of losing it to her rivals. Moreover, the North of Brazil had brazil wood, which was very much in demand for dyeing, as was indigo in Guatemala. Thus, this now underdeveloped northern part of Brazil was early incorporated into the expanding mercantile capitalist system as an exporter of a primary commodity. The grants of land—*capitanias* and *sesmarias*—made by the King to some of his subjects so that they would colonize the New World appear feudal and do indeed have some feudal background. Their essence, however, was not feudal, but capitalist. They were conceived and functioned as mechanisms in the expansion of the mercantile capitalist system. They were accepted by their recipients with commercial profits in view; and they were financed by them with commercial loans which they received and which they paid back—if they did not fail—from profits earned through the exploitation of others (Simonsen 1962: 80-83).

1. Sugar and the Underdevelopment of the Northeast

More important, in 1500 Portugal was already the world's largest producer of sugar, in the Madeira Islands; but sugar was in overproduction for the European market. After 1530, the flow of gold and then of silver from its colonies to Spain, and through Spain to Northwestern Europe, combined with the Oriental trade of these countries, generated, as is known, inflation and a concentration of wealth in all of Western Europe. The demand for and price of sugar also rose rapidly: sixfold in the course of the sixteenth century (Simonsen 1962: 112). Portugal was able to expand its sugar business, planting cane in Pernambuco in the Northeast of Brazil, which rapidly displaced its Atlantic islands as the most important producer. At the beginning, for the primary accumulation of capital, Portugal used indigenous slave labor (as well as foreign, mostly Dutch, capital). But the Indians did not work well—they were not well organized like the Aztecs. Nonetheless profits were large; Portugal had little population, one million, while Europe had fifty million (Simonsen 1962: 126); and thus it was both possible and necessary to import Negro slaves. Moreover, Portugal owned the West African slave export coast. Sugar production and slavery, therefore, were good business.

The socio-economic structure of the region in its golden years merits examination. Business was concentrated in the hands of a few owners of land and sugar mills, and in the merchants who mostly were not residents in Brazil and often not even Portuguese but Dutch. These were entirely tied to and dependent on the metropolis. The concentration of wealth in their hands, the transfer of much of it to the metropolis, and the structure of production whose greatest profit lay in producing a single product for export led to little domestic investment and production and to the importation from the metropolis of the equipment for the sugar mills and of luxury consumer goods for their owners. The structure of underdevelopment—in its essence the same structure which is still in evidence in Latin America in our day—was impregnated into the social and economic structure of the satellite through its very incorporation during its sixteenth-century boom into the world capitalist system.

After 1600, the power of Portugal declined and was overtaken by that of its rivals. The union of the crowns of Portugal and Spain led the enemies of Spain to attack Portugal as well. Between 1629 and 1654 Holland occupied a half of Brazil's sugar lands. In 1642, 1654, and 1661 Portugal signed commercial treaties giving Great Britain economic concessions in return for political protection; and in 1703 through the Treaty of Methuen, Portugal opened her entire market to British commerce and goods.

At the end of the seventeenth century, after their expulsion from Brazil, the Dutch and later others established sugar plantations in great numbers in the West Indies. The supply of sugar on the world market rose rapidly, and the price declined by one half. Sugar exports from the Brazilian Northeast declined by one half. Per capita income in the Northeast fell by one half (Furtado 1959: 68, 78-79, and Simonsen 1962: 112-114). After 1680, the Northeast of Brazil began to fall into decadence. The relative weakening of its ties with the metropolis forced the Northeast to turn in upon itself; the development of the system as a whole produced the involution of its Northeast Brazilian satellite.

The structure of underdevelopment which had already been implanted during so-called good times did not permit any other course during the bad times to come. Celso Furtado says in this

connection: "there occurred a process of economic involution.
. . . The Northeast was progressively transformed into an economy in which a large part of the population produced only what
was necessary to subsist. . . . The formation of the Northeastern
population and its precarious subsistence economy—basic element of the Brazilian economic problem in later epochs—are
thus linked to this slow process of decadence of the large sugar
enterprise, which in its best years was possibly the most profitable colonial agricultural business of all times" (Furtado 1959:
80-81). Here we have a major example of how capitalist development generates underdevelopment.

Two other aspects of the Brazilian experience of the sixteenth
and seventeenth centuries can be illuminated by our model and
at the same time help to confirm it. The sugar economy—the
satellite which is at the same time a national metropolis—generated a satellite economy of its own: livestock raising. Livestock was used for meat, for hides, for draft animals to run the
sugar mills, for fat to grease their works, for beasts of burden to
carry the huge quantities of firewood used in the boilers. The
livestock economy was much less profitable than sugar growing
and export. The stockmen were exploited by the sugar mills
whose satellite they were. Livestock grazing expanded into
Bahia and toward the North. Livestock came to be the main-
stay of the inland *sertaho* region.

The satellite livestock economy formed a metropolis in turn
with respect to the Indian zones into which its expansion forced
the Indians to withdraw and/or to serve as a source of exploited
labor power. The European metropolis thus affected the life of
the interior through a long chain of metropolises and satellites.
With the involution of the sugar economy of the Northeast, its
growing satellite livestock sector absorbed population which
went over from the declining export economy to this relatively
more subsistence economy (Simonsen 1962:145-148; Furtado
1959:70-76). In this Northeastern region of Brazil today rules
coronelismo (*gamonalismo* they call it in Peru, and *caciquismo*
in Mexico): the kind of all-powerful local economic, political,

social and police chieftainship that the so-called "feudal" landowner represents (Núñez Leal 1946).

The second case to be noted is São Paulo and its famous
bandeirantes or pioneers. São Paulo contained initially nothing
of great interest—nothing suitable for export. Therefore the region received little immigrant population; it had no large capitalist enterprises, and the properties in land (as in other non-
export areas, like the interior of Argentina) were small in area
and largely devoted to home consumption: There were no latifundias. The *bandeirantes* had two supplementary economic activities, neither very profitable. One was to look for gold and
silver mines which, except for a few gold washings, they did not
find. The other was to hunt Indians to be sold into slavery to
the sugar economy; but Indians were unwilling workers. The
São Paulo of the colonial period has always been termed "poor."
No doubt its inhabitants were poor—like the people on the
(non-latifundia) frontier of North America—but not so poor
as the slaves of the "rich" Northeast (or American South) who
had an average useful life of seven years. As my model, but
not the dualist model, suggests, São Paulo, being less tied to
the metropolis, exhibited less of the structure of underdevelopment (Simonsen 1962:203-246; Ellis 1937).

2. Britain and the Underdevelopment of Portugal

Between 1600 and 1750, Portugal itself underdeveloped and
was not able to expropriate so much from its Brazilian satellite.
Portugal was ever more converted into a satellite. The treaties
of the seventeenth century, and especially the Treaty of Methuen in 1703, brought on the destruction of Portugal's textile
industries, the take-over by Great Britain of its foreign and even
domestic trade, and the conversion of Portugal into a mere
entrepôt between Great Britain and Brazil and other Portuguese
colonies. Portugal did become an exporter of wine, in exchange
for the textiles it could no longer produce because of the flooding of its market by British products—which David Ricardo in

1817 had the temerity to interpret as a law of "comparative advantage." Portugal became a satellite-metropolis which took an ever smaller part of the economic surplus of its own Brazilian satellite thanks to the political monopoly position it still retained, while Great Britain took over the economic monopoly and spoils.

Illuminating in this connection are the observations of the Marquis of Pombal, Prime Minister of Portugal and its second Colbert, who clarified the situation and therewith the roots of Portugal's underdevelopment in 1755, some years before Adam Smith inquired into the causes and nature of the wealth of nations, and half a century before Ricardo assured the world that Portugal's production and exchange of wine for Britain's textiles was a universal law for the good of all. Pombal wrote:

> The Portuguese monarchy was in its last gasp. The English had firmly bound the nation into a state of dependence. They had conquered it without the inconvenience of a conquest. . . . Portugal was powerless and without vigor, and all of her movements were regulated by the desires of England. . . . In 1754 Portugal scarcely produced anything towards her own support. Two thirds of her physical necessities were supplied by England. . . . England had become mistress of the entire commerce of Portugal, and all the trade of the country was carried on by her agents. The English were at the same time furnishers and the retailers of all the necessities of life that the country required. Having a monopoly of everything, no business was carried on but through their hands. . . . The English came to Lisbon to monopolize even the commerce of Brazil. The entire cargo of the vessels that were sent thither, and consequently the riches that were returned in exchange, belonged to them. . . . These foreigners, after having acquired immense fortunes, disappeared on a sudden, carrying with them the riches of the country (quoted in Manchester 1933: 39-40).

3. Gold and the Underdevelopment of the Central Interior

At this time, when the price and profit of sugar had fallen to its minimum and Portugal found itself in the straits described by Pombal, gold and diamonds were discovered in large amounts in the interior of Brazil, in Minas Gerais and Goias. The subsequent events left their mark on the international and national level of capitalist development and underdevelopment until our times. The gold flowed through Portugal to Britain. In Brazil, slowly after 1720 and between 1740 and 1760 at its greatest rate, there was a veritable gold rush toward the Central Region. Cities were built in the interior. Slaves were imported from the stagnant sugar economy of the Northeast, and more slaves were imported from abroad. The gold attracted immigration from Europe and migration from São Paulo and the South. The satellite livestock and mule economy was greatly stimulated, particularly in the South of Brazil. The new population, geographically isolated and almost entirely engaged in mining activities, was in need of meat in large quantities. The transport of the gold and diamonds to the coast and of other goods in return required many thousands of mules. Thus, the livestock economy and its grazing regions again were satellites to the export economy of the national metropolis.

This time the expansion of the livestock economy served to link the various regions of Brazil to a much greater degree than before. Previously, except for coastwise shipping, the various regions of Brazil had been semi-independent of each other and each dependent only on the metropolis. Economic activity in the Central Region now grew to such an extent that in 1749, for instance, though the export of Pernambuco in the Northeast declined to £500,000, that of Rio de Janeiro, the port for the Central Region, rose to £1,800,000; and Rio de Janeiro was made the capital of Brazil (Simonsen 1962:362). The level of income in the region and the country rose. This time, however, since the gold appeared in surface washings rather than in great mines as in Mexico and Peru and since the proportion of slave labor used was less than in the Northeastern sugar economy—slaves never accounted for as much as half the population of the mining region—the degree of concentration in the distribution of income was much smaller than it had been in the time of the Northeastern sugar boom. The consequences of this difference in social and economic structure were to appear with the decline of the mining economy.

The age of gold did indeed disappear more rapidly than it

had arisen. From 1760, after only forty years—and only twenty of them with large-scale production—the mining economy of the Center declined rapidly. Oliveira Martins, a historian of the last century, summarizes: "The province of Minas [Gerais] had the appearance of a ruin, its settlements isolated from one another by leagues and leagues . . . it was a sad decadence and general desolation. Brazil began to enter a crisis which lasted a quarter of a century" (Simonsen 1962:292). And Simonsen adds: "But there still exist even today in regions of Minas and other parts of central Brazil millions of Brazilians, descendants of the first settlers, who lead a low level of life, working on poor lands and in the face of complex economic problems" (Simonsen 1962:295). Celso Furtado notes again: "[With] the decline of gold production there appeared swift and general decadence. . . . The whole mining economy came apart, with the urban centers declining and scattering large parts of their inhabitants into an economy of subsistence in a vast region of difficult transport. This relatively numerous population would come to be one of the major demographic centers of the country. In this case as in the Northeast . . . the monetary economy atrophied and [the population] came to work at an extremely low level of productivity in an agriculture of subsistence" (Furtado 1959:102-104). Here we have today the other major region in which the reign of *coronelismo* is important—which is called "feudal" but which is merely the result of the development of capitalism itself and of its internal contradictions.

Brazilian gold reanimated the metropolitan inflation and contributed importantly, just like the riches taken out of India by Clive, to Britain's accumulation of capital immediately before its war with Napoleon and its industrial takeoff. Thus, once more, the unequal development of the world capitalist system created the structure of underdevelopment in another populous region of Brazil—the very region in which in our day the military coup started.

During the second half of the eighteenth century, stimulated perhaps in part by the gold, Pombal tried to derail Portugal's path toward underdevelopment and to stimulate the country's economic development through a nationalist mercantile policy. His efforts, as we know, were in vain. It was already too late. Underdevelopment in Portugal had already struck too deep— and, at least until today, no country in the world has managed to free itself from such underdevelopment through any kind of capitalist policy, mercantilist or other.

4. War and the Underdevelopment of the North

But the attempts of Pombal had further effects on Brazil which also persist to our day. He expelled the Jesuits from Maranhão and Pará in the North and, through the establishment of a monopoly trading company, created another national export metropolis there—that is, another satellite of the world metropolis. During the closing years of the eighteenth century and the opening years of the nineteenth century, when the American Revolution withdrew Carolina rice from the market, when the Napoleonic Wars and the consequent Continental Blockade cut down trade, and the British cotton textile industry began to develop, there was a renewed rise in the demand for and the price of rice, cocoa, and above all, of cotton. Through all these circumstances the North of Brazil became an exporter of these products. Around the turn of the century São Luiz— its very name is today all but unknown outside Brazil—overtook all other Brazilian ports in export volume, was visited by 150 ships a year, sent abroad one million pounds sterling worth of goods, and because of its cultural flowering came to be called the Athens of Brazil (Simonsen 1962:346). After the peace of 1815, the renewed competition of American rice and cotton again did away with the market of the North of Brazil, though the American Civil War did occasion a brief spurt of exports, but not of development, in the 1860's. The North of Brazil underdeveloped until, at the very end of the nineteenth century, it was again awakened by Amazonian rubber. Quickly, half a million inhabitants were imported, mostly from the Northeast;

but just as quickly Brazilian wild rubber gave way to Southeast Asian plantation rubber. The population, whose migration to the North had been financed by the export interests, found itself stranded there, abandoned to the underdeveloped fate in which it still lives today. And here we have the third major region of *coronelismo*.

Returning to the colonial epoch, the Northeast and Bahia were also involved in the boom of the Napoleonic era. This, together with the slave revolt and the independence of Haiti in 1789, produced a new rise in the price of sugar and cocoa and increased demand from Brazilian suppliers. In response to the new demand, cotton was also planted in the Northeast. The economy of the Northeast was revitalized while that of the Central Region declined and decayed. This did not represent real economic development, merely an export boom similar to that of the sixteenth century, though on a much lesser scale. And it was short-lived. The peace of Metternich stabilized the international scene, the price of sugar and cotton again fell while the price of manufactured products rose—and the Brazilian economy, this time in all of its regions, again declined into economic depression, a passive capitalist involution that lasted half a century or more (Simonsen 1962:351-381).

5. Monopoly and the Underdevelopment of Industry

The colonial epoch of Brazil also produced manufacturing industry. The first iron works in the New World, North or South, were constructed in Brazil. There was substantial naval construction, especially for the important coastwise shipping associated with the collection and distribution along the coast of export and import goods. And like the *obrajes* in Spanish America, there was textile production in Brazil. It was to be found in the sugar mills, for the domestic use of the slaves and others, and was especially developed in São Paulo and Minas Gerais and also in Maranhão in the North (Lima 1961:114, 152-156, 166). This fact may be significantly linked with our model and hypotheses. It was precisely São Paulo and Minas Gerais—the first without any export industry and the second situated in the interior far from the overseas goods and after its golden age—which were the principal textile-producing centers of Brazil and which even got as far as exporting textiles to other regions. It is, as my hypothesis suggests, those satellite regions that are less strongly tied to the metropolis which have the opportunity for greater autonomous development, especially industrial development. Mining, as we noted earlier, had not produced so extreme a structure of underdevelopment and so unequal a distribution of income in Minas Gerais as sugar did in the Northeast. The internal market and the productive structure in Minas Gerais were therefore more suitable for an active capitalist involution—for industrial production—after the gold ran out and the ties with the metropolis weakened than had been the case in the Northeast.

Nonetheless the Center of Brazil, like other regions, remained a satellite. In 1786 (at the same time that Portugal tried to close its own doors to British textiles subsequent to Pombal's development efforts and only a few years after Spain had instituted similar measures in its colonies in 1778) the Queen of Portugal took action:

I, the Queen, let it be known . . . knowing of the large number of factories and manufactures which, in recent years, have spread through the various *capitanias* of Brazil, with grave prejudice to the culture and working of the land and of the mineral exploitation of this vast continent; because . . . it is obvious that when the number of manufacturers multiply themselves that much more will the number of the cultivators decline . . . as the extraction of gold and diamonds has already declined since, while they should occupy themselves in this useful and advantageous [agricultural] work, they on the contrary leave and abandon it to occupy themselves in another quite different one as is that of the said factories and manufactures, and since the real and solid wealth lies in the fruits and products of the earth . . . which form the entire basis and base of the relations and of the navigation and the trade between my loyal vassals of these kingdoms and those dominions, which I should stimulate and sustain in the benefit of the ones and the others . . . in consequence of all the above, I deem it well to order that all the factories, manufactures or shops of ships, of textiles, of gold and silversmithing . . . or of any kind of silk . . . or of any kind of cotton or linen, and cloth . . . or other kind of woolen goods . . . shall be extinguished and abolished in any place in which they may be found in my dominions in Brazil (quoted in Lima 1961: 311-313).

Note what the Queen said: The rise of manufacturing occurred when the production and export of gold declined, that is, as my hypothesis predicts, when the ties with the metropolis weaken, rather than strengthen. But since the ties of the satellite with the metropolis continued—as they still continue today —many manufacturing and industrial establishments were closed down and the country underdeveloped further.

6. Free Trade and the Consolidation of Underdevelopment in Brazil

After the Napoleonic wars the Brazilian economy underwent a period of depression, until coffee gave it a new impulse later in the nineteenth century. The invasion of Portugal by Napoleon forced the Regent Dom João VI in 1808 to transfer his court to Brazil under British protection and at British expense—and then to seek still more protection from Great Britain. For this Portugal naturally had to pay a price—with Brazil, as colonial satellite, paying a sizable part of it. In 1808, the Regent opened Brazilian ports to the shipping of all friendly nations. In 1810, he signed a commercial treaty with Great Britain which did away with almost all remaining mercantilist restrictions to trade and opened the ports of Portugal and Brazil to economic liberalism. During the Continental blockade this meant England, and in the nineteenth century it meant British industry.

Dom João VI reasoned and addressed his subjects as follows:

I have been served to adopt the most clearly proved principles of a healthy political economy, liberty and freedom of commerce and reduction of customs duties, joined with the most liberal principles, so that the cultivators of Brazil, promoting commerce, could obtain the greatest consumption of their products and achieve the greatest progress of culture in general. . . . [This is] the best way to make [Brazil] prosper, much better than the restrictive and mercantilist system which is ill adapted to a country in which at this time manufactures, except for the crudest kind, cannot be produced. . . . These same principles are corroborated by the system of free trade which by accord with my old, faithful and great ally, His Britannic Majesty, I adopted in the treaties of alliance and commerce which I have just contracted. . . . Do not worry that the introduction of British goods might hurt your industry. . . . For now your capital is best applied to the cultivation of your lands . . . later you will advance to manufactures. . . . The reduction of import duties necessarily must produce a large influx of foreign manufactures; but who sells much, necessarily also buys much. . . . Experience will show you that expanding your agriculture need not totally destroy your manufactures; and if some of them are of necessity abandoned, you may rest assured that this is proof that this manufacture did not rest on a solid base and was of no real advantage to the state. In the end, there will result great national prosperity, much greater than that which you could get before (quoted in Simonsen 1962: 405-406).

In 1821 the Regent returned to Portugal; and in 1822 Brazil declared its independence with his son, Pedro I, as Emperor. Nonetheless, in 1827 Brazil signed another treaty giving Great Britain full access to the Brazilian market on terms better than those conceded to other countries and, above all, on terms better than those available to Brazilian national industry. It was with this economic liberalism that Britain developed its industry while its satellites underdeveloped their manufacturing and agriculture.

The monopolistic metropolis-satellite structure of the capitalist system did not really change; it only altered its form and mechanism. During the mercantile epoch the metropolis's monopoly was maintained by military force and commercial monopoly; and it was thus that the metropolis developed its industry while the satellites underdeveloped their agriculture. During the liberal epoch, the same monopoly of the now industrially stronger metropolis was maintained and extended through free trade and military force. As Alexander Hamilton and Friedrich List recognized, it was liberalism and free trade which guaranteed Britain its nineteenth-century industrial monopoly over the satellites. When this policy no longer excluded her metropolitan rivals from the world market, liberalism was revised at the end of the nineteenth century by the imperialist colonial policy; and with the Depression of the 1930's Britain and John Maynard Keynes abandoned free trade entirely. It has been exhumed again and re-exported "made in USA" during the postwar era of our own times. Friedrich List, father of the *Zollverein,* had called mercantilist protection the ladder that Britain used to climb up, only to push it away so that others might not follow; and he called free trade Britain's major export good. Our perspective may perhaps be enhanced by the perception of List's American contemporary Ulysses S. Grant, who observed that "for centuries England has relied on protection, has carried it to extremes, and has obtained satisfactory results from it. There is no doubt that it is to this system that it owes its present strength. After two centuries, England has found it convenient to adopt free trade because it thinks that protection can no longer offer it anything. Very well then, Gentlemen, my knowledge of my country leads me to believe that within two hundred years, when America has gotten out of protection all that it can offer, it too will adopt free trade" (cited in Santos 1959:125 and retranslated from the Spanish by the present author).

The economic depression of Brazil in the nineteenth century and its penetration by the advance of British imperialism put Brazil entirely out of the development race of the century and of capitalist development as a whole. But it was the circumstances of colonial times which rendered this underdevelopment possible and necessary while the metropolis developed; and at the same time other previously non-satellized or little satellized countries such as Germany, the United States, and Japan achieved their development. (Japan is the classic case of a country which was not yet already satellized, and therefore underdeveloped, in the nineteenth century.) It was during colonial times, then, that a national metropolis and its bourgeoisie, if we may call it that, was formed. The national metropolis became a satellite exporter of primary products to the world metropolis and in turn depended on it for the import of manufactures and luxury consumption goods. The national oligarchy, be it agrarian, mining or commercial, naturally wants to import these goods at the lowest possible price, that is without tariff protection, just as long as it pays for these sumptuary goods with the economic surplus which it in turn expropriates from its national and provincial satellites. It is the structure of capitalist underdevelopment which, as we saw earlier, was implanted in the Northeast of Brazil with the first sugar plantation in 1530 and which in its essence persists up to our day. This satellite economic structure and resulting political policy is discussed in greater detail in relation to Chile (pp. 1-120).

During Britain's industrial expansion, then, Brazil underdeveloped even more. In "independent" Brazil, political power was of course vested in the large landowners and merchants, domestic and foreign—all of them free traders, naturally. Brazil's terms of trade worsened 40 percent between 1820 and 1850 (Furtado 1959:127). The exchange rate declined; the milrei was worth, in pounds sterling, 70d. in 1808 (Prado 1962: 137); thanks to the Napoleonic War it briefly rose to 85d. by 1814; then it began to fall in earnest, to 49d. by the time of Independence in 1822 and to 25d. in 1860; the American Civil War again brought a brief rise, and then the rate fell to 18d., its low before the end of slavery and Empire in 1888 and 1889 (Normano 1945:253-254). The balance of payments was in constant deficit each year from 1821 to 1860, after which the American Civil War and then coffee exports reversed it (Prado 1962:136). The deficit and other economic activity in Brazil was financed by foreign loans. By the middle of the century, service of the foreign debt consumed 40 percent of the Brazilian receipts (Prado 1962:142). Concurrently, Brazil's foreign and domestic wholesale trade fell almost entirely into British hands.

7. Summary: Passive Involution and Underdevelopment

We may thus draw some preliminary conclusions:

(a) The colonial epoch of Brazil did not have any connection with feudalism, but it did have to do with capitalist development. Furthermore, Brazilian reality is not the survival of a region "isolated" from capitalism; it is rather the product of the development of the capitalist system itself.

(b) What happened in the colony was determined by its ties with the metropolis and by the intrinsic nature of the capitalist system. It was not isolation but integration which created the reality of Brazilian underdevelopment. The life of the interior was determined through a whole chain of metropolises and satellites which extended from England via Portugal and Salvador de Bahia or Rio de Janeiro to the farthest outpost of this interior.

(c) What economic development did take place occurred in places and times in which the ties with the metropolis were less close—contrary to the dualist model, which sees progress as the diffusion from the metropolis outward into the interior. We saw this in São Paulo, Minas Gerais and the North. Development in Brazil was rendered possible to some extent by the fact that Portugal *was* a weak metropolis—too weak to exercise the same control over its colonies that other metropolises did.

(d) The temporary weakening of ties with the metropolis, or the decline of dependence on the export market and the unequal development of capitalism produced a passive capitalist involution in the Brazilian satellite, with the partial exception of Minas Gerais where the productive and income structure was less underdeveloped than elsewhere. It is the passive capitalist involution of the interior—Minas Gerais, Goias, the North and the Northeast—which led to the greatest degree of underdevelopment, not only in relative income but also in absolute social and political structure.

It is these regions in which *coronelismo* today reigns supreme, and in which political life is least ideologically based but instead "client based" and directed to serve immediate local interests. These are the regions of major influence and power of the Partido Social Democrata (PSD), the party of Juscelino Kubitschek, the political party *par excellence* of agrarian and provincial clientelism and opportunism. But these regions are not today politically "isolated." Rather, the clientelism and political opportunism are widely taken advantage of by the national and international metropolis through the chain of metropolises and satellites which reaches to the most supposedly isolated village and farm. The world press coverage of the fate of Governor Mauro Borges of the interior State of Goias in 1964 proves that the peasant of the interior is inevitably linked to the military government of the metropolis.

(e) The renewed strengthening of metropolis-satellite ties represented by free trade consolidated this underdevelopment in the Brazilian satellite. The political independence of Brazil was not enough to liberate it from underdevelopment or the structure that produces it. On the contrary, independence placed political power into the hands of those economic groups whose vested interests were to maintain the Brazilian status quo. Simultaneously the metropolis, now Britain without the mediation of Portugal, replaced the increasingly outdated mercantilist instruments of metropolitan monopoly control by the newer and now more advantageous ones of free trade. The essential metropolis-satellite structure of the system did not change, either domestically or internationally. Thus, political independence did not produce Brazil's economic development; and free trade consolidated its underdevelopment and the structure which inevitably generates it.

C. THE UNDERDEVELOPMENT OF DEVELOPMENT

In the middle of the nineteenth century coffee ushered Brazil into a new epoch, analogous to that of sugar in the sixteenth century and to that of gold in the eighteenth century. Coffee production began slowly in the 1820's. During the 1840's it advanced from Rio de Janeiro upwards along the Paraíba River valley. The capital invested in this coffee expansion was Brazilian. Accumulated and concentrated largely in the gold mining economy of Minas Gerais and the foreign trade of Rio de Janeiro (Monbeig 1952), this capital now began to be channeled into the coffee sector of the East-Central Region. Indeed it was withdrawn from other regions to an extent alarming to the Northeast, where slaves were being bought up at prices the Northeast could not meet and shipped south. Pernambuco tried to invoke the total prohibition of the export of slaves from the region but failed. Several Northeastern states did, however, impose an export tax on the transfer of their slave capital to the South. Thus, we see the rise of yet another Brazilian national metropolis, linked to the world metropolis through the export trade.

1. Coffee and External Satellization

In the 1860's, the world demand for coffee increased substantially; and coffee planting advanced farther into the interior in the direction of São Paulo. Railroads were built during the era of Mauá, the Brazilian Carnegie, largely with Brazilian capital. The improvement of the port of Santos was also necessary; this was financed by the British *after* Brazilian capital had paved the way and shown the profit (Ellis 1937:177-180). Coffee attracted increasing European immigration. Slavery was abolished in 1888 and the Republic proclaimed in 1889.

After this, began the major expansion of coffee in São Paulo. Five characteristics of this expansion are detailed below. Our understanding of later periods of economic expansion will rest in great part on the similarities and differences which they exhibit with respect to this expansion. (a) Domestic inflation: The amount of paper money in circulation increased from 215,000 *contos de reis* in 1889 (197,000 according to Normano 1945:231 and Guilherme 1963:19) to 778,000 in 1898 (Monbeig 1952:95). Inflation is a characteristic that reappears in all the later expansionary periods. (b) Devaluation, as long as

Brazil was more or less on the gold standard, was automatic. The value of the milrei dropped from 27d. in 1889 to 6d. in 1898 (Monbeig 1952:95 and Normano 1945:254). (c) Rise and fall of the terms of trade: The price of coffee rose from 2 cents a pound in 1889 to 9 cents in 1895, then fell to 4 cents in 1898 and to 2 cents by 1903 (Monbeig 1952:97). (d) External finance, especially by foreign banks (Monbeig 1952:90-99). (e) The consequences were foreign take-over, at first of the coffee export trade and later of some of its domestic finance and production as well. Once overproduction began and domestic producers and merchants fell into financial difficulties (previous expansion had been highly speculative), foreign houses began to take over these domestic activities, and even to buy coffee lands. The Banks of London and the River Plate, Rothschild, Société Générale de Paris, and the National City Bank of New York distinguished themselves in this process (Monbeig 1952: 98-99).

Overproduction of coffee began in 1900 and has continued with almost no interruption to our time. In 1905, after some vacillation and political pressure, the government of Brazil began a policy of supporting the price of coffee and stockpiling it—a policy which also continues to this day. This helped the domestic producers somewhat, and the foreign merchants even more. Maintenance of the price support policy without drastic consequences was possible in the short run, because Brazil had a semi-monopoly in coffee production—in the 1920's about 75 percent of the world's output (Guilherme 1963:29-30)—and because the measure was externally financed. In the long run, as we shall see, this policy led to important consequences. Meanwhile, we may briefly observe three developments which accompanied the expansion of coffee in São Paulo.

2. Industry and Internal Polar Satellization

The first of these developments was industry. The number of industrial establishments rose from 200 in 1881 to 626 in 1889,

3,000 in 1907, and more than 13,000 in 1920 (Prado 1960:296-298; Simonsen 1939:25-26, 31). But it was the World War in Europe which occasioned the big spurt in Brazilian industrial development, a fact consistent with my hypothesis. "Three countries came out profiting economically as an immediate result of the War: the United States, Japan and Brazil. . . . 5,940 new industrial firms were established [in Brazil] during the years 1915-1919 compared with 6,946 during the period of 1890-1914" (Normano 1945:137-139). Of the 10,000 new industrial establishments built in the fourteen-year period between the two censal years 1907 and 1920, 60 percent were built during the five war years 1914-1919 (Prado 1960:298; Simonsen 1939: 25-26). Industrial production rose 109 percent from 1914 to 1917, measured in deflated constant prices, or 153 percent, from $956 million to $2,424 million, at current prices (Horowitz 1964: 208), and from 1,350,000 *contos de reis* in 1914 to 3,000,000 *contos de reis* in 1920 (Normano 1945:139). Though still concentrated in light industry making consumer goods, the composition of industrial output changed. In 1889, textiles had accounted for 60 percent of Brazilian industrial production: In 1907, textiles and clothing accounted for 48 percent, which by 1920 declined to 36 percent. Food products increased from 27 percent in 1907 to 40 percent in 1920 (Simonsen 1939:31; Normano 1945:140-142).

The second capitalist development, also in accordance with my model and hypothesis, was the concentration of economic activity and income in one national metropolitan center and the polarization of the economy as a whole. In 1881, the regional distribution of industrial production had been: Rio de Janeiro 55 percent, Bahia in the Northeast 25 percent, and São Paulo 5 percent (Simonsen 1939:23). By 1907 Rio had fallen to 30 percent and São Paulo risen to 16 percent (Simonsen 1939:34). In 1914 São Paulo claimed 20 percent of Brazilian industrial output (Simonsen 1939:34); 1920, 33 percent (Simonsen 1939:34); 1938, 43 percent (Simonsen 1939:34), by 1959, 54 percent (Conselho Nacional 1963:267), and today

São Paulo has still more. Bahia in the meantime has fallen to 1.7 percent in 1959 (Conselho Nacional 1963:267).

3. Foreign Investment and Underdevelopment

The third capitalist development is also in accordance with my model and hypotheses: The world capitalist metropolis recovered, its ties with the satellites were again strengthened, and national development in Brazil began to be strangled and misdirected. The 1920's witnessed an expansion similar to that of the 1890's, complicated by the government's coffee price support and stockpiling policy. The features again were (a) inflation, (b) devaluation, (c) first an increase, and then a decrease, in the terms of trade, (d) external financing, and (e) the inevitable consequences: Increasing foreign domination of the Brazilian economy and its eventual strangulation. The external financing of the coffee program brought foreign exchange, money which was spent on the import of foreign goods which competed with those produced by Brazilian industry. The price support program spurred internal inflation and domestic demand, thus attracting foreign firms which produced in Brazil, in competition with Brazilian firms. The deflation, moreover, helped the foreign firms to buy Brazilian money and installations and thus to establish themselves cheaply. This entire capitalist development adversely affected Brazilian industry and economic development. Furthermore, Brazil had to spend an ever greater share of its foreign exchange earnings to service the foreign debt. In addition to hurting Brazil's immediate import capacity, this development was and remains self-aggravating and self-defeating: To repay past debts, Brazil became still more dependent on new loans, and thus more dependent on the metropolis, now increasingly the United States. This dependence inevitably brought further developments which were advantageous to the metropolis and prejudicial to the interests of its Brazilian satellite—particularly Brazilian industry. There are thus fundamental similarities between the situation and events of the first half of the nineteenth century and the second half of the twentieth century.

But there is now a difference: There have been new mechanisms of satellization developed by the imperialist metropolis, the United States. J. F. Normano (1931) summarized these developments following the First World War with considerable insight and great foresight—as post-Second World War events such as those reviewed in my "On the Mechanisms of Imperialism" (Frank 1964b) were to prove.

An inspection of the industrial enterprises of the United States in South America reveals that they are mostly affiliates and subsidiaries of corporations in the United States. . . . [It] is the great United States concerns which have organized these enterprises with their own funds, neither offering the stocks for sale to the general public, nor issuing certificates representing their holdings in these companies. . . . But a part of the so-called foreign capital is in reality native. A large portion of these deposits in the foreign banks of South America is of local origin, while the investments and loans of these banks are considered foreign. . . . This method is now used on a large scale by branches of the United States banks.

Today the investors of the United States in South American industry are the world's greatest industrial giants. The industrial investments of the United States . . . however, are direct, and originate in the quest of ultra-modern mass production for new worlds to conquer. Here, on the other hand, is not the financier, but the industrial corporation which organizes and leads these developments. So in this sense we cannot speak of pure financial capitalism in the United States. There are altogether, perhaps, thirty great— nay, greatest—corporations of the world officially domiciled in the United States, which direct the industrial investments of the United States in South America. . . . The South American company is really in this case a local extension of the parent corporation, and constitutes a point of expansion of industrial United States abroad. Such world expansion is typical of the modern stage of capitalism, for national boundaries are too narrow for world enterprises.

The United States' success is almost entirely a question of noncompetitive exports of manufactures under United States massproduction methods. . . . The *exports* from the United States in the main include a few articles of modern mass-production. Motor-cars, radios, phonographs, machines are a few products of the newly organized large-scale industries. . . . Who produces these articles? Mainly the same "Big Thirty." . . . The *imports* of the United States from South America are mainly vegetable, mining, raw materials, such as petroleum, tin, coffee. Who produces them in South America? Mainly the affiliated organizations of the same "Big Thirty" of the United States. Their investments virtually lie in factories which engage in an export business. Much of the foreign trade of the United States with South America is dominated by the same firms which are regular investors in the local South American industries. These mammoth concerns seem to be foremost not only in investments but also in foreign trade.

The entire economic intercourse with South America seems to be mainly a result of an incessant expansion of the industrial giants. "Trade follows the flag"—the policy of conquest—has been replaced by the new formula, "Trade follows capital"—the policy of economic penetration. The slogan which came into fashion is: "Foreign loans promote business at home." In our case this formula is erroneous. For the moving force in capital exports is large-scale industry, mass-production at its height, the "Big Thirty" concerns which operate throughout the world, but have their official domiciles in the United States. It is they who manage the investments, and through these investments direct the export of materials of production such as machines and installations of various kinds. It is they who supervise the production itself, and through it the distribution of the manufactured articles. They rarely work for the local market. They operate for the market of the world (Normano 1931: 57, 224, 60-61, 41, 64-66).

The imperialist metropolis has further developed in these directions since Normano's time. The foreign monopolies have learned to use Brazilian national capital by recourse to sources other than Brazilian branches of metropolitan banks, and they have come to satellize not only their own manufacturing affiliates in Brazil but previously independent Brazilian firms and increasingly most of Brazil's national industry.

In the 1920's the political consequences of American penetration and of the Brazilian economy's renewed postwar incorporation into the imperialist metropolis-satellite structure were a Brazilian government dedicated to serving the interests of the imperialist metropolis. The government of President Washington Luis in the late 1920's represented the agricultural, commercial, and industrial coffee interests; and Washington Luis proclaimed himself a great friend of the United States. He "practically was his own Minister of the Treasury" (Normano 1945), and his "Brazilian" economic policy sparkled with features we will readily recognize. His main concern was with the balance of payments and with prompt Brazilian payments on its foreign debt. And the President gave his full support to the entry of foreign capital, especially American. His government declared the Brazilian currency convertible. What happened?

4. Crisis in the Metropolis and Active Involution in the Satellite

In 1929 came the crash. The price of coffee and the demand for it fell sharply; exports declined from 95 million pounds sterling in 1929 to 66 million in 1930 (Normano 1945:257). Convertibility now permitted a major capital flight, and the inflow of capital of course stopped altogether. The government, now short of funds to pay its creditors abroad, tried to find them in the national economy. Following classical prescriptions—still followed by his successors today—President Washington Luis, who wavered between the "banking school and the monetary school" (Normano 1945:240), cut domestic government spending. Like his mentor, the American government of the day, he even reduced the money supply—by 10 percent (Guilherme 1963:32). The result was highly prejudicial to Brazilian national industry, whose orders fell off and whose production declined. At the same time agricultural producers, especially those who had been working with a long line of credit, suffered similarly.

The result was the successful "Revolution of 1930." This political and economic movement was supported by the national industrial bourgeoisie, whose interests had been prejudiced by preceding events; and it was directed against the agrarian, commercial and metropolitan interests which had shaped and benefited from previous governmental policy. The Revolution was also supported by political elements from the State of Rio Grande do Sul in the South, whose economy was less linked to the export trade and the imperialist metropolis; and it was directed against the traditional centers of political power—coffee and commercial São Paulo and agricultural, mining and banking Minas Gerais. These two states had traditionally exchanged the Presidency of the Republic back and forth between them. It is no accident that the new President, Getulio Vargas, came from Rio Grande do Sul, which had been settled more by homesteaders than by latifundists and in which a new regional manufacturing center had sprung up. Some observers have called this event "Brazil's bourgeois revolution." But this change of government did not bring with it the expulsion from power of the agrarian interests which had "traditionally" held it and which had been plainly capitalist, rather than "feudal," all along. Instead, the new government meant the accession to power of a new group, the industrialists and Southerners, who now rose to share the privileges with the former beneficiaries.

The "Revolution" was immediately reflected in a new government policy. The old policy of supporting the domestic price of coffee was of course continued and, because of the Depression, even stepped up. But this program was now financed internally instead of externally, a change which was to have far-reaching economic repercussions in Brazil. The government also instituted a policy of tariff protection, though the economically depressed metropolis was not then exporting much anyway.

The result was an economic expansion quite different from previous expansions. Its characteristics were, briefly, the following: (a) Domestic inflation and an increase of internal demand, as in all previous and later expansions. (b) Revaluation, instead of devaluation. (c) Decline in the terms of trade, due to the fall in the price of and demand for coffee and other export products. Brazil's capacity to import declined by one third between 1929 and 1937 (Furtado 1959:223), while the economically depressed metropolis exported fewer industrial goods. (d) Internal finance instead of external. (e) In consequence, instead of increased metropolitan control and strangulation of the Brazilian economy, there arose an unparalleled growth of national industry.

During the economic depression of the world capitalist system, in accordance with my model and hypotheses, the Brazilian satellite experienced a very active capitalist involution. The internal inflation accompanied by internal finance and relative isolation from metropolitan competition led to a sharp rise in the prices of and demand for Brazilian industrial goods. Brazilian industry responded with a rapid and large increase of industrial output. Industrial production rose some 50 percent between 1929 and 1937 (Furtado 1959:224) and some 100 percent between 1931 and 1938 according to Roberto Simonsen (1939:44), then President of the Brazilian Industrial Association. Between 1934 and 1938, industrial output rose some 60 percent (Simonsen 1939:44). The increase of production was at first achieved by fuller use of installed capacity, which had been idled during the "boom" which brought increasing foreign presence in the late 1920's and the bust of the early 1930's. The same presumptive, idle, excess industrial capacity shown in subsequent output increases not matched by increases of installed capacity is also found in the 1910's, when wartime industrial output rose faster than industrial capacity (Normano 1945:139-142). In the late 1930's Brazil, relying on profits from this output and from the high incomes of industrialists and agriculturists, began to install new industrial productive capacity, taking advantage also of the facilities for the purchase at low prices of used equipment idled in the metropolitan countries by the Depression. Brazil substituted domestic production for consumer goods previously imported and increased its basic industry even more. Nonetheless, in 1938 textiles, clothing and food products still accounted for 56 percent of industrial output and basic industry for only 13 percent. And, unlike the Soviet

Union's contemporary expansion, Brazil's iron and steel output still covered only one third of her consumption of these products (Simonsen 1939:44).

Let us pause to analyze this development. Economically, why was this a period of active capitalist involution in the face of the Brazilian satellite's weakened relations with the metropolis, instead of passive involution as before? Politically, why did the agrarian, commercial, and imperialist interests allow the sharing of their power and influence with the newer but still quite weak national industrial interests? In other words, why was the Revolution of 1930 possible and successful? (There had been previous unsuccessful challenges to the government in power during the 1920's.)

My model, it may be remembered, emphasizes the historical transformation, particularly of the basis of metropolitan monopoly, within the capitalist system. The fundamental metropolis-satellite structure has remained the same throughout, but the basis of metropolitan monopoly has changed over the centuries. During the mercantilist period, the basis of metropolitan monopoly was military force and mercantile monopoly; the satellites were denied freedom of trade. During the nineteenth century, the basis of metropolitan monopoly increasingly became industry, light industry and textiles. This metropolitan monopoly, called "liberalism," permitted or even enforced the satellites' freedom of trade but denied them freedom of industrial production. By the first half of the twentieth century, the basis of metropolitan monopoly increasingly shifted to capital and intermediate goods. The satellites were now increasingly free to produce textiles and other light industry consumer goods— indeed they were even forced to do so by imperialism's metropolitan factories set up on their soil—but they were denied the freedom to establish their own capital and intermediate equipment industry. For these products, on which they were more and more dependent since these were the necessary input for their light industrial output, the satellites were still dependent on the monopoly of the metropolis. Then in the second half of the twentieth century, the basis of metropolitan monopoly was to shift again, now increasingly to technology, combined with still greater penetration of metropolitan international monopoly corporations into the satellite economies.

The active involution of Brazil in the 1930's may thus be explained by the fact that Brazil, like some other satellite countries, had in earlier years been able to establish some industry, and therewith the accompanying economic and social structure and nascent industrial bourgeoisie, partly independently during the First World War and in dependence on the metropolis during the 1920's. In 1930, therefore, the social and economic structure of São Paulo was more propitious to responding to the relaxation of metropolis-satellite ties through active capitalist involution than had been the case in Minas Gerais at the end of the gold rush or in the Northeast or North at the times of their passive capitalist involution. Nonetheless, as my model suggests and as later events were to show, as long as Brazil remained a capitalist satellite, such active involution, however much of a takeoff into development it might seem at the time, had to be short-lived.

But why was it politically possible for the Revolution of 1930 to succeed and for the coalition of agrarian, mercantile, imperialist and national industrial interests to prosper? Why was so weak a national industrial group permitted to share power and the formulation of policy? In a word, because the "traditional" capitalist interests had little capacity and less reason to resist this turn of events. The imperialist metropolis was less able to intervene because of the Depression. And if the agrarian, mercantile and metropolitan interests were not so well served by the events of the 1930's, if it was less possible to sell coffee to the metropolis and to import manufactures from them, this was due not so much to the Brazilian public policy adopted in concert with Brazilian national industrial interests as it was to the unavoidable Depression in the world capitalist metropolis. Moreover, the domestic coffee interests were not seriously disadvantaged by the intervention of the industrialists in policy making; through the government's continued coffee price support policy, these interests were still able to sell their coffee on the artificially created domestic market, if not on the depressed world market. The wedding of potentially conflicting interests was, for the time being, not too unhappy.

But in a capitalist satellite this kind of honeymoon cannot last forever. It lasted about two decades in Brazil, because the natural pressures to break up the marriage were diminished again by the recession of 1937 and soon after by the war and its immediate aftermath. Tensions soon began to appear—there was an attempted "counter-revolution" in 1932 and another in 1937—but these were held in check politically by Vargas's dictatorship under the *Estado Novo* (New State) and economically by events in the metropolis. Though to my knowledge no economic interpretation of the political circumstances of the *Estado Novo* has appeared in print, I would venture the following interpretation:

The years 1934 to 1937 witnessed a partial recovery in the metropolis—especially in Germany, which came to replace a significant part of the United States' share of Brazilian trade (Guilherme 1963:43). The price and demand for Brazilian exports began to rise again, and these exerted pressure to raise the exchange rate again. The government seems to have at least partially acceded to this pressure, to the dismay of certain interest groups in Brazil. A British student of Argentina, referring to the period preceding the First World War, summarizes the interests at stake in this sort of situation: "[The] dominant political group, the export-producers and landowners . . . in favorable years had a distinct interest in exchange stability, for it prevented the adverse shift in income distribution which an appreciating exchange rate would have brought, and in unfavorable times [had] a bias in favor of the depreciating exchange rate, which shifted the distribution of income in their favor" (Ford 1962:192). That is, devaluation shifts the burden to others; and exchange stability maintains it there. Wanderley Guilherme observes: "When the exchange rate was revalued, during the recovery of the world capitalist system between 1934 and 1937, the two leading groups of Brazilian society were decidedly opposed to our money's recuperation of international purchasing power, given that this meant the decline in profits of one of the groups—the coffee growers—and the threat of low-priced competition of foreign products for the other—the industrial bourgeoisie" (Guilherme 1963:41). In consequence, the Government fixed the exchange rate.

The agrarian interests, however, had a much stronger and more immediate interest in preventing revaluation, which cut into their current income, than did industrialists who had other means of protecting their sales and who were also importers of foreign equipment. These externally produced circumstances, in combination with the domestic agrarian interests' dislike of industrial demand for their labor supply, probably helped lead to renewed attempts to activate the traditional agrarian-commercial-imperialist political alliance and to reinstitute the traditional economic policy of devaluation, external finance, etc. In 1938, the Integralists, an outspokenly fascist movement of admitted Italian and German inspiration, attempted a coup against Vargas; but the attempt was frustrated by the recently installed "new state." Six months previously, Vargas had assumed dictatorial powers and instituted the *Estado Novo*. This was partly an attempt to contain this pressure from the Right as well as pressure from the Left which had manifested itself in 1935 in a frustrated Communist-led coup (perhaps motivated in part by the prejudicial effect on labor income of revaluation), and also an attempt to maintain by force the agrarian-commercial-imperialist-national industrial bourgeois marriage. Vargas lasted until 1945. He was aided in containing the internal opposition by the 1937 recession, which removed the pressure to revalue again, and by the war, which again removed some of the external pressure on this unstable marriage.

The Second World War, as my model would predict, resulted in renewed or continued active capitalist involution in Brazil. The terms of trade rose. But it was difficult for Brazil to take "advantage" of these by importing more, since the metropolis itself of course needed all it could produce. The foreign exchange earned was sterilized abroad; and even its amount was less than it might have been, since Brazil, together with other satellite countries, agreed to keep down the price of its exports to the Allies as its "contribution to the war effort." At the same time, excess capacity disappeared, due to the output increases of the previous decade, so that internal demand exerted pressures to increase both prices and the amount of goods supplied. President Vargas identified himself more and more with the national industrial bourgeoisie and the unionized workers who were the social product of this industrial expansion. His government instituted several "progressive" measures, such as support for unionization and minimum wages, while President Vargas himself founded the *Partido Trabalista Brasileiro* or PTB (Brazilian Workers Party). Over the long run, this labor policy, like that of Perón in Argentina, results in an alliance between the industrial workers and the national industrial bourgeoisie, which amounts to the pacification of the workers and their unions by that bourgeoisie. Insofar as the potpourri Brazilian political parties represent any particular groups, in recent times the PTB has become the instrument of the more nationalist wings of the more industrialist groups of the Brazilian bourgeoisie swinging labor votes. But this "national" bourgeoisie, and therewith its organized labor support, has itself become less and less independent of the metropolis.

5. Recovery in the Metropolis and Resatellization of Brazil

In 1945, at war's end, Vargas was thrown out. As long as the metropolis had not fully recovered and needed all it could produce, its contradictions with the satellites remained relatively dormant. Brazil had large amounts of accumulated foreign exchange; its terms of trade were high and the exchange rate as well. The economy appeared to be developing well, relying on its foreign exchange and some selective import controls to substitute domestic production for consumer goods imports and importing more equipment for its growing industrial installations. All imports rose 83 percent between 1945 and 1951, but equipment imports rose 338 percent (Furtado 1959:243). Nonetheless, Vargas' populism was eliminated and oppression of the labor movement was reinstituted.

In 1951, Vargas returned to the Presidency, elected by popular vote. His campaign had had a markedly populist, nationalist, anti-imperialist tone. He appointed his fellow Southerner João (Jango) Goulart to the Labor ministry (though, on threat of being forced out of the Presidency himself, he later removed him); he created Petrobras, the Brazilian state petroleum company; and he threatened to create an electric companion, Electrobras. The metropolis recovered after the Korean War; the metropolis-satellite contradictions again became more acute; and Vargas killed himself, leaving a now famous suicide note charging that foreign and domestic right-wing interests and pressures had forced him to his death.

Vargas was replaced by President Café Filho and his ultra-reactionary government, reminiscent of Washington Luis and foreshadowing the present gorilla government of Castello Branco. Café Filho's government is best remembered for and characterized by the Monetary and Credit Authority's Instruction 113, on which the President of the Federation of Industries of São Paulo commented, "Foreign firms can bring their entire equipment in at the free market price . . . national firms, however, have to do so through exchange licenses established in import categories. In this way, there was created veritable discrimination against national industry. We do not plead for preferential treatment but for equal opportunities" (Brasil 1963:125 and Frank 1964b:289). They did not get them, of course; on the contrary, national industry was required to import only new equipment while foreign firms were permitted to import used equipment, which allowed them to produce at a cost the national firms could not meet. This instruction and policy remained in force throughout the following government of Juscelino Kubitschek until it was modified by President Janio Quadros in 1961.

After two attempted military coups, in which the backers of the above policy tried to prevent him from taking office after his election, Juscelino Kubitschek became President from 1955 to 1960. He built Brasilia. But he did a lot more than that. He tried to stem the tide of Brazil's full reincorporation into the recovered and expanding imperialist metropolis-satellite system, by resorting to externally financed internal expansion. The expansion, like earlier ones, was financed through inflation. But, unlike some earlier expansions, this one was accompanied by devaluation, declining terms of trade, and external finance. The cost of living rose; workers complained and were pacified by wage increases. Import costs rose; imports were financed by foreign loans and direct investments: Instruction 113 was still in force. Foreign monopolies established themselves in the Brazilian market with even greater speed and force than during the previous government. Corruption flourished on all sides. Everybody got a rake-off. And the per capita growth rate actually rose from 3 percent per year during the governments of Dutra and Vargas to 4 percent per year under Kubitschek (computed from APEC 1962:27). But it was all strictly a policy of *après moi le déluge*. And the deluge came. In 1961 the per capita growth rate was still above 4 percent (APEC 1926:27). But in 1962 it fell to 0.7 percent, in 1963 to minus 1 percent (*Conjuntura Económica* 1964:15), and in 1964 to minus 6 percent—a 3 percent absolute decline combined with a 3 percent increase of population (*Conjuntura Económica* 1965: 11). And the growth rate is the least of it: It is only the symptom of the ever more acute structural underdevelopment of Brazil, which its continued participation in the capitalist system necessarily produces.

The political events of these years are well known. Kubitschek's now famous policy of "developmentism" was followed by President Janio Quadros's populism. Though supported only by the right wing *União Democrática Nacional* or UDN (Democratic National Union), which represents primarily the commercial export and other interests tied to imperialism and centered in São Paulo (whose governor Quadros had been), he swept away the combined electoral opposition of the PTB laborists and the PSD agrarianists with the same symbolic broom with which he promised to sweep away corruption once elected. In office, Quadros tried to rely on the popular support to the exclusion of the support of the economic interest groups whose party ticket he had headed. Far from mending political fences, he broke up the fences that remained. And more foolhardy still, he reacted to Brazil's increasing satellization and began what came to be known as Brazil's "independent" nationalist foreign political and economic policy. He established diplomatic and trade relations with the socialist countries to expand Brazil's export markets and lessen its dependence on American markets; he opposed the United States position at the Punta del Este conference; he even decorated Che Guevara at the close of that conference. Two days later, in August 1961, Quadros was no longer President. He resigned under pressure, tried to rally the country around him and his populism, but was prevented from doing so by the same domestic and foreign economic, military and political forces, nominally headed by Carlos Lacerda, which had already driven Vargas to suicide and were to make their presence felt again in April 1964.

These same interest groups tried to forestall the accession to the Presidency of Vice President Jango Goulart and tried, by force of arms, to install in 1961 the regime which they finally succeeded in establishing in 1964. They failed only because of a popular uprising against them, organized by elements of the national bourgeoisie—which, in contrast to April 1964, still had an interest in doing so. Goulart had made his political career in the PTB on the shoulders of the more nationalist elements of the bourgeoisie and the labor unions; over the latter he had come to have a large measure of personal control. Both groups now came out in force, especially in his and Vargas's home state of Rio Grande do Sul, to support him and the Constitution.

The economic situation which Goulart's government had to face was ever more critical. Prices rose and the exchange rate fell faster than ever before, while production declined or at least failed to rise. The foreign debt had risen to the astronomical proportions of U.S. $3,000 million, half of it due within two years. It was too late to remedy the situation through simple measures of economic policy. President Goulart faced the choice of either giving in still more to domestic and foreign commercial interests, in the vain hope that they would bail out Brazil and himself, or following the advice of his brother-in-law, Leonel Brizola (whose resolute political action in Rio Grande do Sul had permitted Goulart to assume the Presidency in the face of the attempted August 1961 military coup), by calling a halt to concessions which only suck Brazil and its President ever deeper into troubled waters. That is, he could try to begin an about-face and take some measures, however limited, to bolster up some national and popular interests.

Goulart, whatever his personal qualities, is a typical representative of the national bourgeoisie which was standing on ever weaker economic ground and which in a satellite country cannot take really independent action. He vacillated and gave in ever more to the increasing pressures from the domestic and foreign Right. Unable to face the growing economic problems and instability, Goulart was kicked out and forced into political exile by the same Carlos Lacerda and his imperialist, militarist and commercial-agricultural supporters who had already dispatched Presidents Vargas and Quadros. The national bourgeoisie, this time caught in a vise between the imperialist-generated decline in their profits and labor union pressure against the trend of declining real wages—which if reversed would cut into their profits still further—did not rise to defend Goulart. He and all serious pretense at democracy, populism or national development were sacrificed by all sectors of the Brazilian satellite bourgeoisie acting in concert with the political, military and economic representatives of the American metropolitan bourgeoisie.*

The military government of Castello Branco now took over, reminiscent of the governments of Washington Luis and Café Filho which had served imperialist and reactionary interests under similar circumstances; and this Brazilian government handed the Brazilian economy over to the Americans lock, stock and barrel. Some sectors of the Brazilian bourgeoisie undoubtedly do have contradictions with the imperialist metropolis, but they and the remainder of the bourgeoisie have still more pressing contradictions with the satellites and the proletariat from whose exploitation they live. The Brazilian bourgeoisie, national and otherwise, with its perspectives for profitable national development now ever more limited by the international and national capitalist metropolis-satellite structure, now tries to maintain its immediate economic position by resorting to still greater exploitation of its domestic labor and satellites and by vain appeals to metropolitan capital to bail it out.

In August, 1964, the Mexican government's Foreign Trade Bank reported in its monthly review *Comercio Exterior:* "[The] political events that have recently developed in Brazil are strongly reflected in the economic situation. . . . The economic activity of the country has slowed down. . . . Bank credit to the private sector has been restricted. . . . Government expenditures, especially investments, have been severely cut. . . . For the first time there exists the spectre of unemployment in alarming proportions coming to several hundreds of thousands." The military government's economic policy, though supposedly combating inflation through a tight money policy, has been to increase the exploitation of labor through rising prices and falling real wages. Inflation in 1964 was greater than ever before, greater than under the Goulart government—which was

* These economic consequences of American imperialism in Brazil are examined in greater detail in my "Exploitation or Aid" and "On the Mechanisms of Imperialism" in Frank 1963 and 1964b and the political background of the April 1964 military coup in Frank 1964a.

accused of economic mismanagement by those now in power. During the first six months of 1964, the official rate of inflation, which according to Governor Lacerda himself far understates the real rate, was 42 percent, compared to 30 percent in the corresponding months of 1963.

At the same time, "the government sent businessmen a circular in which it recommends that they abstain from granting wage increases which they think distort the wage structure. . . . The circular holds . . . that wage raises in line with the increase in the cost of living encourage inflation. . . . Moreover, banks have been instructed not to grant . . . loans to those firms whose wage agreements are not in accord with the standards established by the government" (*Comercio Exterior* 1964: October). To prevent union pressure which might result in such "inflationary" wage agreements, the government has taken over and installed military overseers in 409 labor unions, 43 federations of labor unions and 4 confederations of labor unions. Brazilian steel output had fallen 50 percent (*Comercio Exterior* 1964: August). By January 31, 1965, the major Rio de Janeiro daily *Correio da Manha* reported that 50,000 of Brazil's 350,000 textile workers were unemployed. "The Brazilian press announced on February 12 that numerous industrial and commercial enterprises of the country, particularly in São Paulo, have declared themselves bankrupt or are about to do so. . . . Brazilian textile producers also warn that all of the textile factories of the country will soon have to close their doors for lack of markets" (*Comercio Exterior* 1965: February). On March 25, the General Director of the National Department of Employment and Wages of the Ministry of Labor told the Rio de Janeiro daily *O Globo:* "In São Paulo all of industry is in crisis, and the metallurgical and textile industries in particular produce 1,000 new unemployed per day . . . business declines day by day . . . not only in São Paulo is there economic crisis and growing unemployment, but also in the whole of the Northeast" (Quoted in *Prensa Latina* 1965: March 26).

None of this was an accident. It followed from the policy of the new Minister of Planning, Roberto Campos de Oliveira, successor to Celso Furtado:

> In truth, production is declining. But, unfortunately, with it is also declining one of the world's great nations. . . . As may be verified, everything was done calculatedly, coldly, with the purpose of reducing production, which on the one side is affected by the drastic shortage of current capital (absorbed by the government) and by the abrupt reduction of bank credit and, on the other side, by the reduction of consumption forced by the merciless rise of all prices. Ministers of State and public officials then run to the television to try to explain what nobody understands (*Correio da Manha* 1965: January 31).

We have seen part of the explanation: to meet falling profits by squeezing more out of the workers. *Comercio Exterior* (1965: March) supplies another part: "As everything seems to indicate, the economic-financial policy directed by Professor Roberto Campos foresaw but one possibility for its success, though it be partial: that of a large investment of foreign, especially American, capital in the Brazilian economy." To this end, the Brazilian military government opened all doors. Like the government of Café Filho with its Instruction 113, it granted foreign capital renewed special privileges; and it removed the legal though very weak restrictions on the transfer of profits abroad. To placate American business interests and their government, the military government now purchased—for U.S. $135 million, plus U.S. $17.7 million of compensation for not doing so earlier, plus interest, or an estimated total of about U.S. $300 million—the almost worthless, antiquated Brazilian installations of the American and Foreign Power Company; the same Roberto Campos had without authorization agreed earlier to purchase these for about U.S. $70 million while he was Ambassador to the United States under the government of Goulart (*Comercio Exterior* 1964:September).

At the same time, the military government granted the American Hanna Mining Company the authorization, which they had long been seeking, to build a private port to export iron ore from the high-grade ore deposits, said to be the world's largest, which the company had acquired in Minas Gerais. *Comercio Exterior* (1964:December) notes the significance: "The government has authorized the construction of a private seaport by the American mining company, Hanna. . . . This constitutes a privilege which will transform the Hanna Company into absolute master of the internal mineral market of the country, and which will moreover end by eliminating the firm Vale do Rio Doce, a public enterprise of mineral production which occupies the seventh rank in the world in terms of export volume." Nonetheless the door was open in both directions, and "the law about the remittance of profits abroad [and other measures] did not result in the foreseen entry of dollars but rather in their substantial exit. . . . During the first half of the year, the capital inflow was less than the capital outflow" (*Comercio Exterior* 1964:October).

The immediate squeeze on Brazil's domestic satellites and labor and the accompanying short-run halt to economic development is reflected by the decline in the "growth" of per capita national income from an annual 4 percent between 1957 and 1961 (*Plano Trienal* 1962) to zero in 1962, to minus 1 percent in 1963 (*Conjuntura Económica* 1964:15), to minus 6 percent in 1964 (*Conjuntura Económica* 1965:11). This trend and policy has also brought with it the wholesale handing over of the Brazilian economy, not merely in mining, to the American metropolis in the short run and the certain portent of still deeper structural underdevelopment in the long run:

The press of São Paulo reports on February 4 that much ill feeling has been caused by the news that the national firm, Mineração Geral do Brasil, is to be liquidated, following the steps of other Brazilian industrial firms which are being sold to foreigners. . . . The owner . . . [pleaded necessity] in view of the crisis that the firm had to face because of the weakening of the internal market. The sale, which will be to the Continental Company [a Bethlehem Steel affiliate in Cleveland], will be for 70 million dollars, with guarantees by international financial organs. To justify himself, the owner of Mineração Geral said that in a weak market like the Brazilian one, the decline in supply which would result if the firm were to leave the market would produce unforeseeable consequences for the economy of the country. To avoid having to close his business, he chose to convert into dollars the most important steel company in the country, which has an annual production of 300,000 tons of steel, more than 12 percent of the national total" (*Comercio Exterior* 1965: February). (For a more detailed treatment, see Frank 1965b).

6. Internal Colonialist Development and Capitalist Underdevelopment

The causes and nature of ever deeper underdevelopment in Brazil, however, lie not in these immediate policies and events but, as we have said, in capitalism itself. To understand the real nature of the contemporary crisis of Brazil, we may again go over the years past to examine the contemporary capitalist metropolis-satellite structure and process of polarization, focusing first on its national and then on its international manifestations.

The polarization on the Brazilian national level appears perhaps most glaringly in the concentration of economic activity in São Paulo and the increasing relative and absolute impoverishment of the rest of the country. The concentration of industrial production in São Paulo has progressed as follows: 1881, 5 percent; 1907, 16 percent; 1914, 20 percent; 1920, 33 percent; 1938, 43 percent; 1959, 54 percent (page 170 above). In the period 1955-1960, despite the construction of Brasilia and the establishment of SUDENE (Superintendencia do Desenvolvimiento do Nordeste), the Economic Development Authority for the Northeast, 75 percent of both domestic and foreign investment in Brazil was channeled into São Paulo (Conselho Nacional 1963:112). And we may presume that the degree of concentration of industrial production in São Paulo continues to proceed apace.

In the meantime the state of Bahia in the Northeast, which accounted for 25 percent of Brazilian industrial output in 1881, dropped to 3.1 percent by 1950, and to 1.7 percent in 1959 (pp. 170-171 above and Conselho Nacional 1963:267). Indeed, the eleven states of the North and the Northeast combined, with 32 percent of the country's population in 1955, produced 12.4 percent of Brazil's industrial output in 1950 and 9.9 percent in 1959 (Conselho Nacional 1963:267); and they received 20 percent of Brazil's national income in 1947, 16.1 percent in 1955, and 14.5 percent in 1960 (computed from APEC 1963:14). This decline in their *relative* income is but part of it. Even the absolute income per capita of the same eleven states also declined, from 9,400 cruzeiros in 1948 to 9,200 in 1959; while the per capita income of Guanabara, which includes Rio de Janeiro, rose from 63,000 to 69,000 cruzeiros (APEC 1962:page 24 and Anexo 2-VII). The poorest state, Piauí in the Northeast, had a per capita income of 4,000 cruzeiros in 1958, while Guanabara had 52,000 in current prices (APEC 1962:24). Clidenor Freites, a psychiatrist from Piauí who built a mental hospital there before he became head of Brazil's social security system, assures me that Piauí has the highest index of mental illness in Brazil—illness caused principally by malnutrition.

The distribution of personal income, both nationally and regionally, is becoming more and more unequal, the greater the inflation. This benefits owners of property, since property values rise, and penalizes earners of wages and salaries, which do not keep up with prices. Thus, a small decline in average per capita income like that in the North and Northeast means a large decline in the absolute income of the great majority.

The working or unemployed population of the industrial center of São Paulo does not necessarily also benefit from this shift in the distribution of income. The bourgeoisie and its metropolitan allies benefit, while the former peasants and un-employed workers find their incomes reduced by price inflation and economic stagnation. Since the capitalist system is split not only by colonial metropolis-satellite but also by class relations, the fact that the propertyless live in the metropolis of São Paulo or Rio de Janeiro instead of in the provincial satellites scarcely protects them from capitalist satellitization and exploitation.

How does this polarization in the Brazilian domestic capitalist economy take place? Among its salient features are: (a) Private investment, both national and foreign, is concentrated in the national metropolis. (b) Public investment is also concentrated in the national metropolis, and, analogous to the global picture, in some of the immediately outlying areas which supply electricity or raw materials to the national and international metropolis. (c) The tax structure is regressive, taxing the poor proportionately more than the rich. (d) There is systematic and almost continuous transfer of capital or economic surplus from the Northeastern and other domestic satellite regions, as our model suggests, which is appropriated by the national metropolis in the South for the use partly of its own development and primarily of its own bourgeoisie. This transfer of capital, or appropriation/expropriation of economic surplus, may conveniently be discussed under the following divisions: (a) internal terms of trade, which turn against the satellites and in favor of the national metropolis; (b) transfer of foreign exchange, from the satellites which earn it to the national metropolis which spends it; (c) federally controlled structure of import prices, which subsidizes foreign imports into the national metropolis relative to those imported by the satellites; (d) transfer of human capital, from the satellites which invested in it to the metropolis which benefits from it; and (e) services which account for an "invisible" transfer of capital from the domestic satellites to the national metropolis. Combined with such other mechanisms as the structure of taxes and public expenditures, these mechanisms result in a large transfer of capital from the domestic satellites to the national metropolis. This transfer is slowed down or reversed only in years of "bad" depression. These aspects of the domestic metropolis-satellite structure are in turn analogous to the international one.

(a) Internal terms of trade: The American economist Werner Baer notes:

The Northeast . . . had to turn to the Center South's [São Paulo's] new high cost industries for its supplies. This has meant, in effect, that the Northeast's terms of trade declined, causing a resource transfer effect within Brazil which Prebisch has so often mentioned in connection with the total position of Latin America vis-à-vis the developed world. . . . [The practice] which has led the Northeast to buy in the South instead of abroad at less favorable terms of trade, implies a transfer of capital from the poorer to the richer section of the country. It has been claimed that the magnitude of the capital transfer implied can be estimated (Baer 1964: 278).

Over the period 1948 to 1960, the ratio of the index of the Northeast's export prices (measured by Brazilian export prices excluding coffee) to the index of wholesale prices fell from 100 to 10. If this decline is corrected for changes in the exchange rate against the dollar, the decline in the Northeast's terms of trade was from 100 to 48 (Baer 1960:279-280). At the same time, the international terms of trade also declined to the prejudice of the Northeast.

(b) Transfer of foreign exchange: In the study which led to the establishment of the famous SUDENE, the Conselho do Desenvolvimento do Nordeste reported:

The Northeast did not use the total of foreign exchange earnings generated by its exports. About 40 percent of such foreign exchange earnings were transferred to other regions of the country . . . by supplying foreign credits to the Center-South, the Northeast has been contributing to the development of the former, with a factor which is scarce for Southerners, capacity for importing (1959: 18, 24 quoted in Baer 1960: 278).

The average value of [foreign] exports from the Northeast rose from U.S. $165 million in 1948-1949 to U.S. $232 million in 1959-1960, while during that time the average value of [foreign] imports of the Northeast fell from U.S. $97 million to U.S. $82 million. During many of the postwar years, the Northeastern foreign trade surplus was enough to cover the deficits incurred by the rest of the country in its trade balance and, at times, was even large enough to cover other deficits in the balance of payments" (Baer 1964: 278).

Using the Conselho's estimates and other data, Baer estimates that over the period 1948 to 1960 U.S. $413 million were transferred from the Northeastern satellite to the Southern metropolis by this mechanism alone for an average of $38 million a year, which rose to $74, $59, and $84 million respectively in the years 1958, 1959, and 1960 (Baer 1960:280).

(c) Federally controlled structure of import prices:

A further burden on the Northeastern economy of Brazil, which SUDENE officials have not discussed explicitly, is the effect of the "Agio" system in Brazilian exchange rates. For the imports that come into the Northeast, importers have to pay fairly high rates relative to rates for "subsidized" imports like capital goods [used mainly in the South]. Proceeds of these rates have been used by exchange rate authorities to prop up the coffee economy, which is centered mainly in the South. Excess balances from the Agio system also increased the capacity of the Banco do Brasil to make loans, a high proportion of which are made in the South. The degree of "taxation" of the Northeast implied in this operation can be estimated (Baer 1960: 281).

(d) Transfer of human capital: Baer claims that "not enough data is available to judge whether migrants [from the Northeast to the South] are the more skilled and talented ones of the Northeast, who would thus also constitute a net drain on the region. It is known that the best talent in the professional groups have migrated South and have thus caused substantial shortages [in the Northeast]" (Baer 1960:276). Some professional people migrate to the national metropolis; others do not stop there but migrate right on to the international metropolis, the United States. Though the data are admittedly not conclusive, there is substantial reason to believe that this pattern of internal migration from satellite to metropolis does hold true (Hutchinson 1963). One thing is sure: the migrants were fed and educated—insofar as they received any education—in the satellite region at its own expense during their nonproductive childhood, only to leave and spend their productive adulthood in the metropolis.

(e) Services which account for an invisible transfer of capital: Brazilian data for this "invisible" item are of course inadequate. But this does not make it any less important. The International Monetary Fund and the United Nations Economic Commission for Latin America do provide data (exclusive of Cuba), showing that Latin American expenditure of foreign exchange on these "invisible" services purchased from abroad—transport and insurance, profits transferred abroad, servicing of debt, travel, other services, donations, funds transferred abroad and errors and omissions—absorbed and transferred to the metropolis 61 percent of all of the foreign exchange Latin America earned during the period 1961-1963 (Frank 1965a:43). These service items have counterparts in domestic transactions, and there is presumptive evidence that they account for a substantial transfer of capital from satellite to metropolis within Brazil just as they do between Brazil or other satellites and the international capitalist metropolis (Frank 1963, 1964b). Without the complement of such transfers from satellite to metropolis on service or financial account, it would be difficult to account for the perennial balance of trade surplus (of exports over imports) of the domestic satellites and the balance of trade deficit (imports exceeding exports) of the national metropolis or for the difference between the national metropolis's domestic balance of trade which shows a deficit and its balance of payments which shows a surplus.

As a result of the aforementioned and other mechanisms, and in accord with my model and hypotheses, São Paulo had a balance of trade surplus with respect to other regions of Brazil and the world, as shown in the excess of exports over imports (presumably of goods), through its port of Santos during the second half of the nineteenth century, while it was not yet the national metropolis of Brazil (Ellis 1937:426, whose data cover the years 1857-1862 and 1877-1886). In the twentieth century (the data in Ellis 1937:512 begin with 1907), São Paulo shows, on the contrary, a consistently large balance of trade deficit, that is, a surplus of imports from other regions over exports to other regions through the port of Santos's coastwise shipping until the year 1930. This terminal date is of considerable significance. São Paulo had become the national metropolis. It systematically imports more from other regions in Brazil than it exports to them through Santos.

How can São Paulo import more goods than it exports, and pay for them year in and year out? Ellis answers that it is due to its large export earnings. Part of the answer must lie in export earnings of São Paulo which do not show up in shipments out of the port of Santos: earnings on the export of "invisible" service items. But São Paulo does not have a balance of payments surplus on loan or any other service account with foreign countries: Like all satellites, it has a balance of payments deficit and a service account deficit with the world capitalist system and its metropolis. We may also discard the possibility of an excess of overland exports over imports from neighboring regions in Brazil during this period (it was probably also an import surplus instead). We are thus left with the explanation that São Paulo pays for its excess of goods imports over goods exports to other regions in Brazil (as well as perhaps some of its balance of payments deficit with abroad) with earnings that São Paulo derives from capital transferred to and appropriated by it from other regions in Brazil. The question which remains is whether this drain of capital from its satellites to the national metropolis in São Paulo should be called payment or earnings from services rendered.

This flow of funds on the service account of "invisible" items from satellite to metropolis is so large that it permits the São Paulo and Rio de Janeiro national metropolis to pay for its large excess of domestic imports over exports, and also it converts the metropolis's domestic balance of trade deficit on goods account into a large balance of payments surplus. The Brazilian domestic satellites have a systematic balance of payments deficit with respect to the national metropolis, notwithstanding the fact that the Northeast has a balance of trade surplus with respect to São Paulo and an even greater surplus with respect to the world abroad: "[The] Northeast has had perennial [balance of payments] deficits with the rest of the country [in the postwar period], mainly the Center-South, and

. . . these deficits have been growing in the latter part of the fifties. These deficits have averaged about 25 percent of its exports or 20 percent of its greater amount of imports of goods and services from other regions" (Baer 1964:278, 279).

Another observation seems to be consistent with my model and hypotheses: When the Depression hit, São Paulo switched from having a domestic goods export deficit to having a surplus on goods account with other regions of Brazil. Until 1929, coastwise shipping imports far exceeded corresponding exports except in recession years like 1923 and 1924. In 1930, imports dropped sharply; in 1931 they were nearly equal to exports; and in 1932 and 1933 (the end of the series) exports to other regions exceeded imports from other regions into São Paulo (Ellis 1937:512). When times are "good," the satellites are exploited more by the metropolis; when they are bad, they are exploited less.

One might think that agricultural, and even more, oft-called "feudal" regions like the Northeast would be self-sufficient in food. On the contrary, like the "agricultural" capitalist satellites of the world capitalist metropolis, such as Latin America and Brazil as a whole, its "agricultural" single-crop export regions in fact import food. The Brazilian Northeast spends 30 to 40 percent of its expenditures for regional imports on food products (*Desenvolvimento & Conjuntura* 1959:47). Does this make the Northeast an isolated, "feudal," pre-capitalist region, as the dual society model has it? Or does it leave it, as it has always been, an exploited capitalist satellite region?

The role of commerce and finance throw some additional light on this question. It is primarily through commercial monopoly that the contemporary national and regional metropolises (and the international metropolis) exploit and appropriate the economic surplus from their satellites. The evidence here is of many kinds. (This problem is discussed in greater detail below, pp. 247-277.) In Brazil as a whole the 23 percent of the population in the tertiary sector receives 47 percent of the national income; in the "isolated subsistence agriculture" Northeast the 15 percent in the tertiary sector receives 46 percent of the income; in the North they receive 49 percent (*Desenvolvimento & Conjuntura* 1958:52, APEC 1963:17, and Baer 1964:274 give similar data on the sectoral income breakdown). The important tertiary income recipients are of course not white collar workers or clerks in service establishments, but merchants and financiers. In the Northeast, 21 percent of the income goes to commerce, financial intermediaries and rents; of this total 17.6 percent went to commerce in 1958-1960 (Baer 1964:274, APEC 1963:17). A very small number of large merchants receives the lion's share of this 46 percent of the regional tertiary sector income. Moreover, the large landowners, whose income is officially attributed to agriculture, actually receive the largest part of their income from commerce and finance; thus the real share of income "earned" in commerce and finance is much higher than the figures indicate.

The commercial monopoly aspects of the capitalist system in rural areas are intimately tied to the structure of landed property. In Brazil in 1950, 80 percent of those dependent on agriculture owned 3 percent of the land. The other 97 percent of land was owned by 20 percent of the agricultural population, 0.6 percent of which owned over 50 percent—including the best land (see pp. 248-254 below). This monopoly control over land in turn permits these few owners to participate, often primarily, as commercial monopolists in the monopolistic structure of capitalism as a whole.

That the supposedly pre-capitalist or even feudal economic and social structure of rural areas is an integral part of the entire capitalist metropolis-satellite structure is further shown by the changes in concentration of landownership and of living standards of the rural population over time and place. The land in the South, especially in the state of Paraná and earlier also in São Paulo itself, which was divided into relatively small homestead properties, came to be concentrated into large holdings precisely when it was invaded by the capitalist expansion of coffee and other cash crops. In consequence, the standard of living of a large part of the landed population fell in the train of this capitalist development. It was during the capitalist expansions of the 1920's and the 1940's and the lesser expansion of the 1950's that the concentration of landownership increased, tenant farmers were transformed into agricultural wage workers, and the level of living of the majority declined. During the 1930's, on the contrary, and in some places during the 1950's, these trends were in the reverse direction: deconcentration of landholding, increased small holders and tenants, higher standards of living for the rural population. But when the United States withdrew its sugar quota from Cuba and parcelled it out among its "friendly" nations, Brazil among them, and in consequence the demand for Northeastern sugar briefly rose again, sugar was planted right into the peasants' houses, in the words of the now imprisoned Governor of Pernambuco; and their living standards suffered accordingly. Thus Brazilian agriculture, far from being a feudal, pre-capitalist, isolated subsistence sector, as the dualist model suggests, is and reacts like the part of the capitalist system whose behavior is predicted by our hypothesis: Involution in response to lessened ties with the metropolis, and underdeveloped development in response to renewed stronger ties with the metropolis.

This same monopolistic metropolis-satellite structure is not limited to the interregional level but extends to the intersectoral level. Thus, the relations between one industry and another and also between one firm and another within the same industry can be said to correspond to the metropolis-satellite structure. The technologically advanced sectors or firms have either their own sources of capital or relatively easy access to external capital, and they maintain a monopolistic metropolis-satellite relation with those which lack this technology and capital and which work with more labor-intensive techniques. This is particularly evident in the contrast between the large foreign firms, which rely on the technological and credit facilities of their world-wide operations, and Brazilian firms on the other hand. But much the same relationship also exists between the few large Brazilian firms, which are moreover usually tied to foreign firms in one way or another, and the many medium and small Brazilian firms in the same industry.

The relationship may be seen in the structure of their buying and selling operations with each other; and it becomes particularly evident when, as under the present military government, foreign firms are granted special privileges and national firms are starved for credit. This gives a strongly increased competitive advantage to the foreign firms and to technologically and financially relatively stronger national firms over the medium and small firms which are forced out of business, their assets being taken over by the large or foreign firms.

The present military government is adding still another mechanism to the advantage of the big firms: It makes business taxes depend not on company earnings but rather on the company's wage bill. Since large companies have relatively large earnings while small companies, being less capital-intensive, have a relatively larger labor force, the result is obvious. Little wonder that foreign and Brazilian Big Business and its associated bourgeoisie do not complain about a monetary and fiscal policy which might appear to hurt business: Like all else in the capitalist structure, it hurts unevenly.

All these kinds of commercial, one might say mercantilist, appropriation of the economic surplus and/or surplus value from the agricultural and industrial producers and consumers is of course possible, I should say necessary, only because exploiters and exploited alike are part of the same highly monopolistic system. The local metropolitan landlords and merchants who exploit their satellite agricultural workers and consumers, serve as instruments of the regional metropolis whose satellites they are, whose regional bourgeoisie in turn serves as the instrument of exploitation of the national metropolis and bourgeoisie—and on up to the world capitalist metropolis and bourgeoisie, whose instrument in the exploitation and increasing underdevelopment of the satellite countries is inevitably the national bourgeoisie.

All minor contradictions notwithstanding, the bourgeoisies of these local, regional, national and world capitalist metropolises have a stake in the preservation of this system. The initiative and effective political action to transform this society to permit genuine economic and human development must necessarily fall to the exploited classes of the capitalist satellites, rural and urban.

7. Imperialist Development and Capitalist Underdevelopment

To complete our analysis of Brazilian underdevelopment and the country's contemporary political crisis, we must proceed to a more analytic examination of Brazil's recent international relations with the capitalist metropolis and of their bearing on our problem. Again, it is well to keep in mind that although I take them up separately, the international and national metropolis-satellite structure of capitalism is inseparably intertwined.

While always referring back to my model and hypotheses, I shall try to proceed step by step from more superficial to deeper lying structural causes of this underdevelopment. An observation and explanation of "the economic causes of the present crisis" was made by Celso Furtado in his book, *Dialectica do Desenvolvimento* (The Dialectics of Development), published in the spring of 1964 at the time of the coup:

The exhaustion of the factors which supported the process of industrialization occurred, apparently, before the formation of capital reached the necessary degree of autonomy with respect to the external sector. This fact appears to show that the difficulties which the country has been facing during recent times are deeper than was at first suspected. There is ample evidence that industrialization brought Brazil very close to the point at which development is a cumulative circular process which creates its own means to keep going. It may even be said that if it were not for the large decline in the terms of trade beginning in 1955, Brazil would have reached this decisive point in the course of this decade of the sixties (Furtado 1964: 120).

Translated into our terms, Furtado thus maintains that Brazil almost managed to escape from the vicious circle of capitalist metropolis-satellite ties, their relaxation and their renewed strengthening; that through a rising national capitalism Brazil almost got out of the grip of the world imperialist system; and that it failed only because after 1955 its terms of trade fell.

This stress on the quite real and important adverse change in the satellite's terms of trade, which is universally emphasized in official publications of the satellite countries and of international organizations and even in the learned studies of economists from the capitalist metropolis, often serves to divert attention from the fundamental problems and causes of the growing underdevelopment and poverty of the satellite countries. Moreover, Paul Baran, among others, pointed out that for those countries whose export trade is largely in foreign hands, a fall in the prices of their export products does not necessarily harm them much since the gains from that trade, reduced or not, go to enterprises from the capitalist metropolis anyway (Baran 1957:231-234). Brazil is not in quite so unenviable a position in this respect as some other primary-goods exporting countries. Nonetheless, the importance for Brazil of changes in the price of coffee are, as we have seen, to some extent subject to this reservation.

The following explanation of Brazil's renewed turn into underdevelopment attempts a broader comprehension. We can recognize this turn of events as still another example of a characteristic of the capitalist system and its development: The reappearance of the pattern of renewed strengthening of metropolis-satellite ties which accompanies the recuperation of the metropolis. This is accompanied by the necessarily fruitless attempts of the satellite to meet this threat, which aggravate the condition, the consequent strangulation of the more autonomous development which the satellite had undertaken in the previous period, and its misdirection into further underdevelopment.

In the 1950's, after the period of active capitalist involution during the Depression and the War, we saw the renewed appearance of essentially the same pattern as during the Brazilian depression of the first half of the nineteenth century, during the last years of the nineteenth century after the coffee expansion, during the 1920's after the involution of the first World War, and again in our day: (a) inflation, (b) devaluation, (c) rising and then falling terms of trade, (d) external finance, and (e) reintegration of the satellite economy into that of the metropolis, the renewed exertion of metropolitan monopoly power, and metropolitan takeover of the satellite. These identical characteristics we have also observed in our review of the years recently past.

Celso Furtado himself points out that inflation, when combined with the circumstances of devaluation and falling terms of trade, cannot possibly play the same role of stimulating development that it did during the 1930's and 1940's when Brazil's exchange rate and its terms of trade rose, and, so to speak, provided impersonal, automatic external finance for this inflation (Furtado 1964:117-118). He points out further that under these same circumstances of devaluation and falling terms of trade in the late 1950's, external finance in the form of foreign loans and investment cannot possibly save the situation but rather only make it worse. Recourse to external finance through loans and investment is no substitute for external finance through rising terms of trade, least of all when these same terms of trade are falling. Under these circumstances, inflation and external finance can only lead to the inevitable consequences of imperialist takeover.

This was the consequence of the same pattern of economic and political forces at the turn of the century, in the 1920's under the guiding hand of Americanophile President Washington Luis; and it was inevitably the consequence of the economic development and policies of political economy of Presidents Café Filho, Juscelino Kubitschek, and their successors, all other circumstances notwithstanding. Thus, my model and hypotheses offer at least an approximation to an explanation of the renewed strangulation of Brazil's development and its misdirection into further underdevelopment accompanied by the relapse into an ultra right-wing government which seeks (at a payoff for itself) the help of the wolf's paw to protect the Brazilian people from the wolf's ravenous appetite.

But there are other circumstances which reinforce this trend. There have been important transformations not of, but within, the structure of the capitalist system on the international and on the Brazilian national level since 1929, the starting date of the active involution in Brazil which has now given way to renewed underdevelopment.

An excellent review of the situation was recently published by self-proclaimed Brazilian enthusiasts for foreign capital and for the closest of relations with the United States, APEC Editora, S.A.:

> Thanks to its passive dependence on the balance of payments, sustained by centuries of single crop culture, the Brazilian economy has earned the term "reflex" economy. At the present time, it is with coffee that we buy our bread, fuel, and civilization. During the last thirty years, and especially with the Second World War, the process of industrialization and diversification of the economy intensified; but the decline of agricultural production relative to population and the progressive deterioration of the terms of trade are evidence that we have not freed ourselves from this vicious circle. Industrialization substituted much local production for imports; but at the same time it imposed on us an even more rigid exchange dependence in the form of raw materials, fuels, spare parts, equipment, technology and capital. In recent years, instead of giving way to the natural limitations of the economy, this spurt of industrialization was extended by an inflow of foreign capital which was attracted not so much by a good investment climate as it mostly was by absolute tariff advantages, reasons of market policy and of national defense. The most important aspect of this industrialization is that which imposes a deeper integration and interconnection of the economy [with the outside], rendering it more vulnerable to changes of fortune (APEC 1962: 93).

This short summary contains the germs of several important truths about the deplorable state and trend of affairs in the Brazilian economy. But the authors in general refer all the causes of Brazilian dependency back to the problem of the terms of trade and the import vulnerability to which Brazil thus becomes exposed. The poor terms of trade are thus made to bear much more of the responsibility for underdevelopment than they in reality have. The other circumstantial causes that are summarized by these observers have even greater importance in their own right than they do in relation to the problem of the terms of trade.

Let us examine the problem of import substitution. The largest part of the process of industrial expansion in Brazil during the past decades has been one of the substitution by production in Brazil of products that were previously imported or of products new to the world market that would otherwise have been imported. Import substitution, now that the source of metropolitan monopoly no longer lies so heavily in industrial production itself as in particular kinds of industry and technology, has been widely hailed by metropolitan economic advisers to the underdeveloped countries as the first and major step toward their industrialization and development. Such import substitution, however, when undertaken within the framework and structure of the capitalist system, cannot afford the advertised salvation, but must instead be but another step into greater dependence on the metropolis and deeper structural underdevelopment. And so it has been in Brazil.

The choice of products whose importation is to be substituted by domestic production is based on several criteria: relatively low capital cost and simple technology (this is usually the advice of economists from the metropolis); goods whose domestic prices are high and in the production of which there is little or no competition precisely because their importation is restricted by a protective tariff against "non-essential" imports; but, above all, import substitution is of consumer goods for the high income market, which in a capitalist economy is about the only one that can provide a demand for them. This kind of industrial production can result in the short run in some higher income and demand on the part of some of the producers; but it evidently is not the kind of supply which could, in analogy to Say's Law, create much further demand for internal production in the long run.

This kind of import substitution, far from reducing the satellite economy's overall need and demand for imports, necessarily increases them. Evidently, the more domestic import substitute production is limited to consumer goods, though the output of these may rise, the more equipment and raw materials to produce them are needed and must be imported. The further this process is extended and the longer it continues, the more technically complicated and costly the equipment that must be imported and the more limited the income range and number of potential domestic consumers who can buy the final products.

The internal contradictions of the national capitalist metropolis-satellite structure place severe limits on the extension of this process of import substitution; and the contradictions of the international capitalist metropolis-satellite structure render ever more costly and impossible the continuance of even the degree of import substitution already reached. The domestic capitalist structure necessarily channels this supposedly development-producing process of industrialization and import substitution into ever greater polarization between the national metropolis and its privileged groups on the one hand and the satellites and national metropolitan low income groups on the other. These last never come to enjoy the benefits of this sort of industrialization but, through the various polarizing mechanisms as well as through inflation in general, are forced to pay for the major share of its costs. Moreover, these same exigencies of the productive process of capitalist import substitution generate an increasing degree of monopoly even within the industrial sector itself, as expansion becomes more difficult and weaker firms are forced out, which in turn aggravates the problem still further.

Though Brazil, as we saw, devoted its industrial production not only to these consumer goods, its pattern of import substitution has not substantially deviated from the extreme case dis-

cussed here; and its industrial development has met the indicated fate. To adopt a substantially different pattern of import
substitution and to avoid this fate by beginning with heavy
producer goods industry and intermediate equipment manufacturing instead of light consumer goods industry, as the Soviet
Union did, Brazil would have to have an income distribution
and therefore pattern of consumer demand other than that of
a satellite capitalist country and/or a distribution of political
power and the consequent ability to allocate investment in
response to criteria other than immediate consumer demand.
This too is quite foreign to the essential nature of a capitalist
country.

This import substitution process, instead of reducing import
requirements, thus increases them. Moreover, it tends to raise
the cost of imports as it becomes necessary to import ever more
technically complicated, advanced, *monopolized,* and thus
costly equipment from the metropolis. Yet this import substitution cannot reach the point at which the satellite ceases to be
dependent on the metropolis for equipment, technology, and
critical raw materials, since this industrial blind alley leads the
satellite country away from rather than toward the domestic
production of these necessities. Thus, the United Nations
Economic Commission for Latin America notes that although
"In the post-war period . . . limitations on the external sector
were considerably less in Brazil than in other countries of the
[Latin American] region . . . in the light of the study of the
main sample items, it may be concluded that no real substitution process took place in respect of capital goods as a whole"
in Brazil (*Economic Bulletin* 1964:38).

At the same time, the import pattern comes to be extremely
rigid. Thus, while in 1952, its best postwar year thanks to the
Korean War, Brazil's external payments for essential imports
of fuels, wheat, newsprint and financial payments accounted
for 25 percent of its export earnings, by 1959 these same demands on foreign exchange used up 70 percent of export earnings, leaving only 30 percent for all other imports combined

(*Economic Bulletin* 1964:15). In this same year, Brazil devoted 50 percent of its imports to industrial equipment and metal intermediate products, and another 25 percent to non-metal products; it may thus easily be seen that absolutely essential imports which have been structured into the economy by its satellite underdeveloped development exceed its import capacity (*Economic Bulletin* 1964:22). Brazil is thus prohibited from importing new types of equipment it might need to develop in a different and more advantageous direction and must have recourse to external finance to cover even its most essential existing import needs.

These contradictions in satellite attempts to industrialize through import substitution, serious enough in themselves, are rendered still more acute and generative of underdevelopment by their inevitable combination with other facets of the exploitative metropolis-satellite relationship. One of these is the declining terms of trade. Evidently the import substitution difficulties due to increased costs and other factors are aggravated when the terms of trade fall, as they have since 1955, and the means of payment for imports decline or fail to rise enough. The inevitable result is resort to foreign loans. But these, in Brazil, can only keep the wolf from the door temporarily while rendering him more rapacious in the long run. Foreign borrowing brings with it the necessity to devote an ever higher share of foreign exchange earnings to servicing the debt. It also places the debtor ever more at the mercy of the creditor who then uses this satellite dependency to obtain ever more and greater concessions, on threat of failing to renew loans or to extend the dates of repayment when, as is inevitable, Brazil cannot pay. Thus Brazil has been placed in a position of debt bondage to the United States creditor which becomes lord of the land—and this bondage does not differ in any essentials from the debt bondage of peasants the world over to their landlords and moneylenders.

Two other forms of metropolitan monopoly control are foreign investment and technology. Each of these separately would be enough to engender increasing underdevelopment in the Brazilian and other satellites. Combined with each other and with the factor of import substitution within the total structure, they doom Brazil to capitalist underdevelopment.

Contradicting his earlier attribution of renewed Brazilian underdevelopment to the decline in the terms of trade, Celso Furtado refers to the role of foreign investment:

> The new capitalist industrial class . . . found . . . in concessions to foreign groups the path of least resistance for the solution of problems that arose from time to time. . . . There has been a widespread process of de-Brazilianization of the economy which, independently of the effects of other factors, inexorably leads to external strangulation. . . . There thus arose contradiction between the broadest interests of national development and the private interests of thousands of firms controlled by foreign groups which worked with costs tied to more or less stable kinds of foreign exchange costs. . . . It is still common to suppose that this problem can be solved by "regaining foreign confidence" and attracting new foreign capital. . . . This is undoubtedly the most acute internal contradiction of Brazilian development at the present time and also that for whose solution the governing class is least prepared (Furtado 1964: 133).

There can be no doubt that Furtado has here placed his finger on a part of the underdevelopment-generating metropolis-satellite relationship which is all too often conveniently forgotten or left unmentioned.

Domestic industry must not be confused with national industry as long as the former contains a significant and ever growing share of foreign companies and therefore control. Foreign and especially American firms, as we saw, entered Brazil to establish themselves in the country's domestic industry in the 1920's. Even during the Depression of the 1930's, this kind of penetration went on apace. In 1936, for instance, 121 Brazilian firms were incorporated while 241 foreign firms, among them 120 American, were incorporated (Guilherme 1963:41). This process took on ever greater speed and proportions in the 1950's and in the present decade. The foreign firms are almost always very large ones which are vertically and horizontally integrated on a multinational basis and therefore have substantial monopoly power even in the world market. Little wonder that they quickly come to absorb smaller Brazilian rivals and to convert Brazilian competitor, supplier and customer firms into their economic satellites. I have discussed this process in greater detail in "On the Mechanisms of Imperialism: The Case of Brazil" (Frank 1964b).

The behavior of these foreign monopolies within Brazilian industry therefore serves substantially to reinforce the satellite status and dependency of the latter and of the economy as a whole. Moreover, the nature and extent of foreign investment and productive activity in Brazil structures into Brazilian industry and the economy in general import needs of a kind and quantity which greatly increase the rigidity of Brazil's import selection and even take the selection of products to be imported out of Brazilian hands. Foreign investment thus aggravates the import substitution problem by the control it comes to exercise over Brazilian industry, while at the same time withdrawing substantial amounts of capital—always more than is contributed, as I showed in the just-mentioned article and in an earlier one entitled "Aid or Exploitation" (Frank 1963b)—or Brazilian-created economic surplus which is thus not available for investment in Brazil and whose withdrawal from the country still further aggravates the balance of payments and import substitution problem.

These ties between foreign and national firms in the domestic Brazilian economy, not to speak of mixed enterprises of foreign and national capital—which always end in converting the national part into a satellite of the foreign part while the latter is saved the expenditure of the capital contributed by the former—of course also tie the domestic bourgeoisie, including the national bourgeoisie, to the imperialist metropolis. More often than not, they produce common interests in the common exploitation of the Brazilian people and in the increasing satellization and underdevelopment of its economy; and however much the interests of the stronger foreigners and the

weaker Brazilians may conflict in one case or another, it renders
the weaker ever more dependent on and satellized by the
stronger. Nonetheless, this foreign investment and control,
which Celso Furtado rightly sees as strangling development, is
but one element in the whole of the ever more underdevelopment-generating monopolistic metropolis-satellite structure of
the contemporary capitalist system.

Technology intercedes in the metropolis-satellite relationship
and serves to generate still deeper satellite underdevelopment.
It is technology which is rapidly and increasingly becoming
the new basis of metropolitan monopoly over the satellites.
The significance of this development may be seen more clearly
in reference to my model and the transformation within the
metropolis-satellite system to which it refers.

During the mercantilist era, the metropolitan monopoly lay
in commercial monopoly; in the era of liberalism, the metropolitan monopoly came to be industry; in the first half of the
twentieth century the metropolitan monopoly switched increasingly to capital goods industry. It then became more
possible for the satellites to produce light industrial consumer
goods at home. In the second half of the twentieth century,
the basis of metropolitan monopoly seems to be switching increasingly to technology. Now the satellites can even have
heavy industry at home. Such heavy industry might, 100 or
even 50 years ago, have freed a satellite from dependence on
the metropolis; it would have converted the satellite into still
another part of the metropolis and would have made it an
imperialist power. But no satellite was then able to break
through the metropolitan monopoly of heavy industry. Only
the USSR did so by abandoning the imperialist and capitalist
system altogether and going over to socialism.

In our time, however, heavy industry no longer is enough to
break out of this metropolitan monopolist domination, for the
domination has come to have a new base, technology. This
technology is variously represented in automation, cybernetics,
industrial technology; chemical technology—the substitution

of the satellites' raw materials by metropolitan synthetics; agricultural technology—the importation of food by the "agricultural" satellites from the industrial metropolis; and, as always, military technology, including nuclear and chemical as well as anti-guerrilla warfare technology. For a capitalist satellite country to develop competitive technology in our day is even more difficult and unlikely than it was for the same country to develop its own light or heavy industry at the time when these were the basis of metropolitan monopoly. Within the structure of the capitalist system, therefore, Brazil and other satellites are now even more dependent on the metropolis than they were before. And there is no reason to believe that the capitalist metropolis will use its monopoly power over its satellites in the future any differently than it did in the past. On the contrary, the evidence is already coming in that in this respect also monopoly capitalism will develop in the future as it did in the past.

So far, the evidence seems to have been best documented by the Europeans, for they have been the first to become aware of and alarmed by the problem of technological monopoly. The United States magazine *Newsweek* reports:

A Chase Manhattan official in Paris has estimated that two-thirds of the total of U.S. investments in Europe belongs to fifteen to twenty giant companies. . . . Americanization or not, many Europeans are seriously worried by the flood of dollars and the growing power of U.S. companies in Europe's economy. Especially in France, nationalists led by President Charles de Gaulle warn of the danger of "satellization"; almost daily, politicians and publishers tell the Yankees to take their dollars and go home. . . . To knowledgeable Europeans, in fact, the technical lead of the big U.S. companies is the most disturbing fact of the dollar invasion. In the future, a French study committee recently concluded, competition over prices will give way to competition in innovations, and the pace will be so hot that only firms of international size—"that is, American ones, chiefly"—will survive. . . .

In the vanguard of European opposition, French politicians and publications of the Right, Left, and Center have been accusing the U.S. of economic colonization, satellization, and vassalization for nearly three years. . . . U.S. firms now control almost the whole electronics industry, 90 percent of the production of synthetic rubber, 65 percent of petroleum distribution, 65 percent of farm machinery production. Even a few of the subcontractors for President de Gaulle's top-secret *force de frappe* are U.S. subsidiaries. . . . "Unless Europe reacts and gets organized," warns Louis Armand, the man who turned the French railroad system into the world's best, "we are condemning ourselves to industrial colonization. Either we counterattack or we sign our vassalization warrant."

There is a steady flow of mergers and acquisitions enlarging the U.S. dollar stake. One of Germany's most prominent bankers complains: "The rate at which the Americans have been gobbling up small European companies is positively indecent." "We can't survive this sort of one-sided competition," says a Belgian petro-chemical executive. "Our American rivals are a thousand-odd patents ahead. Long term, we are bound to be absorbed. . . ." A company chairman in Brussels sums up: "We are becoming pawns manipulated by the U.S. giants. . . ."

But in the new sophistication of European industry, sheer size is sometimes less important than the research that makes it possible. This was spelled out by an Olivetti executive discussing alternatives to the GE deal. "We studied a European solution very carefully," he said. "But even if we had merged with Machines Bull in France and Siemens in Germany [which later signed a licensing agreement with RCA], we still would have been dwarfed and eventually put out of business by the U.S. giants. There is no European solution to these problems. Research costs are too high. The transatlantic technological gap is a fact of life" (*Newsweek* 1965: 67-72).

If the patent transatlantic technological gap is a fact of life and if it promises to condemn the strong industrially developed countries of Western Europe to economic colonization, satellization and vassalization, then what hope does the weak, industrially underdeveloped economy of Brazil—to say nothing of the still weaker parts of the capitalist world economy—have of escaping this same or a worse fate and further underdevelopment? None—within the system which produces it.

D. CONCLUSION

In conclusion, then, the Brazilian economy has recently become ever more intimately integrated into the metropolis-satellite structure of the world capitalist system.

The implications of this recent capitalist development and underdevelopment are far-reaching. Even if the metropolis were to experience another period like the Depression of the 1930's or the War of the 1940's in which its immediate ties with its satellites became weaker, it would be much more difficult or even impossible for Brazil to react with a similar active capitalist involution and another push toward industrialization. Even Brazil's industry will have become too dependent on the metropolis to permit it such independent capitalist development.

If domestic Brazilian industry is ever more dependent on the imperialist metropolis, then so is the Brazilian bourgeoisie. If the development of capitalism in the world and in Brazil renders a truly national industry ever less possible, then it similarly precludes the development or even the continuance of a national industrial bourgeoisie. The structure and development of the capitalist system are therefore converting the Brazilian and other satellite industrial bourgeoisies into bourgeoisies dependent on the imperialist metropolis—like the commercial bourgeoisies of the satellites before them. Thus the Brazilian "national bourgeoisie," if it can be said to exist at all, thrives only on its exploitation of the Brazilian people through the maintenance of the domestic capitalist metropolis-satellite structure and its generation of regional and sectoral underdevelopment; it persists only through its dependence on the imperialist metropolis in the world capitalist structure. Since these structures are, as we have seen, indissolubly interlinked, since they are in reality one and the same, it can be only the vainest, most futile, and most disastrous of hopes to expect the national bourgeoisie of Brazil to take any action which might significantly help to stem the growing tide of Brazilian underdevelopment on all levels.

The recent political and economic events in Brazil can be understood only against this background. The contradictory and discontinuous development of the capitalist system and particularly the withdrawal from its exploitative grasp of the new socialist countries, combined with the postwar recovery of the world capitalist metropolis within the economic space remaining to it, have further limited the development possibilities of the Brazilian economy and the progressive perspectives of the Brazilian bourgeoisie. The entire Brazilian economy and bourgeoisie are hemmed in by the structure and development of the capitalist system and by its old and new monopolistic instruments of property, trade, loans, investment, technology and the rest.

The most exploited and weakest sectors of the Brazilian bourgeoisie strike out against one or another of these foreign or domestic instruments which limit their own exploitative capacity. But their efforts are in vain even in the short run. The range of possibilities for this "national" bourgeoisie is limited by its economic and political contradictions vis-à-vis the people whom it exploits at home and vis-à-vis the stronger bourgeoisies at home and abroad which exploit the same people and also exploit the national bourgeoisie itself. This bourgeoisie's dependence on capitalist exploitation and weakness in the face of foreign and domestic interests that exploit it in turn—these very contradictions, which now and then, here and there, lead the "national" bourgeoisie to pursue national capitalist policies, also guarantee that this pursuit will be futile and short-lived. Thus the nationalist and relatively progressive elements of the Brazilian bourgeoisie are overcome by the same contradictions that create them.

The largest and strongest sectors of the Brazilian bourgeoisie, which are the most dependent on the imperialist metropolis, try to overcome the imperialist and self-created limitations to their economy's development and their own perspectives by sticking their head still further into the jaws of the imperialist lion. Thus, their future is inevitably cut short in the long run too. And as the lion, whose prey elsewhere is increasingly escaping him, is becoming more and more rapacious, that future is becoming shorter and shorter.

Both sectors of the Brazilian bourgeoisie, the "national" and the "international," are bourgeois: They are instruments and executors of the exploitative capitalist system which gives them their economic existence and permits them their political survival. They are necessarily allied in the economic exploitation of the people and in the political maintenance of the system. The less the "national" elements can gain by fighting their foreign enemy and the "international" ones by joining him, the more do both sectors try to cut their losses by exacting a still higher toll of exploitation from the people and the more does the stronger bourgeoisie try to eliminate the weaker so as to monopolize the field of exploitation for itself. The more the people resist this process, or even the nationalist sectors of the bourgeoisie oppose it, the more does the dominant bourgeoisie of Brazil seek the aid of its natural, though exploitative, ally in the imperialist metropolis.

And so came the military coup of 1964, supported by the imperialist bourgeoisie, the Brazilian "international" bourgeoisie, and most sectors of the "national" bourgeoisie and the "petty" bourgeoisie or "middle classes." If some parts of the last two sectors have since become unfriendly to the gorilla government and its foreign and domestic backers, it is only because they are now suffering the inevitable consequences—increased exploitation of themselves and decreased opportunity for the exploitation of others. Thus the bourgeois daily *Correio da Manha,* in whose pages we have read such disrespectful report and commentary on the current management of the economy, has become the "nationalist" mouthpiece of the medium and small bourgeoisie whose possibilities and perspective have been limited by events. And even Carlos Lacerda, Governor in Rio de Janeiro, aspirant to the Presidency and ultra-reactionary or outright fascist traditional mouthpiece of the rural and urban petty bourgeoisie, has grabbed a nationalist, or rather national socialist, flag under which to run for President.

What then are the perspectives? For the bourgeoisie, as limited as ever—and because of the increased dependency and deeper underdevelopment of Brazil's economy, even more limited than before. The perspective of the return to the "developmentism" of Juscelino Kubitschek or the "Jangismo" of João Goulart offered by the circles around the *Correio da Manha* in Rio de Janeiro and around the exiled Goulart himself in Montevideo can, for those who would learn the lessons of history both recent and remote, represent nothing but the worst kind of confusion or illusion at best, and the most disastrously irresponsible political opportunism at worst. If history teaches us anything at all, it makes it clear that no bourgeois capitalist regime of any kind can possibly take significant and still less, decisive, steps toward the elimination of Brazil's long-standing development of underdevelopment and toward the solution of its consequent contemporary economic and political problems. At this juncture of the development of capitalism, even the most nationalist and progressive sectors of the Brazilian bourgeoisie are unable to follow a movement toward national liberation and economic development except at rare times and places. Nor, evidently, can the petty bourgeoisie or the "middle classes" take such independent steps or lead this movement. Though increasingly pauperized, they remain characteristically volatile and opportunistic. Both the forces of reaction and those of revolution will seek to harness sectors of the petty bourgeoisie in the future as they have in the past. Whatever the outcome of these efforts may be, the initiative, vanguard and future of Brazil's movement out of capitalism and underdevelopment must lie with the masses of its people.

The contradictory and discontinuous historical development of capitalism and underdevelopment in Brazil reached a new crisis with the military coup of 1964 and the events that followed it. For all the damage to its economy and suffering to its people that this development of capitalism in Brazil has brought, it is accelerating the political process in Brazil at the same time that the deepening contradictions of the capitalist system have quickened that process elsewhere. As the solutions to the problems of underdevelopment become ever more impossible within the capitalist system which creates them, and as the bourgeoisie is less and less able even to face these problems with bourgeois programs, the long exploited people themselves are being taught and prepared to lead the way out of capitalism and underdevelopment.

IV

CAPITALISM
AND THE
MYTH OF FEUDALISM
IN
BRAZILIAN
AGRICULTURE

A. THE MYTH OF FEUDALISM

Agriculture is in crisis. Everyone agrees. And the crisis of agriculture is the crisis of Latin America and of Brazil. But what about the sources, nature and solution of the crisis? The standard Western bourgeois view is that Latin American agriculture is feudal and that it is this feudal structure of agriculture which prevents economic development. The consequent solution proposed, following the Western example, is to destroy feudalism and substitute capitalism. Curiously, this explanation of "feudalism" is almost equally widespread among Marxists. According to their analysis, feudalism persists at least in large sectors of the agricultural countryside, although these are being progressively penetrated by capitalism. And these Marxists propose essentially the same solution for the crisis as their bourgeois antagonists: Accelerate and complete the capitalization of agriculture.

The purpose of this study is to suggest that the causes and explanation of the agricultural crisis must be sought not in feudalism, but in capitalism itself. The Brazilian economy, including its agriculture, is part of a capitalist system. It is the development and functioning of this system which produce both development and underdevelopment and which account for the terrible reality of agriculture in Brazil—and elsewhere.

1. The Bourgeois Thesis

In the Western literature, both popular and scientific, it is a commonplace to maintain that Latin America began its postdiscovery history with feudal institutions and that it still retains them today, more than four centuries later. The thesis is so widely accepted among politically conservative writers that there is no need to quote them here. But the same interpretation of the facts, though not of the solution, is also reflected by so knowledgeable a writer as Carlos Fuentes of Mexico.*

---

* In quoting the various authors below, I do not wish to imply that they subscribe to the feudalism thesis in its entirety. In fact, I have selected

We were founded as an appendix of the falling feudal order of the Middle Ages; we inherited its obsolete structures, absorbed its vices, and converted them into institutions on the outer rim of the revolution in the modern world. If you [North Americans] come from the Reformation, we come from the Counter-Reformation: slavery to work, to religious dogmatism, to latifundia (enormous expanses of land under the same landlord), denial of political, economic or cultural rights for the masses, a customs house closed to modern ideas. Instead of creating our own wealth, we exported it to the Spanish and Portuguese metropolis. When we obtained political independence, we did not obtain economic independence; the structure did not change.

You must understand that the Latin American drama stems from the persistence of those feudal structures over four centuries of misery and stagnation. . . . The formulas of free-enterprise capitalism have already had their historical opportunity in Latin America and have proved unable to abolish feudalism. . . .

This is what Latin America is: A collapsed feudal castle with a cardboard capitalistic façade. This is the panorama of the historical failure of capitalism in Latin America: *Continuous monoproductive dependence. . . . A continuous system of latifundia. . . . Continuous underdevelopment. . . . Continuous political stagnation. . . . Continuous general injustices. . . . Continuous dependence on foreign capital. . . .* Agrarian feudalism is the basis of the wealth and political dominion of the governing classes in Central America, Chile, Peru, Argentina, Brazil, Venezuela, Colombia, Ecuador. . . . (Fuentes 1963: 10-14).

Even the Second Declaration of Havana of 1962, undoubtedly the most incisive and important contemporary document on Latin American economic and political reality, calls Latin American agriculture "feudal."

Where it is not all of Latin America that is termed "feudal," it is its agriculture, or its provincial regions, or large parts of them. It is this which many observers express or imply when

---

Marxist authors who are among the least inclined to the whole feudal thesis. Yet conversation with several of them suggests that their espousal of part of the thesis involves their unconscious agreement with other parts. For "feudal" and "capitalist" are not just convenient words; they are names for concepts whose implications, often unconsciously, affect the user's perception of reality well beyond the immediate context in which the words are used.

they note that 1.5 percent of the owners own 50 percent of the land, on which various conditions of servitude still prevail. And this was substantially my own view until recently, as expressed in an article on land reform in *Monthly Review* (Frank 1963a). Brazil's former Minister of Planning, Celso Furtado, says: "The non-existence of a modern agriculture, based on capitalism and tied to the internal market, is in large part responsible for the permanent tendency toward disequilibrium observable in this country" (quoted in Paixão 1959: 32n).

This interpretation of Brazilian society as feudal is linked with the still more widespread and fundamentally even more erroneous "dual society" thesis. One statement of this view which has found broad acceptance is that of Jacques Lambert in his *Os Dois Brasis.* *

> The two Brazils are equally Brazilian, but they are separated by several centuries. . . . During the long period of colonial isolation, there was formed an archaic Brazilian culture . . . a culture which . . . in the isolation that still continues has the same stability as the indigenous cultures of Asia or the Near East. . . . The Brazilians are divided into two systems of economic and social organization, as different in their methods as in their level of living. . . . It is not only the states of the Northeast . . . but also the rural areas very near [São Paulo] whose structure in closed societies makes them penetrable by external circumstances only with difficulty. . . . The dual economy and the dual social structure that accompanies it are not new, nor characteristically Brazilian—they exist in all unequally developed countries (Lambert 1961: 105-110).

Several important interpretations of historical and current reality are inherent in this general view, and most of them are seriously mistaken. The standard Western bourgeois analysis might be said to begin with feudalism in Western Europe. This

---

* Though written by a Frenchman, the book was published by the Brazilian Ministry of Education. Moreover, its earlier French edition was commended by Brazil's outstanding Marxist sociologist, Florestan Fernandes, as "one of the best sociological syntheses so far written about the formation and development of Brazilian society." The Brazilian edition, used here, was characterized three years later by Wilson Martins as "one of the most intelligent studies yet written about our country."

feudalism, it is held, was transplanted to Latin America, while it was supplanted in Europe by capitalism. Thus Europe and later its Anglo-Saxon offshoots took off into economic development, leaving Latin America and other now underdeveloped areas still behind in the feudal state. To the extent that Latin America has now become "semi-feudal" or "pre-capitalist," and hence shows some scattered signs of economic development, this is because the developed countries dragged or helped the others up behind them. Aside from this drag-help relationship, however, economic development and underdevelopment are seen as being caused independently of each other by capitalism and feudalism respectively. Insofar as Latin American cities are more "advanced" and the countryside more "backward," more or less the same argument is applied—with the notable exception that, although nobody argues that the development of the metropolitan industrialized world is determined or even seriously hampered by the peripheral underdeveloped agrarian countries, it is argued that the backward feudal provinces do determine and prevent the economic development of their respective urban industrializing centers within the underdeveloped world!

The policy conclusion logically derived from this analysis is of course to abolish feudalism and to follow the same general course of development as the developed countries. The exact dose of the anti-feudal remedy prescribed varies from one doctor to another: Sometimes it is the abolition of all large landholding; sometimes only of "unproductive" lands; sometimes it is only colonization of new lands; always it is the creation with government technical and financial help of an independent yeoman small-farmer middle class (cf. Frank 1963a). Unfortunately, each step of the diagnostic analysis is mistaken; and therefore, logically, so is the proposed remedy.

2. The Traditional Marxist Theses

The interpretations of the agricultural crisis in Latin America and Brazil which I here call "traditional Marxist" may be conveniently summarized in three theses: (a) feudalism predates capitalism, (b) feudalism coexists with capitalism, and (c) feudalism is penetrated or invaded by capitalism. These theses are not mutually exclusive; they complement each other; and several writers subscribe to two or more of them and their subtheses.

(a) *Feudalism Predates Capitalism.* This thesis involves in Brazil the further pre-existence of slavery. The problem comes when we ask what produced this slavery, what determined the functioning of the slave society, what caused slavery to disappear, and what replaced it. Nelson Werneck Sodre thus discusses the first two questions:

> Simonsen . . . rejects the idea of colonial feudalism and raises that of capitalism. He thinks that even in Portugal, in the period of the discoveries, feudalism did not exist. The capitalist thesis is also espoused by students of [Latin] American history, like Sergio Bagú. . . . Celso Furtado denies the colonization's feudal character and defends the slavery thesis as explaining the hermetic nature of the regime. Other students turn to devote themselves to the feudal traces in the legislation, in which planning had a subordinate place. It is not difficult to conclude that such legislation showed definite feudal marks. Nor could it have been otherwise, given that the dominant class in Portugal at the time was one of feudal nobles. . . . The slave regime here did not rise out of the disintegration of the primitive community. The slave regime here is established by nobles who previously lived in a world, the metropolitan world, in which a more advanced form of production, the feudal one, predominated. . . . Those who subscribed to the thesis of the existence of capitalist characteristics in the colonization enterprise were undoubtedly led to do so by the confusion, long current, between the notion of commercial capital, a characteristic of the mercantilist phase, and capitalism. Today it seems clear that . . . commercial capital was far from giving rise to, and further still from characterizing, the above method of production [slavery]. Thus, the conclusion to which the examination of reality brings us is that Brazil started its colonial existence under the slave productive system (Sodre N.D.: 82).

Examination of other parts of Sodre's argument suggests that, far from deriving this conclusion from an "examination of reality," he really gets its from his own mechanical application to Brazil of Marx's argument about the development of capitalism in Europe. Since Marx notes that mercantilism (trade) was not sufficient to give rise to capitalism in Europe, and that industry (production) was necessary, Sodre argues that mercantile trade could not produce capitalism, or even slavery, in Brazil. The same unfounded, and un-Marxist, argument appears to be behind his claim that mercantilism could not have been dominant in Portugal at the time, and that feudalism therefore must have been. He does not consider the possibility that feudalism may have reigned in Portugal and that nonetheless its mercantilist sector opened up Brazil. And he cannot of course explain why his feudal nobles would have had the desire, to say nothing of the ability, to conquer a new continent.

The argument is extended further by Paul Singer: "The import of Africans represents 70 percent of the total Brazilian purchases. It appears it is not the monoproduction for the metropolitan market that determines the regime of slave labor, but rather the latter that presupposes the former." Turning to the period of the abolition of the slave trade and later of slavery itself, Singer notes that two possible paths were open to Brazil, "feudalization" or "capitalization." Although he says that both found application in different regions, he concludes: "As is evident, the abolition of slavery did not generate a capitalist agriculture; nor could it have been so under a structure of land-ownership whose formation was based on slave labor and which was not directly affected by the abolition of captivity" (Singer 1961:65, 69, 72).

(b) *Feudalism Coexists with Capitalism.* The second traditional Marxist thesis, referring to recent and current times, is that feudalism and capitalism coexist. The thesis takes many forms, only a few of which can be cited here.

Thus we come to a conclusion of extraordinary importance for us: The existence of a dualism in the revolutionary process of Brazil. . . . It is that our society is open for the working class, but not for the peasant class. In effect, our political system permits the working class to organize to carry forward. . . . Brazilian society is rigid in a large segment: that formed by the rural sector (Furtado 1962: 28).

This political analysis, paralleling the theory of the dual society in underdeveloped countries (Boeke 1953), comes not from a Marxist but from a leading ideologist of the bourgeoisie, Brazil's recent Minister of Economic Planning. But essentially the same interpretation is to be found among important Marxist analyses of Latin America and Brazil:

Thus in some underdeveloped countries capitalist industrial production, regionally limited, coexists with a semi-feudal system of large latifundias. Both structures (or substructures) of the society are characterized by their own productive relations, and therefore by their own class structures. But insofar as the economic development of these countries is a capitalist development, the fundamental classes are, or will become, the classes of the capitalist system (Stavenhagen 1962: 2).

They [regional differences] reveal different stages of evolution in the direction of capitalist economic-social structure. In brief, whereas in certain regions traditional forms of work predominate, like subsistence economy, tenancy, or traditional forms of rental and sharecropping, in other regions we find work for money wages. At one extreme we find the traditional rural complex, while at the other we have the capitalist system in development (Ianni 1961: 33).

Brazilian agriculture . . . is a formally capitalist structure which appears in two forms: direct employment of agricultural wage workers or leasing of lands in tenancy. But under its capitalist appearance, that is, of economic relations . . . appear in reality the elements of personal subordination . . . an extension of servitude. . . . Finally, the feudal residuals, which reduce the tenant to the condition of a serf, are more common than one thinks (Singer 1961: 71-72).

(c) *Feudalism Is Penetrated by Capitalism.* The third thesis is that capitalism is slowly but surely penetrating the countryside. This process brings with it blessings, the rationalization of agriculture and the liberation of the economy and the peasant from their feudal shackles; but they are mixed blessings, for the same process involves the proletarianization of the peasant.

As I see it, the central point for visualizing land reform in Brazil is the description of the process of penetration of the capitalist form of production in the countryside and the transformation it produces in the old patrimonially based agrarian structure. In this discussion, the problem of the forms of property and of economic organization is decisive (Cardoso 1961: 8).

Stimulated by the growth of the consumer market for agricultural products, provoked by the expansion of industrialization, agriculture modifies itself to become adjusted to the conditions of work. . . . The agricultural enterprise changes, promoting in turn the expulsion of part of the workers. . . . There is a continuous, progressive, and cumulative interaction between the different socio-economic systems involved in the Brazilian reality. The subsistence economy is continually affected and modified by the already more vigorous market economy; and the latter in turn finds itself periodically or continually stimulated by international trade. The interrelations between them therefore are leading to the extension of capitalist forms of production among agricultural activities that are still embedded in the molds of subsistence economy . . . it transforms the manner of using work, provoking proletarianization (Ianni 1961: 45).

The substitution of a capitalist structure for a colonial, semi-feudal, pre-capitalist structure, and the specific features of each, are summarized by Singer in a later article:

Brazil . . . continued practicing a traditional colonial agriculture, geared to export, with substantial subsidiary subsistence production, methods of extensive cultivation, of land rotation, with plow and fertilizer unknown, devastating lands, deforesting large areas offered up in a holocaust to erosion. . . . The very economic development of the country also brings about a series of qualitative transformations in the structure of the agricultural economy. . . . These transformations are essentially a change from a traditional agriculture of the colonial type, with the characteristics described above, to a modern agriculture of the capitalist type. . . . The passage of a colonial agriculture to a capitalist type implies a transformation of all aspects of agricultural activity. The productivity of the land and of labor increases: Of land, because fertilizers and other methods that can raise and preserve soil fertility are introduced. Of labor, because, along with human energy, animal and mechanical energy as well as mechanical agricultural implements are introduced. The technique of cultivation changes, passing from rotation of lands to rotation of crops. Similarly, the technique of livestock raising changes, now no longer depending on natural pastures but on artificial pastures or on stables. Finally, the productive unit loses a large part of its self-sufficiency and comes to depend on inputs [consumption] acquired on the outside; and it enters a larger whole in which the division of labor and the specialization of tasks are propelled by the expansion of the market and by the increase in scale of production. . . . A larger share of capital is used for the same amount of land and labor. For this to occur, capital has to become relatively cheaper; and land and labor have to become more expansive. Both conditions occur during the process of industrialization (Singer 1963: 25-28).

3. Critique of the Myth of Feudalism

(a) *Comparison with Reality.* We may begin our evaluation of the traditional Marxist theses by taking the particular features they attribute to feudal and to capitalist organization and comparing these with the realities of Brazilian agriculture. This examination may, as in Table 1 (p. 230), be conveniently divided into three major parts: (i) the organization of agricultural production, (ii) the condition of agricultural workers and (iii) changes in these over time. We will find that the greater part of the features attributed to the "feudal" and "capitalist" sectors or forms of productive organization are not indeed true to the facts.

(i) *Organization of Agricultural Production.* Though "feudal" concentration of land is certainly large, "capitalization" of agriculture, far from decreasing it, increases the concentration still further. During the "capitalist" expansion phase, notably between 1920 and 1930, and again between 1940 and 1960, the concentration of agricultural holdings increased (Prado 1960: 207). Between 1940 and 1950 holdings of over 1,000 hectares increased their share of total agricultural land from 48 to 51 percent (*Folha de São Paulo* 1963). During the world crisis of the 1930's, concentration decreased, a matter I discuss below.

In São Paulo, the most "capitalist" state with the most commercial crops, coffee and cotton land concentration also increased with development (Paixão 1959:33, Schattan 1961:101).

)

Table 1

Features of "Feudalism" and "Capitalism"
(according to traditional Marxist theses)

Feudalism	Capitalism

A. ORGANIZATION OF AGRICULTURAL PRODUCTION

Feudalism	Capitalism
1. Large size of landholdings (latifundia)	1. Landholdings smaller?
2. Extensive agriculture	2. Intensive agriculture
3. Low and inefficient land use	3. Greater, more efficient land use
4. Migrant and slash-burn agriculture	4. Crop rotation
5. Land-exhaustive and eroding techniques	5. Land conservation and maintenance
6. Extensive livestock grazing	6. Intensive livestock raising
7. Capital-poor agriculture; no fertilizer, machinery, or investment	7. Capital-intensive agriculture; fertilizer, machinery, investment
8. Self-sufficiency sector; subsistence	8. Specialization, outside dependency, commercialization, no subsistence
9. Non-rational mentality	9. Rational, capitalist mentality

B. CONDITION OF AGRICULTURAL WORKERS

Feudalism	Capitalism
1. Serfdom	1. Proletarianization
2. Tenancy, sharecropping, unpaid labor; payment in kind and in tokens	2. Contract work with pay in money wages
3. Unfree existence even behind money-payment façade	3. A certain liberty
4. Low income	4. Labor more expensive; workers less poor?
5. Workers tied to farm	5. Expulsion of agricultural workers

C. CHANGES OVER TIME

Feudalism	Capitalism
1. Continuous de-feudalization	1. Continuous capitalization
2. Total disappearance of feudal agriculture	2. Total proletarianization of agriculture; irreversibility of defeudalization/capitalization process
3. Unresponsiveness to demand changes	3. Responsiveness to changes in market demand

Similarly, for the state of Rio de Janeiro, Geiger (1956: 50, 74) reports that resident and absentee landlords, individuals and corporations, buy up land right and left with economic expansion. Or to quote Guimarães (1963), writing in the *Jornal do Brasil:*

> Economic development might lead us to suppose a less unjust regime of land distribution. Far from it, what the high percentages of families without land indicate, as observed particularly in São Paulo and Rio de Janeiro, is that economic development does not lead spontaneously and by itself to a redistribution of the agrarian structure and to the solution of the land problem in our country (Guimarães 1963).

Nor does the expansion of the agricultural frontier help to eliminate land concentration. Although the states of Rio Grande do Sul and Santa Catarina were settled during the nineteenth century with a pattern more resembling one of smaller homesteads, land concentration there is today not notably different from other regions. As Cardoso (1961: 13) notes, in the "new zones" such as Northern Paraná where coffee agriculture started on the basis of small properties, regrouping of these into large properties by the most prosperous local owners, or into the hands of others from São Paulo who have bought into the area, is already widespread. Nor does the current expansion of the agricultural frontier in Goias, Matto Grosso or anywhere else inhibit concentration. As the daily press reports indicate, although these lands are often opened up by small settlers, they are soon grabbed by large so-called *grilheiro* owners who in one way or another force out the small owners.

Contrary to the traditional Marxist thesis, there is no consistent pattern of extensive and intensive agriculture in the "feudal" and "capitalist" sectors respectively. The patterns of resource use summarized in Table 1 (A: 2 to 6), especially, are not determined by these supposed principles or organization but, as we will see later, by other considerations. Therefore we find that small but "feudal" tenant farms are generally much more labor-intensive—and maybe even more capital-intensive —than large farms, be they "feudal" or "capitalist." (See, for instance, the analysis of farming in the lower half of the state of Rio de Janeiro by Geiger 1956, especially 75-81, 128-152.) The excellent study of agricultural organization and production in São Paulo by Salamão Schattan (1961) shows that smaller and medium agricultural holdings are more intensively cultivated, devote less land to relatively wasteful forest and pasture lands, have a higher human and animal population per hectare, a greater work force per hectare, produce more income per hectare, including from animal products, but of course less income per inhabitant (103-114). The same relation between land size and production holds true in the state of Rio de Janeiro (Geiger 1956: 76-77). On the other hand, migrant agriculture, soil exhaustion, underutilization and undercapitalization of lands, and other "pre-capitalist" features are, as Paixão suggests (1959: 33-34), "most pronouncedly reflected" in the "capitalist" coffee and cotton economies of "capitalist" São Paulo. And the Instituto Brasileiro do Café (1962) recognizes these effects of coffee culture, and even asks for government aid to promote and extend them. Ianni (1961: 29n) observes that increases in agricultural output in Brazil have typically been due to the opening up of new lands and not to increase in agricultural productivity.

As to the supposed intensification of livestock raising, it does not appear for São Paulo from Schattan (1961: 105-107) and is explicitly denied for Rio by Geiger (1956: 59, 121). A study by the Agriculture Ministry's Comissão Nacional de Política Agrária (1955) shows that burning is nearly as common in the "capitalist" South as in the "feudal" Northeast, being used in 87 percent and 98 percent of the municipios respectively. For São Paulo and for Piauí, respectively the most advanced and most backward states, the percentage relation is the same (103-118). "Three years or more fallow" and "fallow land devoted to pasture use" occur respectively in 55:80 percent and 64:88 percent of the municipios of the South and the Northeast (103-118), but in this case much of the difference is possibly due to the difference in crops between the two regions—permanent (coffee) crops and pasture in the South and not in the Northeast. The same study, however, does indicate a more notable difference between the two regions in regard to capital invested in fertilizer (103-118) and traction (127-133); but also, not surprisingly, an even greater difference—and one that can go a long way to explain the difference in capital—between the amount and source of credit available in the two regions (85-94). The fact that, as Singer posits, capital may with development become more plentiful and cheaper relative to land and labor in the economy as a whole does not mean that agriculture, or any particular part of it, will therefore receive concomitantly more capital investment. In fact, little investment flows into agriculture: Indeed, the opposite is probably true; it still flows out. In the most capitalist state, São Paulo, when demand for a particular agricultural product rises, any response in supply is due less to an increase in total resources than it is to the withdrawal of resources from another crop—usually a non-cash crop (Schattan 1961: 88, Prado 1960: 205-207).

As to self-sufficiency and subsistence production versus specialization and dependence on outside suppliers, there probably is in fact some such pattern in the two sectors. But the reasons are not necessarily those implied by the traditional Marxists. Thus, the fact that a greater area is devoted to food crops in coffee regions than in sugar regions (which does not even support the feudal/sugar, capitalist/coffee argument) may be due more to the fact that interplanting other crops with coffee does not necessarily reduce, and may increase, coffee yields, while the same is not the case with sugar. Moreover, the "feudal" Northeast devotes 30 to 40 percent of its total imports into the region to food (*Desenvolvimento & Conjuntura* 1959/4: 71); since its settlement, of course, this area has been an exporter of commercial products. Subsistence and specialization can be found intermixed in all parts of Brazil; moreover, their importance relative to each other varies back and forth over time (Prado 1960: 205; Geiger 1956: 128), an important part of reality not explained or explicable by traditional Marxist analysis.

Finally, if "rationalist" mentality refers to serving one's own interests well, it will be difficult to accept without further proof that people in the "feudal" sector serve their own interests less well than people in the "capitalist" sector, or that the former will do so increasingly thanks to the penetration of capitalism into their lives. It all depends on what their particular circumstances and interests are, a matter I examine in the next section. And if "rational" refers to the common or public welfare, then it remains far from obvious that the better (for the producers) *variety* of crops on more traditional farms (Geiger 1956: 76, 129) is a non-rational or irrational disadvantage.

(ii) *The Condition of Agricultural Workers.* If all non-cash-nexus relations in agriculture are by definition non-capitalist and all money-contract payments capitalist, then the traditional Marxist theses about the conditions of agricultural employment are of course true by definition. But in that case they teach us nothing about reality. And the reality of Brazilian agriculture is that the thousand and one variations and combinations of agricultural working relations are intermixed in all areas. Any number of forms of tenancy and hired labor may be found in the same region, the same farm, the same part of a single farm; and they exist almost entirely at the pleasure of the farm owner or manager. How this pleasure is determined will appear from the discussion beginning on p. 242. These relationships, rather than being caused by feudal mentality or colonial traces, are determined by hard economic and technological considerations. They differ by crop, for instance. Thus, permanent and semi-permanent harvest plants, like trees and bananas, evidently do not permit harvest sharing; and in their cultivation sharecropping is accordingly not found (Geiger 1956: 80). It is common that a family will be paid in two or more forms for work on different crops. And changes in the form of employment and payment will follow shifts in the crops or livestock produced.

Another evidently crucial determining factor is the degree of fluctuation in production and the amount and reliability of available labor. The more variable the production and the more plentiful and secure the supply of labor, the less, evidently, do the owners "tie" the peasants to the farm—that is, the more proletarianized they become. Payment by token at the "company store," far from being evidence of a feudal relationship, is a function of the commercial activity of the farm and the monopoly position of the company owner. It can be found in the most "modern" farms and at the doorstep of Rio de Janeiro (Geiger 1956: 86). We find in the "feudal" Northeast 12 percent, and in the "capitalist" South 14 percent, of all municipios reporting payments in kind rather than in money. Even for the most "feudal" state, Piauí, and the most "capitalist," São Paulo, the comparison is only on the order of 26 percent and 10 percent respectively. And we may note that São Paulo is a permanent crop producer, while Piauí is not (Comissão Nacional 1955: 149-156).

Though Singer (1961: 71) maintains that money payments are often a façade for a semi-feudal relationship due to the owner's colonial-derived social and political position, the reverse is shown by Prado (1960: 214-224), Costa Pinto (1948: 165-168) and Ianni (1961: 41), namely, that various "feudal" features of the owner-worker relation are façades for essentially commercial economic exploitation. A change from one form of employment to another—or to unemployment—does not give the agricultural worker "a certain liberty" if the exploitative economic power of the owner over the worker remains unchanged or is increased. And such a change often deprives the worker of security which does offer a certain degree of freedom of action.

However low the income and living standard of the various kinds of tenants, the study of rural living conditions in 1836 of Brazil's 1,894 municipios demonstrates that agricultural wage workers quite consistently suffer from lower incomes and worse living conditions than tenants and sharecroppers (Comissão Nacional 1955: 9-39). Francisco Julião (1962: 58) confirms that the agricultural wage workers, in terms of freedom and income, are culturally poor and economically both poor and dependent.

As to the expulsion of agricultural workers from the land and their migration to other areas and to the cities, it is not the substitution of "capitalist" relations for "feudal" relations on their accustomed lands which is determinant, but rather the capitalist development of the national and international economy as a whole. Interestingly enough, if the data can be relied upon, there may be relatively more outmigration from Northeastern municipios among workers of the 11-20 cruzeiro income group than among those of the 0-10 cruzeiro group (Comissão Nacional 1955: 41-48; 1952 prices).

(*iii*) *Changes Over Time.* Most serious of all the deficiencies of the traditional Marxist theses and analysis, aside from fundamental considerations of theory and policy (of which more later), is their inability adequately to account for the changes that have occurred over time. The "pre-existence of feudalism" thesis introduces difficulties from the very start. Apart from the moot question of to what degree Europe or the Iberian peninsula was feudal at the time of the conquest, there arises the problem of how feudalism got to the New World to begin with. Even though the prevailing social relations in the metropolis may have been feudal, the sector which was determinant for opening up the New World could have been mercantile. Otherwise why would or could a feudal society take steps to conquer and open to trade a whole new continent? And further, would the metropolis, feudal or mercantile, have an interest in, or the capacity to, set up a feudal system in the New World? Thus, why one feudal system would carry another, or transplant itself, to a new continent is doubly inexplicable.

The "coexistence of feudalism and capitalism" thesis leaves in serious question where capitalism in Latin America or Brazil is supposed to have come from. Did it arise out of pre-existing local feudalism as in Europe? In the face of the evidence, to which Sodre and Singer also subscribe, that Latin America and Brazil from the beginning had strong mercantile ties to the metropolis, such an answer would evidently merit little support. If feudalism first pre-existed and then coexisted with capitalism in the New World, we must still ask where the capitalism came from. The "capitalist penetration of feudalism" thesis raises still further difficulties. In its more extreme versions it refers to "continuous, progressive and cumulative" penetration and proletarianization and holds that this process will "lead to the complete and definite expulsion of the *colono*, tenant, and sharecropper, etc., from the interior of the hacienda or latifundia, that is, to his proletarianization" (Ianni 1961:45, 36).

We are supposed to be witnessing, in other words, a process in which capitalism is irreversibly extinguishing feudalism in the countryside and finally incorporating agriculture into the capitalist national economy. Moreover, it is frequently claimed that the feudal sector, apart from and before its penetration by capitalism, is quite unresponsive to long-term and short-term changes in demand, and indeed unresponsive to changes in circumstances of any kind, whereas the capitalist sector is responsive to and apparently capable of filling the demand and need for agricultural products. But if these "penetration" theses be true, they cannot account for the factually quite frequent substitution of "feudal" and "capitalist" features back and forth over time (cf. Prado 1960: 205-207). Moreover, the most casual observer can note, as testified by the serious analyses of Caio Prado (1960, 1962), Schattan (1959, 1961), Paixão (1959), Geiger (1956) and others, that the "feudal" sector does make continual adaptations to circumstance, including changes in demand, while the most "capitalist" and most "rationally organized" sectors of agriculture fall far short of responding to society's demands and needs.

In fact, the very duality of the feudalism-capitalism approach fails to account for much of either the "feudal" or the "capitalist" aspects of agricultural development, let alone providing an understanding of their combination. The feudalism thesis does not even explain events in the "feudal" sector: It does not account for the introduction of "feudalism," nor the historical development of the "feudal" sector, nor its many short-term changes. Nor does it account for the "capitalist" sector, although some professed Marxists go so far as to argue that "feudal" owner-worker relations "internal" to the farm determine the farm enterprise's behavior in the "capitalist" market outside the farm; and there is even wider agreement that the "feudal" sector holds back, and at least in this sense determines the development of, the progressive "capitalist" sector. This view, purportedly based on the Marxist tenet that internal and not external relations are determinant, is, so far as I can see, a result of its proponents' inability to tell inside from outside.

The "capitalist" part of the thesis, insofar as it refers not to the whole economy but only to its "capitalist" sector, suffers from similar, if less severe, shortcomings. We must ask again: If agriculture, including export agriculture, was "feudal," then how and why did capitalism arise? Finally, if capitalism is only just penetrating agriculture, how do we explain the relation of agriculture in its entirety to the national economy? And, if the national economy is not wholly capitalist, how then do we understand the Brazilian—or any other national—economy and society as a whole?

(b) *Theory and Policy Conclusions.* There is a remarkable similarity in all fundamentals between the bourgeois and the Marxist analyses—both metropolitan born. Both maintain that the society consists of two substantially independent sectors. The one is more modern because it took off more or less independently and is capitalist; and the other, the agrarian sector, still holds back both its own progress and that of the modern sector because it remains feudal. Therefore, destroying agriculture's feudal structure and introducing or extending modern capitalist organization will simultaneously solve two problems ——the crisis of agriculture and the development problem of the national economy. Thus we need only change some things in the agricultural sector without overhauling, much less replacing, the total capitalist mechanism. The easy identifiability of feudal and capitalist features will facilitate that separate surgery in feudal agriculture which will heal the body as a whole.

This dual society interpretation rests on important confusions. One relates to the use and semantic content of terms like "feudal" and "capitalist." Almost every time the quoted writers and others use these terms, they are referring to features such as those listed in Table 1—types of relations between owners and workers, behavior and motivation of people, productive and distributional techniques, etc. But they often go beyond these features to conclude not only that feudal relations are being or should be replaced by capitalist relations, but that the feudal system is being or should be replaced by the capitalist system. Their conclusions often are derived by confusing the system with its various features.* This might be avoided by reserving terms such as "feudal" and "capitalist," as they were classically used, to refer to what is really central, the economic and social *system* and its structure itself, rather than applying them also to all sorts of supposedly associated features.

A more significant source of confusion concerns the real nature of a feudal system, and, most importantly, of the capitalist system. Whatever the types of personal relations in a feudal system, the crucial thing about it for our purposes is that it is a *closed* system, or one only weakly linked with the world beyond. A closed feudal system would not be inconsistent with—though it need not follow from—the supposition that Brazil and other countries have a "dual society." But this cloture—and the duality as well—is wholly inconsistent with the reality of Brazil, past or present. No part of Brazil, certainly no populous part, forms a closed, or even an historically isolated, system. None of it can therefore in the most essential respect

* Since writing this, I have found that Silvio Frondizi makes essentially the same point referring to Argentina: "the existence of pre-capitalist forms as the fundamental characteristic of an economy—such as in pre-revolutionary Russia—is one thing; and another and totally different thing is the existence of pre-capitalist forms that are inserted into an entirely capitalist economy and which are the expression, [only] apparently different, of the capitalist system of production" (Frondizi 1956, II, 168).

be feudal. On the contrary, all of Brazil, however feudal-seeming its features, owes its formation and its present nature to the expansion and development of a single mercantilist-capitalist system embracing (the socialist countries today excepted) the world as a whole—including all of Brazil. The essentials of feudalism have never found any existence in Brazil, as Roberto Simonsen, the leading Brazilian industrialist of his time, made clear in his monumental and path-breaking *História Económica do Brasil 1500-1820* (1962).

Most important, we must try to understand the real structure of capitalism, not merely some of its features and symptoms. Nor should the capitalist system be confused with its manifestations only in the most developed—or modern, or rational, or competitive—sector of the European-American or São Paulo metropolis. Capitalism is embodied and developed as one single capitalist system: "Brazilian" or "Paulista" or "American" capitalism are but sectors of this single world-embracing system.

This capitalist system has at all times and in all places—as in its nature it must—produced both development *and under-development.* The one is as much the product of the system, is just as "capitalist," as the other. The underdevelopment of Brazil is as inherent to the system as the development of the United States; the underdevelopment of the Brazilian Northeast is no less capitalist-determined than the development of São Paulo. Development and underdevelopment each cause and are caused by the other in the total development of capitalism. To call development "capitalist" and to attribute underdevelopment to "feudalism" is a serious misunderstanding, which leads to the most serious errors of policy. If feudalism does not exist, it cannot be abolished. If the present underdevelopment and ills of agriculture are already due to capitalism, they can scarcely be eliminated by "extending" capitalism still further. In that case it is capitalism, not feudalism, that needs to be abolished.

The theoretical foundation on which the "feudal" analysis of agriculture is based turns up again in attempts to understand

and resolve other facets of the problems of Brazil and other underdeveloped countries. Both the bourgeois and the traditional Marxist interpretations, as we have seen, assume two sectors of a supposedly single society, which are either independent and each self-determined, as in Sodre and Singer, or at least quite separate, as Cardoso and Ianni suggest. This split-in-the-middle duality, which admits of a separate dynamics for separate sectors and denies a common dynamic to both of them together, negates the very basis and heart of the Marxist theory and method. It necessarily prevents any adequate understanding of a single, total capitalist society. Consequently it leads to the most disastrously wrong political policy.

This analysis has its counterpart in the same kind of approach to the international part of the same economy and the problem of imperialism that it poses. For apparently in the opinion of some Marxists, that part of the economy is separable, and the problem it poses separately resolvable, just like its agricultural counterpart. Thus, the national capitalist economies in Latin America, leaving feudal agriculture behind, somehow took off and described their own independent development, not unlike their European forebears. Then, somewhat as national capitalism began to invade provincial agriculture, so did international capitalism begin to invade the national economies—but with undesirable results. Thus, surgery again becomes indicated, this time to cut out the cancer of imperialism and thereby let the national economy proceed on its otherwise relatively healthy way.

There are of course doctors of political economy in the so-called vanguard of the national bourgeoisie who prescribe precisely these operations. What is surprising is that some professed Marxists, especially the old-line Communist parties, should believe that all the bourgeoisie, or even all the "national bourgeoisie," should wish to resolve the problems of agriculture and imperialism, and thus of national development, in this way; that the "bourgeois revolution" hence has still to be made and that the bourgeoisie should be supported in this task. And these Marxists maintain that the bourgeoisie actually has not only the will but the capacity to do this; they offer the bourgeoisie their unqualified support in freeing the underdeveloped national economic body of its inappropriate feudal agricultural and imperialist international sectors; and they denounce as adventurist, divisionist or revisionist-reactionary all who do not join this front. This disastrous policy will appear less surprising if we recognize that it arises out of a totally *un-Marxist* theory and analysis which admits two, and even three, autonomous sectors, independently or separately created—and separately destroyable.

B. CAPITALIST AGRICULTURE

1. Capitalism and Underdevelopment

Really to understand underdeveloped agriculture, we must understand underdevelopment. And for this, we must investigate the development of that underdevelopment. Yes, *development of underdevelopment*—because underdevelopment, as distinct perhaps from *un*development, did not pre-date economic development; nor did it spring up of itself; nor did it spring up all of a sudden. It developed right along with economic development—and it is still doing so. It is an integral part of the *single* developmental process on this planet during the past five centuries or more. Unfortunately, attention has hitherto been paid almost exclusively to the economic development part of the process—maybe because our science, both its bourgeois and its Marxist branches, developed in the metropolis along with economic development itself.

It is not possible of course to elaborate here a whole theory of underdevelopment, but it is essential to take note of some fundamentals of the process. The first is that this process took place under a single dominant form of economic and political organization known as mercantilism, or mercantile capitalism. A second fundamental is that each step of the way this form of organization concentrated economic and political power, and also social prestige, to an extremely high degree—what has come to be known as monopoly. Thirdly, the effects have been widespread, one might say universal; and while they have been quite different from one place and group to another, they have everywhere been extremely unequal. It is the third factor (universality) which lends to the second (concentration) its importance. For concentration also exists, for instance, in feudalism. But feudalism concentrates land in each separate feud rather than in any wider economy; whereas monopoly in the modern sense refers to concentration in a universally inter-related whole. Further, it is this combination of universal relations with monopoly which necessarily produces inequality, not only of the monopolized factor but of other relations as well. Fourthly, we are dealing here with a *process:* It continues, and so do its effects. Thus, inequality is still increasing (cf. Myrdal 1957), and so are both economic development and underdevelopment.

Capitalist development has involved monopolization of land and other forms of capital, and of labor, commerce, finance, industry and technology—among other things. In different times, in different places, monopoly has taken various forms and effects in adapting to differing circumstances. But while it is important to distinguish peculiarities, such as those of Brazilian agriculture, it is still more important to keep in sight fundamentally similar aspects. Above all, it is important to take into account, where possible, how other parts of the capitalist process in the world determine the one under study, and vice versa.

The development/underdevelopment duality or contradiction of capitalism of course receives its greatest attention today on the international level of industrialized countries and under-developed countries. The European metropolis began seriously accumulating capital several centuries ago. Its expanding mercantilist system was spread to other continents, where it imposed forms of economic organization differing in place and time according to circumstance. In the American elevation running from the Sierra Madre in the north across the Isthmus to the Andes, it found highly organized empires of civilized peoples—with existing mineral wealth ready to be taken home. In Africa, it found human labor which it then used to open up the Latin American lowlands, notably Brazil. This expansion not only contributed to the economic development of the metropolis; it left its marks on other peoples, the effects of which we are still witnessing today. Among the Aztecs and the Incas whole civilizations were destroyed. But, although capitalism did penetrate these lands and tie them to metropolitan forces that have determined their fate, some of their people found partial protection by retreating into a mountainous isolation. In Brazil, a whole new society was implanted, mixing three races and countless cultures, all as grist for the expanding metropolitan capitalist mill. Whatever institutional forms were transplanted or grew up in the New World, their content inevitably was mercantilist- or capitalist-determined.

Later, when metropolitan industrialization and urbanization began to demand more raw materials and foodstuffs, the now underdeveloped regions were called upon—that is, forced—to supply that part which the metropolitan primary producers could not produce, or were thus spared from having to produce. Countries like India and China, which had not yet been thus exploited, received their turn in the imperialist phase when their rural industries, if not their agriculture directly, were destroyed so that they might more effectively absorb the metropolis's surplus industrial goods. In our day, the capitalized metropolis is investing its capital in producing technology and synthetics which substitute for some raw materials, and even produce surpluses of other primary products (wheat, etc.), which the now-specialized primary producing countries are also forced to absorb. Throughout, the peripheral countries have been the tail which has been wagged by the metropolitan capitalist dog: They developed underdevelopment, particularly underdeveloped agriculture, while the metropolis developed industry. Current analyses of this process may be found in Baran (1957), Myrdal (1957) and Lacoste (1961).

This simultaneous development of unequal wealth and poverty may also be seen between regions of a single country. The relationship between the North and South in the United States, and in Brazil between the South and the Northeast, is fundamentally the same as that between the metropolis and its underdeveloped regions. But the Northeast's relation to the South is a supplement to, not a substitute for, its relation with the metropolitan world; that world has not ceased to exist and can never have its effects undone.

The Brazilian Northeast, one of the world's poorest and most underdeveloped regions, has a per capita income about one fourth that of the South; Piauí, its poorest state, one tenth that of Guanabara, the seat of Rio de Janeiro (*Desenvolvimento & Conjuntura* 1959/4: 7-8). The Northeast (including Sergipe and Bahia), with 32 percent of Brazil's inhabitants, in 1955 earned 75 billion cruzeiros out of the national total of 575 billion. And the income at the disposal of its inhabitants was even less, since the area shows an outflow of capital to other regions (*Desenvolvimento & Conjuntura* 1957/2: 18-19). In fact, the capital-poor and starving agricultural Northeast earns foreign exchange which is spent for the capitalization and welfare of other regions, from which it in turn imports the foodstuffs which represent 30 to 40 percent of its regional imports (*Desenvolvimento & Conjuntura* 1959/4: 71). Even its expenditure on maintaining and educating its young people goes to the development of other regions, for its most productive workers migrate to areas of greater opportunity.

It is enlightening to examine the historical course of the Northeast's underdevelopment. During the sugar era its coast was the leading sector; and its interior was the sugar export sector's peripheral, underdeveloping, cattle-raising meat supplier—as the sugar sector was itself an underdeveloping periphery of the European metropolis. With the decline of the Northeast's sugar fortunes, the entire Northeast became fully underdeveloped. The subsequent rise of the national metropolis in São Paulo further decapitalized the Northeast, as it has much of the rest of the economy. There are Paulistas who say that São Paulo is the locomotive that draws twenty-one cars (the twenty-one states); they neglect to add that these are its fuel-supplying coal cars. To regard the one region as more "feudal" and the other as more "capitalist," however, serves only to obscure their common capitalist structure, which generates this inequality between them.

This development/underdevelopment duality or contradiction of capitalist society is universally accompanied by monopoly concentration of resources and power. In the United States, the contradiction appears in the large cities and metropolitan areas, between regions like North and South, between sectors like industry and agriculture, within sectors in industry. In agriculture, 10 percent of the farms in 1950 produced 50 percent of the output, whereas 50 percent of the farms produced 10 percent of the output—while 1 million of the 5 million farm families live at a mere subsistence level. And the United States never underwent feudalism in any form. Western European industry exhibits at once the most advanced technology, incorporated in international cartels, alongside factories which are more family than business and artisan shops that take us back to the Middle Ages. We find the same thing in all parts of the Brazilian economy, as in the urban properties of Porto Alegre in which 0.5 percent of the population accounts for 8.6 percent of the proprietors who among them own 53.7 percent of the real estate (*A Classe Operária* 1963).

2. The Principles of Organization

Brazilian agriculture can thus only be understood as an outgrowth of world capitalist development/underdevelopment. A rigorous demonstration of this thesis and a full analysis of Brazilian agriculture are beyond the scope of this study. For one thing, the available theory and methodology of capitalist development/underdevelopment are themselves still underdeveloped. The varieties of capitalist development and underdevelopment, their changes over time, indeed the total social reality, are more complicated than the relatively simple economic theory available to interpret them. There is a concomitant dearth in the collection and prior analysis of data, notably on the monopolization of the commerce in agricultural products, especially foodstuffs. There are, moreover, the limitations of my own theoretical development and familiarity with the realities of Brazilian agriculture. I can only try here to point out some major directions for further study.

The three principles of organization adopted here for the analysis of Brazilian agriculture are: (a) Subordinate determination, (b) commercial or market determination and (c) monopoly. These are of course interrelated and mutually supporting. I name them separately partly to distinguish them from other principles or emphases in social organization, such as superordination or independence, productive or cultural determination, equality or competition.

(a) Subordinate Determination. Brazil and Brazilian agriculture have traditionally been subordinate. Celso Furtado (1959: 13, 15) tells us: "The economic occupation of the American lands was an episode of the commercial expansion of Europe. . . . America becomes an integral part of the European reproductive economy." And Caio Prado Junior carries us through Brazil's history:

If we seek the essence of our development, we will see that we formed ourselves to supply sugar, tobacco, some other products, later gold and diamonds, and still later cotton and then coffee for European commerce. No more than that. It is for this end . . . that the Brazilian society and economy were to be organized. Everything occurred in this sense: The social structure, as well as the activities of the country. . . . This beginning . . . lasted until our own time, in which we are only just starting to free ourselves from this long colonial past (Prado 1962: 23).

When in this century industry and commerce rose to power in the South, these sectors have come to share, but still not to substitute for, the determination of Brazil's agricultural production, life and fate.

Within the agricultural sector itself the same principle of subordinate determination obtains. Cash crops and commercial, especially export, agriculture completely dominate and determine the activities in the essentially residual subsistence sector. This was true in the past, and Furtado (1959: 79) shows the retrenchment into a relative subsistence economy of the Northeast as a result of the declining value of its sugar exports during the eighteenth century. The same is true today, as Caio Prado (1960: 201, 205) and Geiger (1956: 81) note when discussing the shifting fortunes of commercial agriculture and its effects on the subsistence sector.

(b) Commercial Market Determination. As to the dominant commercial influence in Brazilian agriculture, Caio Prado (1960: 199) is quite explicit: "Brazilian colonization . . . was always, from the beginning, and essentially still is today, a mercantile enterprise." This judgment is amply confirmed by two geographers' current "rural study" in the state of Rio de Janeiro, which becomes, as well as a study of economic geography, an exercise in the analysis of commercial agriculture in sometimes non-commercial-seeming form (Geiger 1956). Even subsistence agriculture and "feudal" productive relations are in essence commercially determined—though previous studies seldom bear explicitly on this problem.

(c) Monopoly. Everything connected with Brazilian agriculture is monopolized to an extreme degree. It is a commonplace that land, the principal factor in agricultural production, is concentrated in few hands. But Table 2 (p. 250) suggests that the degree of concentration of ownership and control is considerably higher than is often believed and than appears in the usual presentation of landownership statistics. Conventionally, concentration of landownership is shown by comparing the number of agricultural establishments or owners with the amount of land owned, which Table 2 presents in columns 1 and 2. This procedure suggests that 51 percent, some half of

the establishments or owners (col. 1), accounts for 3 percent of the land (col. 2), while the other half has the remaining 97 percent of the land; and that among these latter, 1.6 percent of the total owns 51 percent of the land. These figures, with certain reservations noted below, are accurate enough to indicate what they are intended to show—the distribution of landownership among that part of the agricultural population which owns land. But this form of presentation leaves out of account the most numerous and productively important part of the agricultural population, the 62 percent who are dependent on agriculture and who work on the land but who do not own any land— the landless agricultural workers.

To take a first major step toward reflecting more accurately the true monopoly concentration of landownership, I have therefore added to Table 2 a third column of agricultural "population" or families. This procedure permits us to compare the distribution of land held, not only with the distribution among owners, but also with the much more significant population and workers dependent on agriculture, whether they own land or not. Table 2 also seeks to distinguish between those agricultural families and workers who own a large or *viable* enough amount of land to earn a living from it and those others whose properties are too small or *unviable* to permit them to live without earning additional income—generally by selling their labor power to those who do have enough land. These "apparent owners" of unviable land, as Engels called them, really belong in a class with the propertyless agricultural workers insofar as in the capitalist system both depend for their bare survival on employment given by the large owners of capital, including land. The non-owners and the apparent owners together comprised 81 percent of Brazil's agricultural families and labor force in 1950.

The addition of the category of agricultural population in column 3 and its division into economically viable and unviable permits a clearer view of the property structure and shows that

Table 2

Monopoly Concentration of Agricultural Landownership in Brazil 1950 (Thousands)*

Category of Those Dependent on Agriculture	Establishments (1)		Land (2)		Population (3)	
	Number of Owners	% of Total	Number of Hectares	% of Total	Number of Families	% of Total
Economically Viable	1,009	49	224,242	97	1,009	19
Owners of Over 1000 Hectares	33	1.6	112,102	51	33	0.6
Owners of Over 20 Hectares	976	47	106,140	46	976	18
Economically Unviable	1,056	51	7,949	3	4,397	81
Owners of Less than 20 Hectares	1,056	51	7,949	3	1,056	19
Non-Owners	0	0	0	0	3,341	62
Total	2,065	100	232,211	100	5,405	100

* The source for the data on agricultural establishments and agricultural land, in columns 1 and 2, is the Instituto Brasileiro de Geografia e Estatística (IBGE), VI Recenseamento do Brasil, Censo Agrícola (1950), Vol. 2, pp. 2–3. The source for the total number of families in column 3 is the number of family heads, IBGE, Censo Demográfico (1950).

In the absence of adequate data, the class breakdown of families in column 3 is estimated by applying to it the percentage breakdown of agricultural establishments from column 1. This procedure involves the assumption that there is one family per censal family head, and that each landowning family or its head owns one censal agricultural establishment. This assumption and its implications are discussed in the text. All percentages are computed.

The data used are for all agricultural establishments and their land. The Census also indicates land "owned," "occupied," and "owned and occupied" which together account for 1,856,288 out of the 2,064,642 total establishments and for 214,153,913 hectares out of the total of 232,211,106 hectares of agricultural land. The difference between the two categories consists almost entirely of land owned by the state. The use of the more restrictive category which excludes this state-owned land and confines itself to privately-owned land would, however, leave the percentage breakdown virtually unaltered; I have therefore chosen to use only the simpler and more conventional data in the Table. Similarly, the Census uses two categories, "Agricultural Population" and "Persons Dependent on Agriculture." Their totals differ so slightly that the percentage breakdown is almost identical; I have therefore used the catgory "Persons Dependent on Agriculture" which appears in Censo Agrícola, Table 22, line 7, as though it referred to agricultural population as well. "Persons Active" or "working in agriculture is from Table 29, line 1. Combining this total of 9,966,965 persons active in agriculture and the 29,621,-089 people dependent on agriculture, both from the Censo Agrícola, with the total of 5,405,224 family heads from the Censo Demográfico, we find an average of 6 persons per family, of whom 2 are censally defined as workers.

the effective degree of monopoly concentration is much greater than it appears in the conventional form of presentation. It now appears that not 1.6 percent (col. 1), but only 0.6 percent (col. 3), own 51 percent of the agricultural land. Not one half, but only one fifth (including the above 0.6 percent), as shown in column 3, own 97 percent of the land. And it is not one half but 81 percent, fully four fifths of the population dependent on agriculture, who own only 3 percent of the agricultural land. The 5,405,224 family heads or families correspond to 29,621,089 persons dependent on agriculture, of whom 9,966,965 are actively engaged in agriculture work and the remainder are family dependents. In other words, in 1950 in Brazil in an agricultural labor force of nearly 10 million, over 8 million agricultural workers together with their 16 million family dependents were dependent for work on 1 million owners of land, of which 33,-000 and their families, about ½ of one percent, owned more than 50 percent of the land.

The very small owner with an unviable amount and/or quality of land (they usually go together since the smallest owners also have the worst, the residual, land) is, much like the propertyless worker, directly dependent on larger landowners; he is highly subject to monopoly exploitation. Moreover, his ownership is often unstable; he may have been replaced by another similar small owner before the same plot of land is registered in the next census. Finally, his living conditions approximate, and sometimes even fall below those of non-owning agricultural wage workers. The stability or security of land tenure is here probably crucial. If ownership or control is secure or stable over time, then in Guatemala or Peru at least, the indigenous peasant is totally different from his wage-earning fellow. Such security of tenure, however, is generally achieved only by collective community action which permits only use or control rights but not ownership to individuals or, when permitting ownership, restricts land sale (cf. Wolf 1955).

There arises the problem of where to draw the dividing line between owners of "viable" and "unviable" properties. I have

here drawn it somewhat arbitrarily at 20 hectares per family
—partly, I confess, because it facilitates rounding of numbers.*
The real division between "viable" and "unviable" will differ
with the land, crop, cultural and other circumstances; and the
line should perhaps be drawn at a lower number of hectares.
On the other hand, the Brazilian Three Year Plan states that
"possibilities are severely limited not only in areas of less than
10 hectares" but that "more or less satisfactory results in terms
of income and productivity" require 50 hectares (Plano Trienal
1962: 141). Yet under present Brazilian conditions, 50-hectare
farms import rather than export labor!

Even the Table 2 measure still understates the monopoly concentration of land. As is customary, given the lack of adequate
statistics, it equates for the census category of properties owned
and/or occupied (but not rented) one property for one owner
and one family. Yet some owners are not individuals or families
but corporations or other groups. And more important, one
owner often owns several properties. There are no reliable overall statistics for this; but Geiger (1956: 49-68), in his careful
study of the state of Rio de Janeiro, shows that ownership of
several properties is common; and he cites various examples of
owners with three or more large properties. Many are owned
by absentee city capitalists. Thus, 11 percent of the properties
with 30 percent of the agricultural land in the state are run by
administrators. Sugar mills, which by law may grow on their
own land no more than 30 percent of the cane they process,
own land through agents in order to bypass the legal limit.
Other owners register their properties in the name of family
members, thus also invalidating the one family/one property
index. Additionally, since large properties include the best land
and small properties the worst, concentration of land still understates the concentration of values. To the extent that Rio's
pattern of ownership of multiple properties is common in other

* For a further partial justification of this figure, see Postscript, pp.
270–271.

states, effective monopolization of land is clearly considerably higher than statistics suggest.*

Monopoly concentration in agriculture is not limited to land. All capital is concentrated. Costa Pinto (1948: 184) estimated 78 percent of the value of farms to be accounted for by land in 1940. Census data suggest that other capital is even more concentrated.

The transportation, commercial distribution, and financing of agricultural products is also monopolized, especially in large-scale cash crops and export crops. And these monopolies are moreover predominantly foreign. Of the ten largest coffee firms, which export 40 percent of the crop, eight are foreign, of which seven are American (Vinhas 1962: 64). Two American firms, the worldwide cotton monopoly Anderson & Clayton, and SANBRA accounted for 50 percent of the cotton exported from Brazil in 1960 (Vinhas 1962: 64). According to the Brazilian Congressman Jacob Frantz (1963), the same two firms in 1961 received 54 billion cruzeiros of the total 114 billion which the Banco do Brasil (the national central bank) loaned out for all agricultural and livestock activities combined. In meatpacking, four foreign firms, the three famous Chicagoans, Swift, Armour, and Wilson, plus Anglo, account for some 12-15 percent of all animals slaughtered in Brazil, but at the same time for 80 percent of those slaughtered and processed through the large modern slaughterhouses which principally serve the large urban and export markets (*Conjuntura Econômica* 1962: 50). Sugar is controlled through the public Institute of Sugar and Alcohol (IAA) which supposedly serves the public interest but is actually controlled—as is usually the case in the capitalist world —by the sugar producers themselves. They thus avail themselves of state protection and price support, like their colleagues of the Brazilian Coffee Institute.

For other crops, principally staples, information on monopo-

---

* For substantiating data from other states concerning multiple ownerships, from the current study by the Comité Interamericano de Desarrollo Agrícola, see the Postscrip below, pages 270–271.

lization of transport, commerce and finance is less readily available. But the conservative daily *Folha de São Paulo* (1963) states that producers and consumers of agricultural products are subjected to a network of monopolists and speculators which doubles and triples prices. The equally conservative *Correio da Manha* (1963) reports products from the state of Rio de Janeiro actually being sold with a 1,500 percent markup in the city. And Geiger (1956) throughout his study confirms the universality of such monopolization of agricultural products.

Monopoly is thus ubiquitous in Brazilian agriculture, and one concentration reinforces another. Through commercial and other relationships, monopoly determines subordinacy and permits exploitation, which in turn produces development/underdevelopment. It is the combination of all these that produces Brazil and its crisis in agriculture.

3. Determination of Agricultural Production, Organization and Welfare

The determination of production, organization, and welfare in agriculture may for convenience be divided by topics: (a) Large-scale commercial agriculture; (b) residual agriculture, including primarily subsistence and small-scale production; (c) underproduction and non-production of some goods in combination with overproduction of others; (d) organization of production on the farm through varieties of owner-worker relationships; and (e) contradictions in welfare, in the agricultural sector and in the economy as a whole.

(a) Commercial Agriculture. It is often argued that the commerce in agricultural products is necessarily secondary to their production—a matter of disposing of them after their production has been determined by other, that is productive and "internal" considerations, which are in turn determined, or "limited," by the "feudal" or "pre-capitalist" productive relations between owner and worker on the farm. It is of course the thesis of this study that commercial determination is paramount instead. All the initiative and capital for large-scale commercial

production came originally from commercial interests across the seas. With the development of a relatively independent Brazilian market and commercial interests, these interests came to play a role in the determination of agricultural production. But fundamentally this did not change anything in agriculture itself.

Commercial interests were and are the source of capital and credit for commercial agricultural production. An early example of this occurred in the development of livestock to serve the once dominant gold- and diamond-mining sector and to some extent, even earlier, the sugar producers. With continued trade with the overseas metropolis and the new development of a Brazilian metropolis, the commercial determinant of large-scale agricultural production persisted. This does not mean, of course, that the productive source of this capital need be outside of agriculture. It means only that its ultimate control is in the hands of those for whom commercial considerations predominate. Similarly, when in recent times agricultural prices have risen more than industrial prices, this also does not mean that capital is being transferred from the non-agricultural sector to agricultural production or even to the consumption of agricultural producers. In the first place, prices of agricultural goods reflect production considerations much less than they do commercial considerations, precisely because of the high degree of monopolization of the economy. The higher price of agricultural goods therefore remains largely in the hands of the commercial sector. And even the part which gets into the hands of "agriculturalists" does not necessarily flow into their production expenditures, or even their consumption.

For the question arises as to what extent these owners are primarily producers and to what extent primarily "commercialists." The cocoa growers of Bahia are notorious for being businessmen much more than growers, for watching stock quotations more closely than cost schedules (Prado 1960: 203). According to Geiger (1956) it appears that almost all owners of any size in the state of Rio de Janeiro are above all businessmen and speculators. This is doubtless true in other states to a much greater degree than is commonly realized.

Additionally, we must take account of the crops produced by entrepreneurial renters of large amounts of land for contract and commercial production of agricultural goods, such as rice in Rio Grande do Sul. Moreover, Geiger (1956: 72-74, 81-85) reports that landowners are at the same time the commercial traders and financers of their tenants' products, just as sugar mills, packing houses and other commercial enterprises are for their commodity suppliers. Finally, Vinhas de Queiróz, reporting on his preliminary sample of 50 out of the 800 economic groups (10,000 firms) that his Institute is studying, found that 35 percent of the Brazilian and 70 percent of the foreign economic groups own agricultural enterprises of some sort, while 30 percent and 40 percent respectively also own storage or distribution businesses, "which indicates that among their principal or secondary activities may be found commerce in agricultural products" (Vinhas de Queiróz 1962: 10). Vinhas's principal finding is the great degree of monopolization of the Brazilian economy, including the production and distribution of agricultural products.

The relevant weight and determination of commerce in agriculture may be found also in the relation between employment and earnings throughout the economy. Table 3 shows that income from industry is twice the percentage of the total, both in Brazil as a whole and in the Northeast. In agriculture the percent of income is of course lower than the percentage of employment. But people employed in the tertiary sector earn twice their proportional share of the national income, and in the agricultural "feudal" Northeast three times their share. Since the bulk of this income is from finance and commerce, and since many of the "farmers" (*agricultores*) in the primary sector are really chiefly commercial people, we get some idea of the weight and influence which commercial considerations must have in agriculture. There is, of course, substantial responsiveness of commercial agricultural production to changes in supply of credit, and in demand for products, from the financial and commercial sector. The major crop and regional shifts over time in Brazilian agriculture can only be understood in this way (Furtado 1959; Prado 1960, 1962, etc.)

Table 3

Distribution of Employment and Income by Sectors
(In percentages)

	Primary Sector (Agriculture)		Secondary Sector (Manufacturing and industry)		Tertiary Sector (Service, finance and commerce)	
	Population employed	Income	Population employed	Income	Population employed	Income
Brazil, total	66	33	11	20	23	47
Northeast	78	42	6	12	15	46

SOURCE: *Desinvolvimento & Conjuntura* 1958/7: 52.

According to the Instituto Brasileiro do Café (1962: 5), coffee contributes 5.5 percent of the Brazilian national income and this rises to "about 10 percent" if we include also its transport, commercialization and export. But even the 5.5 percent includes much more than costs of production, and "coffee" is thus relatively little "agriculture" and quite a lot of commerce. Similarly, Schattan in his various works on cotton, wheat and agriculture in São Paulo (principally 1961), Paixão (1950), Singer in his recent work (1963), Rangel (1961), Geiger (1956) and others all analyze the response to changing commercial considerations of the expansion and contradiction in the production of particular crops in particular areas.

It has been argued that, notwithstanding all this, commercial agriculture is insufficiently responsive to changes in demand and need for agricultural products, principally because the supply of foodstuffs to the cities is inadequate, causing a rise in food prices. But while food shortages may indicate unresponsiveness to *social* needs, they should not be interpreted as the result of unresponsiveness of the agricultural enterprise to *commercial* effective demand. Far from it: They are, precisely, evidence of agriculture's response to the high degree of monopoly in the organization of production and distribution. Any elementary economic text, Marxian or Western neo-classical, shows that the economic consequence of monopoly is high prices and low output.

(b) Residual Agriculture. While subsistence agriculture and much of small-scale agriculture might seem by definition not "commercial," they *are* commercially determined because they are residual to commercial agriculture. They are residual in every way imaginable—residual land, residual finance, residual labor, residual distribution, residual income, residual everything. Residual agriculture and commercial agriculture are like the two parts of an hour glass. The connection between them may appear small, but the resources do flow from one to the other with each turn of the hour-glass economy. What determines this flow of resources? Evidently not the changing fortunes of the subsistence sector, at least in Brazil. (The agricultural reform of Bolivia did in a sense turn the subsistence sector at least partially into the primary sector.) The determining forces come either from the commercial sector and its shifting fortunes and/or from the national and international economy as a whole.

The residual nature and commercial determination of small-scale and subsistence agriculture are expressed in manifold ways. Caio Prado (1960) points out that the spearhead of the whole development of Brazilian agriculture has always been large-scale commercial agriculture. Only in its shadow or indeed in its path, on already exhausted land, did it carve out a marginal and subsidiary place for small-scale and subsistence agriculture. Prado notes furthermore than when commercial agriculture's good times decline, as they did during the 1930's, this brings along a period of "good times" for subsistence agriculture. Thus, during that decade the trend toward land concentration was temporarily reversed as large owners sold off parts of their holdings to increase their liquid capital. In such circumstances, tenants are better able to enforce their demands for land and for permission to raise subsistence crops; and the "non-commercial" sector in general grows. But when the demand for one or more commercial crops expands, small owners begin to find themselves squeezed and bought out; and tenants find, as Miguel Arraes, then Governor of Pernambuco, put it in a lecture, that the planting of sugar cane spreads right into the middle of their houses, not to speak of their subsistence plots.

What Caio Prado (1960) and Schattan (1961: 87) discuss on a regional level, Geiger (1956) confirms for particular farms at particular times, such as the decline of cereals production in the face of rising demand for cash crops (72, 129). Moreover, non-cash crops wither from lack of financing (81-84), because tenants and even small owners are dependent on owner-traders first for seeds and circulating capital in general, to produce their output, and then for transport, storage, etc., to market it (74-76). Finally, owners restrict, and thus indeed determine, their tenants' production choices with respect to permanent crops, soil-exhausting crops, livestock and animals, use of already exhausted land, crop rotation, timing of agricultural activities—in short, everything—essentially in accordance with their own commercial economic interests (80-81).

The hour-glass relationship of residual and commercial agriculture thus has a perhaps insufficiently understood additional effect or function—insurance. The interrelation can be viewed as, among other things, a huge insurance scheme for farm owners, for agriculture and for the economy as a whole. The subsistence sector, precisely by being residual in production and earnings, acts as a sort of shock absorber which partially insulates, protects and stabilizes the entire agricultural economy, thereby helping to stabilize the national and international economy as well—all of course for the benefit of those (including the landowner) whose income is derived from commerce and to the disadvantage of the subsistence farmer who does not share in the profits but gets left holding the bag of costs of this arrangement. Far from being a "drag" on the national and international economy, therefore, the subsistence sector, like the springs or a weight in the back of a car, is one thing that keeps it going: It keeps the system from flying apart at the joints as it travels over its bumpy—and self-created—economic road. Thus "non-commercial," "subsistence" agriculture is commercially determined through the medium of monopoly control of land and of other economic resources and institutions.

(c) *Under/Over Production.* Under this heading I include also non-production, under- and over-financing and distribution, etc. By "overproduction" I do not mean too much absolute production but rather too much production, financing, distribution, etc., of one item relative to others. "Under/over production" is hence the agricultural analogue to development/ underdevelopment on the national and international levels; and it too is the necessary result of dominant commercial monopoly capitalism. Underproduction and overproduction, similarly, are not separable from each other in the present economic structure. All this is not to deny that the concentration of ownership and control of land is of crucial importance for this phenomenon. It is only to put it in context and in perspective.

The monopolization of land and other resources necessarily results in the exploitation of the non-monopolized resources, that is, labor, and in the underutilization of all resources. Thus, one primary purpose of the ownership of large amounts of land, both on the individual and on the social level, is not to use it but to prevent its use by others. These others, denied access to the primary resource, necessarily fall under the domination of the few who do control it. And then they are exploited in all conceivable ways, typically through low wages. Thus, monopoly concentration of landownership means monopsony in the labor market which keeps wages and production costs low, not only for agriculture but for industry as well; not only for the national capitalist economy, but for the international economy.

The monopolization of landownership results in land utilization in the interest of the monopolist. He may and generally does face in turn a commercial monopolist. And thus, paradoxically, there exists a whole chain of monopoly/ monopsony or oligopoly/oligopsony bottlenecks on the way from the humble producer to the humble consumer of agricultural products—who often are the same humble and thus doubly exploited persons. This chain of monopoly, in the words of Ignacio Rangel (1961: iii), "methodically organizes scarcity" and thus "imposes extortionist prices on the consumer," not to speak of the analogously low wage or purchase price on the producer. And the large landowners "respond" all too well to these market pressures. They put their perfectly good farmland into extensive livestock pasture, for instance, thus driving off their tenants in a typical "enclosures" movement, either when the prices of other agricultural products fall or when meat prices rise. The meat goes to the relatively high income consumers, while the low income consumers are left without staples. And the landowner has further advantages (Geiger 1956: 122). It is relatively easy to get credit for livestock (according to Geiger, practically every head of cattle in the state of Rio is mortgaged), and the practice also allows the land to recover through lying fallow. The evidence for all this is legion (Geiger 1956: 58-59, 120-122, Schattan 1961: 94, etc.); and the Instituto Brasileiro do Café (1962: 44), in recommending government expenditures for putting into other uses lands they want to take out of coffee production, notes that financing will not be necessary for conversion into pastures because owners do it anyway.

Non-utilization and underutilization also have other sources. Owners wish to hang on to land for possible future use and to rent it out in the meantime. They "use" and buy into land because it is an excellent hedge against inflation, maybe the best one. Thus, in the states of Espírito Santo and Paraná the prices of land have risen faster than the price level in general (Geiger 1956: 63). Appropriately located land serves other speculative purposes as well, being often held for subsequent subdivision, for future sources of wood (54, 179-190), for tax advantages

(*Folha de São Paulo* 1963), and the like. And once you hold land for speculative purposes, then letting livestock graze or fatten on it adds to your income with no added expense or trouble. This is why practically within sight of Rio de Janeiro the same average of 3 to 5 head of cattle per hectare prevails as leagues from nowhere (Geiger 1956: 121).

The monopolistic structure of the economy also has other effects; or, to put it the other way around, other well-known phenomena can also be explained by monopoly commerce without inventing "feudalism." Thirty-two percent of Northeastern municipios and 19 percent of Southern Region municipios (28 percent of all Brazilian municipios) report no agricultural credit available at all, and 39 and 51 percent respectively report the availability only of non-bank, that is, of commercial and "other" credit for agriculture (Comissão Nacional 1955: 85-94). Other studies report the unavailability of credit for small producers, and of course for non-commercially profitable crops. But credit for monopolized and therefore profitable trade and distribution is relatively generously available—as of course also for monopolized industry and super-monopoly foreign cartels. In particular, credit is unavailable for food crops but flows handsomely into industrial (raw materials) and export crops. These are then stocked, because the monopolized industry cannot absorb them; and this creates still further opportunities for speculative gains from the stockpiles. Or, in the more guarded language (but with more illustrative data) of the Three Year Plan: "Between 1952 and 1960, the coffee cultivated area increased by 1,600,000 hectares (57 percent), whereas the total cultivated areas grew by 38 percent, and the growing of food crops increased by 43 percent." In the Plan's accompanying Table LII, however, it appears that the increases in *output*, as distinct from area cultivated, were 150 percent for coffee and 60 percent for foods. "As there was no way of placing the whole of the coffee harvest in the international market, the social productivity of production factors applied to the coffee sector was very low, compelling the Federal Government to pile up great stocks with no prospects of short-term marketing" (Plano Trienal 1962: 134-135).

The pattern is not limited to coffee. The Plan shows that all the yield increases exceeding 5 percent (except potatoes, which rose 15 percent) were in industrial crops: coffee, 87 percent; peanuts, 33 percent; cotton, 15 percent (the world cotton market was particularly depressed during the period); sugar, 9 percent; castor seed, 57 percent. On the other hand, stable yields varying from 1 percent increase to 3 percent decrease appear for corn, rice, beans and bananas; while wheat shows a 20 percent decline. The Brazilian population's staple, manioc (cassava), almost never grown on a large scale because of lack of financing, registered a yield change of zero (Plano Trienal 1962: 139).

The opportunities for higher profits in speculative commerce and industry act as suction pumps that draw capital out of capital-poor agricultural production, especially of mass-consumption staples, exactly the way developed regions and countries suck capital out of the capital-poor underdeveloped regions and countries, thus increasing the inequality still further and increasing in turn the flow of resources—human as well as economic—into socially undesirable channels. The cause of this is not "feudalism" or "pre-capitalism," but capitalism. And the problems of agricultural output and income, if left to run their free course, will become worse, not better (Schattan 1961: 89). The same prospect faces us with the problem of development/underdevelopment in general.

(d) Organization of Production on the Farm. No one questions that owner-worker relations in agriculture are determined by the concentration of landownership. But, as we have seen, some additional considerations are often advanced to explain both their causes and effects. It is said that they have a rationale of their own—a "feudal" rationale—which accounts for their survival and their successful resistance to more rational capitalist forms. It is also said that the various forms of tenancy are all fundamentally different, that each seems to have its own rationale, and that it is these "feudal relations" which determine not only the organization of production in the "feudal" sector but even the economic health of the "capitalist" sector and the economy as a whole.

The analysis of this study rejects these interpretations. Various owner-worker relations are found intermixed all over the country, in each region, on many single farms, within many worker families; and they often change back and forth even from one growing season to another (Prado 1960: 213; Geiger 1956). Is this because the degree of feudalism or of capitalist penetration concomitantly differs from one place, or family, or year to another?* Or is it rather because the changing exigencies of the capitalist economy and agriculture permit or demand from the owner various ways of organizing his production and various forms of exploiting land and labor? We might, in short, ask for each case of owner-worker relations: How long would it resist a change in the capitalist labor and product market which would make its abandonment profitable or economically necessary to the owner?

Even to pose these questions suggests that the owner-worker relationship, far from being the starting point of the chain of determination—or the fundamental contradiction, to use Marxist terms—is only an extension and manifestation of the determinant economic structure and relation. That structure is monopoly capitalism; and the relation, the content of the relation, is the resultant exploitation of the worker by the owner who expropriates the fruits of the worker's labor. What makes this relation possible is of course the monopoly/monopsony position of the owner. What determines the form this relation will take, the exploitative content remaining the same, is above all the commercial capitalist interests of the owner. Not only does he exploit, he dictates the form this exploitation will take.

The monopolization of land forces non-owners, and even

---

* This explanation, logically derived from one part of the "feudalism" thesis, is inconsistent with the other part of that thesis which holds that feudalism disappears and capitalism advances without reversals.

small owners, to buy access to, or the fruits of, that key resource.
Their only means of doing so is to sell their labor to the same
monopolist/monopsonist buyer. Following the discussion of
Costa Pinto (1948), Caio Prado (1960), Ianni (1961), and
others, these forms of sale may be classified as follows:

> Sale of labor for money wages (wage workers)
> Sale of labor for product (payment in kind)
> Sale of labor for using land (tenant)
>   And paying with money (renting)
>   And paying with product (sharecropper)
>   And paying with labor (unpaid, forced labor)

The owner-worker relation may of course involve combinations of these; and also the worker often has to pay the owner
for access not only to land but to his monopoly of credit, storage
facilities, transportation, merchandising of goods required for
production or consumption—in short, monopolization of everything. Thus even when tenants are able to produce a crop in
excess of their immediate requirements, they are often forced—
lacking storage facilities, insecticide, etc., and having immediate cash need—to sell their excess to the owner today, only to
buy the same stuff back six months later at twice the price
(Geiger 1956: 130). If the owner's monopoly of these commercial factors alone does not suffice to force the tenant to "sell"
his product to the owner, then the owner's monopoly of land
and his monopsony of labor, and his consequent power to ex-
clude "uncooperative" tenants from his land, do permit him to
extract this last bit of product from the worker.

Which of these forms of the exploitative relationship, or their
combinations, will obtain in a given case depends above all on
the interests of the owner. And these in turn are determined
by the capitalist economy of which he is a part. In some cases,
it is relatively easy to explain the persistence or introduction
of a given form of relationship. Money wages and short-term
contracts, for instance, serve better if the supply of labor is
large and secure relative to the owner's actual and potential
demand for it, and/or when permanent crops are economically

indicated and when the owner wishes for speculative reasons to make rapid shifts from one crop to another, and when times are good, and when because of inflation the value of money declines, etc. In other circumstances and times, such as when labor is in shorter supply, payment in kind and various forms of tenancy, which tie the worker to a particular owner, are more profitable to the owner.

We must not assume that under capitalism non-cash-nexus contract relations are never indicated. On the contrary, they are often indicated for exploiting the peasant both as a producer and again as a consumer. Even when it is not immediately evident what function is served by a particular form of owner-worker relationship, we should not renounce attempts to discover one. Nor may we argue that because there is only "one" capitalism but several forms of owner-worker relations, we therefore need some extra-capitalist explanations for these relations. Evidently capitalism admits of, nay requires, a variety of such relations corresponding to the variety of capitalist circumstances and development. Nor, if we cannot establish a capitalist determination of owner-worker relations in a given case, should we adopt the strange conclusion that these on-farm and local relationships somehow "determine" the operation of the economy elsewhere in the capitalist structure. To maintain that on-farm owner-worker relations determine off-farm developments on the grounds of the Marxist tenet that the internal relations or contradictions determine the external ones is only to confuse the farm with the economic structure.*

(e) Contradictions in Welfare. Capitalism, therefore, through the three principles of subordination, commercialization and

---

* It once seemed to me useful to distinguish "inside the farm" from "outside the farm," which is not the same as the distinction made in Marxist theory. I thought, and Ignacio Rangel (1961: iiii) seems to think, that this distinction might help avoid the confusion of calling agriculture "feudal" when the "outside" relations are evidently capitalist but the "inside" ones are not. But I now think that all relations are fundamentally affected by the capitalist structure of the economy, and I can thus of course no longer recommend this distinction.

monopolization operates to produce a myriad of welfare contradictions—development together with underdevelopment.
There is too much production of cash crops, especially export
crops and insufficient production of mass consumption foodstuffs. Capitalization of agriculture increases together with
strengthened monopolization. Agricultural output rises, but the
production of staples falters. If wages rise, prices rise faster.
Prices of agricultural commodities rise faster than those of industrial goods, but capital flows out of agriculture anyway.
Income in agriculture may rise (according to Schattan 1961: 88,
its per capita income is declining) but income inequality increases also, and the poorest may become absolutely poorer.
Wage payments replace other forms of remuneration, but agricultural workers earn less. They are forced off the land and migrate to the cities, and end up unemployed in the slums having
to pay higher prices for their subsistence.

Avowedly to correct these aberrations, the government intervenes in the process. But the intervention merely reinforces
them. Public productive investment and supply of technology
for agriculture serve only the landowners, not the agricultural
workers. Agricultural credit flows into the hands of those who
already monopolize the commerce in agricultural commodities.
New storage facilities serve the needs of speculators in agricultural commodities. Public stockpiling and price-fixing mechanisms are controlled by the largest, including foreign, monopolies of finance and commerce in agricultural commodities,
which use them exclusively in their own bourgeois interests.
Minimum wages for farm workers and maximum payments by
tenants, even if enforceable and enforced, prejudice the smaller
and weaker owners in favor of the larger, economically stronger
owners; they are absorbed by the strategically placed commercial monopolies; they reduce the number of workers hired and
increase unemployment; and in general they strengthen the
monopolization of agriculture and the countryside. Public intervention by the bourgeoisie, in a word, strengthens the bourgeoisie—and sometimes also the petty bourgeoisie.

Bourgeois capitalist land reform necessarily does the same. Government purchase of lands turns into a program of disposal of unwanted land at the local discretion of the landowners, permits them to transfer still more capital out of agriculture into relatively more profitable commercial and industrial pursuits, pushes up land prices still further, thus adding fuel to land speculation and inflation, and still further confuses the issue behind the crisis in agriculture—undoubtedly one of its major purposes, as in Venezuela (cf. Frank 1963a). Even the Mexican large-scale land reform, preceded by ten years of bourgeois revolution—by far the most profound in Latin America before the Cuban Revolution—became the primary basis of Mexico's new bourgeoisie and of its current ever-deepening development/underdevelopment (Frank 1962, 1963). Bourgeois reform, to repeat, reforms for the bourgeoisie. It does not resolve the crisis of agriculture or of underdevelopment.

4. Conclusion for Theory and Policy

This analysis requires deepening and extension in the future, and the working out of a full theory of development/underdevelopment taken jointly. My analysis of the supposed coexistence of feudalism and capitalism calls into question the received dualist theory. And since the theoretical and policy implications of this dualism often appear in problems well beyond the range of the present discussion, it is imperative to re-examine our reasoning on underdeveloped countries, to ferret out these implications of dualism, and to elaborate a unitary dialectical theory of the process of capitalist development, and indeed of socialist development. The analysis of past Brazilian development along the lines of Celso Furtado (1959) and Caio Prado (1962), which has been only sketched in here, must be theoretically strengthened and projected to the present and future so that, among other things, we can more readily identify and appreciate the human costs of continued capitalist development/underdevelopment.

The present analysis of the Brazilian situation may also find application elsewhere in Latin America and perhaps even in Asia and parts of Africa. It may demand reformulation for countries like Peru and Bolivia which had and maintain a large preconquest indigenous population and which have been exporters not so much of agricultural products but rather of minerals (in colonial times and today Peru imports food); or for countries like Venezuela which have recently abandoned agricultural exports for mineral exports—or indeed for Brazil and Mexico which may come to substitute industrial exports for agricultural exports. But the essence of the analysis, a unitary theory of monopoly capitalist development/underdevelopment, should serve significantly to reinterpret much of Latin American reality as seen by bourgeois and Marxist students alike.

Particularly necessary is fuller economic analysis of the finance and commerce of agricultural commodities and its connection with agricultural production on the one hand and with commerce and industry in general, Brazilian and foreign. Such analysis might reinforce our understanding of how land reform would strengthen, not weaken, the commercial-financial monopoly sector(s) and the bourgeoisie and petty bourgeoisie it supports. Similarly, the connection between the agricultural situation and imperialism requires analytical extension beyond mere description of this or that foreign interest in agriculture to theoretical formulation of their mutual interrelation, with each other and with the whole capitalist economy.

The analysis here should be specifically related to analysis of class structure and dynamics. Development and underdevelopment, for example, are suggestive of one class and the other. Combined development/underdevelopment reflects the relation between the classes; their mutual and mutually caused development evokes the dialectic development of class relations; the subordination, monopolization and exploitation relations between economic development and underdevelopment parallel the corresponding relations between classes; and more.

Finally, our analysis has far-reaching implications for policy,

for both agriculture and the whole society. The well-known reform policies that deal separately with the agricultural sector—
or even part of it—and separately with the international imperialist "sector" clearly fall far short of the mark. The analysis
here calls into question the theoretical base not only of bourgeois ideology but also of the Communist parties in Brazil and
elsewhere in Latin America, which establish their programs
and alliances with the bourgeoisie on the premise that the bourgeois revolution has yet to be made. It is the naked capitalist
interests of landowner-merchants and financial and commercial
groups, which find their cover in the strategy and tactic of the
bourgeoisie to "reform" capitalism. The strategy and tactic of
the peasants and their allies must be to destroy and replace
capitalism.

5. Postscript: Further Evidence

Since this study was undertaken, the Comité Interamericano
de Desarrollo Agrícola (CIDA, Interamerican Committee on
Agricultural Development) has begun to make available new
evidence which supports some of my interpretations, particularly with respect to the key role of capitalist monopolistic commercial determination in Brazilian agriculture. I am grateful
for the use of their still unpublished preliminary findings, in
which CIDA coordinated the intensive field study of eleven
municipios throughout Brazil.

(a) *Monopoly of Landownership.* Several municipios afforded evidence on multiple ownership of properties by single
owners. Thus Della Piazza (1963: 20) reports from Santarém,
Baixo Amazonas, cases of single owners with 78, 76, and 55
properties each. Medina (1963: 87) reports for Sertãozinho,
São Paulo, that of 323 owners, 40 have 2 properties each, 12
have 3 each, 3 have 4 properties, 3 have 5, and 6 owners have
from 6 to 23 properties each. Thus in this municipio, 64 multiple property owners own 214 of the total of 473 properties.
Distribution by size was not indicated. In Jardinópolis, São

Paulo, the same author found 30 owners with 2 properties each, 9 with 3, 2 with 4, also 2 with 5, and again 2 with 6 properties each of a total of 295 owners. Further scattered evidence from other municipios, and the evidence from Geiger which I have already cited for Rio de Janeiro, suggest therefore that the effective concentration of landownership is considerably higher than indicated by the census classification of "establishments."

The CIDA study also supplies indirect evidence on what I have called owners of viable and unviable agricultural properties. There are repeated references to the practice of small owners working on large owners' land—or even renting out their own—so as to obtain a subsistence income for their families. CIDA's analysts tried to estimate the number of hectares necessary to permit full farm employment to a family of 2 to 4 workers. The estimated ranges are: Quixadá (Ceará) 30-50 hectares, Sapé (Paraiba) 5-20, Garanhuns (Pernambuco) 5-20, Camacarí (Bahia) 7-15, Itabuna (Bahia) 10-30, Matozinhos (Minas Gerais) 20-30, Itaguai (Rio de Janeiro) 10-20, Jardinópolis (São Paulo) 20-50, Sertãozinho (São Paulo) 15-40, Santa Cruz (Rio Grande do Sul) 10-30. The 20-hectare dividing line which I used (page 250 above) between the related but not identical concept of farm families with viable or unviable properties as an all-Brazil average, is maybe somewhat high but clearly of the right order of magnitude. Excepting in Santa Catarina and Rio Grande do Sul, the CIDA study estimates that from two thirds to four fifths of the farm families have insufficient land to support 2 agricultural workers (personal communication).

Thus Table 2 and its discussion (page 250 above), even with all the reservations already made in the text, still probably understate the monopoly concentration of land for 1950. The increase in the number of establishments in the smallest and largest size groups, noted in the 1960 census, which was not available at the time of writing, suggests that today's concentration is still greater.

(b) *Fluidity in Owner-Worker Relations.* CIDA's findings

regarding owner-worker relations, their great fluidity, and the great mobility among workers, reflect the fundamentally commercial determination of production and distribution in Brazilian agriculture. Symbolic are the examples given by Julio Barbosa (1963: 14-15)—i.e., a single worker who is simultaneously (i) owner of his own land and house, (ii) sharecropper on another's land (sometimes for a half, sometimes for a third), (iii) tenant on a third's land, (iv) wage worker during harvest time on one of these lands, and (v) independent trader of his own home-produced commodities. Symbolic in turn are the single-owner farms, medium-sized as well as large, that Medina (1963) analyzes in São Paulo, which have simultaneously administrator(s), tenants, sharecroppers, long-term wage workers, transitory wage workers and various further combinations. The combination of functions that a particular worker fulfills often changes from one growing season to another, as does the landowner for whom he performs these functions, and as do the plots of land within one or more properties on which he exercises them. Similarly, an owner modifies the combination of relations he has with his workers and of course changes the particular workers he uses.

There is in most parts of Brazil a great mobility of workers from one farm to another, and more so from one plot of a single farm to another. This mobility is high not only among wage workers whose contracts run for the season, the harvest, or the day, but also among the various types of tenants. Though there are no systematic data available, the distribution of tenancy turnover rates appears to be bipolar: A few tenant families stay on one property for long periods of years or generations; and many tenants stay for periods of one, two, and up to five years. An average turnover rate would thus be worse than meaningless; it would be misleading. Interviews in the various municipios contain repeated references to half of a farm's tenants—not workers—staying an average of 2 to 3 years. Barbosa reports a continuous movement of tenants among properties that is limited only by their access to transportation.

Even ownership of land is not stable. Though surveys of property registers indicate land transfers of only about 1 percent of a municipio's land per year, interview data suggest that between a quarter and a half of the landowners existing at any one time obtained the land through purchase. Both census and interview data indicate that it is mostly the small and medium-sized farms that change ownership, and that large farms increase in size through the acquisition of smaller farms but are rarely broken up or sold themselves.

The picture of rural Brazil, even omitting rural-urban migration, is thus one of continued irregular flux in space and time of wage workers, tenants, owners, traders, and all their possible combinations and relations. This multiplicity and mobility clearly cannot be due to the weight of "feudal" or traditional factors. It must instead be traced to the commercial considerations which determine the relations and behavior of both owners and workers in a highly monopolistic economic, social and political structure. In a sense, owners and workers alike may be regarded as individual entrepreneurs each trying to serve his own short-term advantage. The owners, reflecting both general changes in conditions and their own changing fortunes, shift around their input mix and especially that of labor and its (forms of) payment to respond to fluctuations in the marketability of particular crops, availability of money, credit, water, transport and other factors. Likewise, workers, tenants, and even small owners are forced to take advantage of increased opportunity elsewhere—or more often of decreased opportunity where they are—and to shift around the only resource they have, their labor and their contractual relations, in a continual battle for survival.

That this same competitive, exploitative pressure of the monopolistic structure embraces everyone is brutally indicated by the fact that small and medium-sized owners, and even tenants themselves, exploit other workers when they can, sometimes even more severely than large owners and commercial firms—for their own weak competitive position relative to these larger enterprises forces them thus to exploit their fellows in order to survive themselves. Once unable to do even this, small owners have to sell their land or rent it together with their labor on it to those who have enough capital to exploit it. For workers and tenants the fluidity of the agricultural structure, though a source of insecurity, is also one of "opportunity," if it can be called opportunity or "freedom" that poor and resourceless workers may move on from one monopolist exploiter to the next. And the various "feudal" and "personal" forms of relations and obligation serve at best to personalize and mask this dog-eat-dog capitalist world in which all, big and little alike, must fight for their existence.

(c) *Commercialization and Credit.* The CIDA study, like most others regarding land tenure as the key to the whole structure of Brazilian agriculture, makes no systematic attempt to shed light on its commercial and finance sectors. Nonetheless, its numerous reports of individual instances of finance, credit, storage, transport, wholesaling, retailing, etc., do help to confirm my thesis that ownership, production and labor relations are intimately integrated into, and largely subordinated to and determined by, the monopolistic commercial structure of agriculture and indeed of the whole national and international economy. José Geraldo de Costa (1963: 19), referring to Garanhuns (Pernambuco), reflects this commercial center of gravity in summarizing that "the precarious social and economic situation of the small producers of the area leads to reflection about the changes that the local agrarian structure needs. But not especially or decisively concerning the *ownership* of land." This observation and judgment does not of course imply any defense of the latifundia but rather the need to transform the remaining (commercial monopoly) structure along with that of the concentration of landownership.

Perhaps one of the best insights into the real nature of the agrarian structure and the need for its total transformation is afforded by following the thread of credit as it weaves through the economy. We have already seen that the principal direct beneficiaries of the "public" credit of the Industrial and Agricultural Portfolio of the Banco do Brasil (the central bank) are the super-monopolies which are largely foreign-owned and international, like Anderson & Clayton, SANBRA, the American Coffee Company (owned by A & P), the Big Four meatpackers, etc. This credit is analogous, and often only supplementary, to the outright gifts that the great monopolies, mostly American-owned, receive from the Brazilian government's price support program and from the American government's Alliance for Progress. These monopolies turn around and lend the same money out again, at higher rates of interest of course, and pocket the difference. And that is the least of it. More important is the effective control they thus obtain and maintain over the supply of agricultural products for the foreign and Brazilian national markets alike. The same money, in chains of varying length, is lent out again to big commercial houses or subsidiaries, then by these to wholesalers, and on to retailers, suppliers, large landowners, small owners, down to the lowliest tenant. If the tenant does not already have his production and its sale limited by and to the large landowner—on threat of expulsion from the land—he has to give his crop and his land (if any) as security and consign it to his creditor to get the subsistence and production loan necessary for survival.

All the way up and down the line, the major profit in "agriculture"—often the only real direct profit—lies in this monopolistic control of credit and other sources of financial capital, together with the associated control of the supply of agricultural produce, control in some cases of its export and/or domestic demand as well, and in the speculation which this control permits. Only a manageable but critical share, not all, of the market supply or demand need be controlled by the monopolists at various levels. The vast majority of the suppliers in agriculture—who after all can only *produce*—are left with next to nothing; and the great bulk of potential consumers are similarly placed.

The principal advantage of large landownership, then, is not that it permits the latifundista to produce, which he doesn't, but that his ownership of a necessary resource allows him to interpose himself as merchant and financier between the real producers and the large financial and marketing monopolies— which would just as soon (and often try to) do without him and pocket also his share of their common monopoly position. Latifundia ownership is often little more than an institutional means of guaranteeing to the owner the supply of commodities necessary for his real "economic" activity—speculation. For it is speculation, combined with monopoly-monopsony manipulation of demand and supply and preferably relying on the capital of others, and not production, which is the true source of profit in the unstable monopolistic market structure which characterizes agriculture—and indeed the entire economy of Brazil and of capitalist world imperialism. Speculation, of course, with the fruits of others' labor.

Essentially, this commercial monopoly organization characterizes all sectors of Brazilian agriculture. Moreover each "separate sector" is intimately linked with all the others through ties of family, corporate organization, trade, and above all political power and finance. Capital, influence and power readily cross all boundaries of latifundia, product, sector, industry, region—as easily as they cross international frontiers. There is, in effect, only one integrated capitalist system. In Brazilian agriculture, I repeat, the development/underdevelopment structure of the capitalist economy as a whole now intervenes through the intermediary of the monopolistic commercial, political, and social structure; and it produces there the exploitation and poverty witnessed by all observers.

To eliminate these symptoms from Brazilian agriculture it would be necessary to isolate the latter from—not to integrate it into, as is more usually held—the development/underdevelopment structure and the exploitation and poverty it generates in the Brazilian economy as a whole. Since this is evidently impossible (though it might occur in part through a Korea-Vietnam type division of Brazil which may yet come to pass), it would and ultimately will be necessary to isolate the Brazilian economy itself from these underdevelopment-generating forces by destroying its capitalist structure. Attempting instead to eliminate exploitation, poverty and underdevelopment in agriculture through "land reform" designed to "integrate" agriculture ever more into the otherwise fundamentally unchanged monopoly capitalist economy can at best alter the particular forms which exploitation and underdevelopment on the land will take. Eliminating monopoly in landownership—setting up "family farms," for instance—but retaining it in the remainder of the economy can only strengthen the position of the commercial monopolies by removing one of their rivals. It can only expose the peasants even more directly to this commercial exploitation; and, if it is not a step to complete transformation of the society, it would in a few years only deprive them of their new-won land again through forced sale or renting out of their land and its product, as has already happened in Mexico and elsewhere.

Only by the destruction of the capitalist structure itself and the liberation of Brazil from the world imperialist-capitalist system as a whole—only by the rapid passage to socialism—is it possible to begin to solve the crisis and underdevelopment of Brazilian agriculture, Brazil and Latin America.

V

FOREIGN
INVESTMENT
IN
LATIN AMERICAN
UNDERDEVELOPMENT

The problem of foreign aid and investment in orthodox analyses appears to be a question of whether the developed countries, as a gesture of good will, should give more to the underdeveloped countries or not. For the underdeveloped countries, the problem is regarded as one of deciding on what terms to accept foreign investment and aid. As commonly viewed, therefore, the problem appears relatively new, while its various solutions appear to depend on the voluntary decisions of the donor and recipient powers. Yet, along with exploitation and capital accumulation, conquest and foreign trade, foreign investment and finance have for centuries been and remain today an integral part of world capitalist development; and all of them are objects not of voluntary decisions (least of all gestures of good will), but of the needs and contradictions of capitalism and their historical resolution.

To appreciate and understand the problem of foreign investment or finance and its relation to economic development and underdevelopment in Latin America (and Africa and Asia as well), it is therefore necessary to examine how foreign finance has been related to other aspects of world capitalist development in each of its historical stages. This essay examines the role of foreign investment and finance in colonial, imperialist, and neo-imperialist metropolitan development and in the simultaneous development of Latin American underdevelopment. Better clarified by historical analysis, the problem of foreign finance will be resolved by man's more adequate intervention in the historical process.

B. FROM COLONIALISM TO IMPERIALISM

1. Colonial Primitive Exploitation and Accumulation

The very conquest and colonization of Latin America were

acts of what today we would call foreign finance or aid. Christopher Columbus, the discoverer of America, had declared: "The best thing in the world is gold . . . it can even send souls to heaven. . . ." Cortés, the conquerer of Mexico, added: "The Spaniards are troubled with a disease of the heart for which gold is the specific remedy." The Franciscan Friars confirmed: "Where there is no silver, religion does not enter." That is, the voyages of discovery and Spanish investment in Latin America, much of it with Dutch and Italian merchant capital, were part of the mercantile capitalist expansion and an attempt to tap colonial satellite natural and human resources—mostly precious metals and labor—so as to plow the proceeds into metropolitan development and consumption. The fortunate combination of silver, Indians, and pre-Columbian social organization in the high civilization areas of Mexico and Peru permitted an immediate high return on limited investments in transport of goods and men. Since Europe lacked the capital and labor to produce the primitive capital accumulation and development that eventually occurred there, the initial capital had to come from the work and foreign finance of the Indians of Latin America and the Negroes of Africa, which cost these regions first the decimation of up to eight ninths of the population (in Mexico), then the destruction of several civilizations, and finally resulted in permanent underdevelopment.

The Portuguese in Brazil and later the Dutch, English, and French in the Caribbean did not find a happy combination of silver, labor, and civilization; and therefore they had to create a colonial economy through foreign finance. Indirectly, it was the previous Spanish-American bonanza that made this finance possible, if not necessary, by concentrating income and raising the prices of sugar and other products in Europe. The metropolitan countries erected plantation economies in these tropical lands, putting African Negroes to work producing Latin American sugar for European tables.

If Spain and Portugal did not benefit from this arrangement

as much as might have been hoped, it was in large measure due to their own satellization through foreign finance by Holland and Britain—colonization without the trouble of colonizing, as Portugal's Prime Minister, the Marquis of Pombal, called it in 1755.

A principal result of this combination of foreign finance and the double triangular trade in slaves, sugar, rum, grains, timber, and manufactured goods is analyzed by the Prime Minister of Trinidad and Tobago, Eric Williams, in his *Capitalism and Slavery*:

What the building of ships for the transport of slaves did for eighteenth century Liverpool, the manufacture of cotton goods for the purchase of slaves did for eighteenth century Manchester. The first stimulus to the growth of Cottonopolis came from the African and West Indian markets. The growth of Manchester was intimately associated with the growth of Liverpool, its outlet to the sea and the world market. The capital accumulation in Liverpool from the slave trade poured into the hinterland to fertilize the energies of Manchester; Manchester goods for Africa were taken to the coast in the Liverpool slave vessels. Lancashire's foreign market meant chiefly the West Indian (and then Brazilian) plantations and Africa. . . . It was this tremendous dependence on the triangular trade that made Manchester (Williams 1944: 68).

Indeed, discounting the hard-to-identify minor capital flows, during the preceding three centuries foreign trade and finance had generated a capital flow to the metropolis from Latin America, Africa, and Asia (about half of which came from Latin America) of approximately 1,000 million pounds sterling, or more than the value of all of Europe's entire steam-driven industrial capital stock in 1800 and half again as large as Great Britain's investments in its metallurgical industry up to 1790. Between 1760 and 1780 alone, Britain's income from the West and East Indies more than doubled the investment funds available for its growing industry (Mandel II, 1962: 72-73).

It is clear, then, that from the beginning the real flow of foreign finance has been heavily from Latin America to the metropolis. This means that Latin America has had resources or investment capital of its own but that much of it has been transferred abroad through foreign trade and finance, and invested there instead of in Latin America. This transfer of capital out of Latin America, rather than its supposed nonexistence there, has evidently been the first cause of Latin America's need for more investment capital, such as that invested by foreigners.

But the development of this colonial relationship between the metropolis and Latin America also had domestic structural consequences in Latin America itself, the essentials of which survive to this day. (See analysis by Aldo Ferrer, p. 26 above.)

The second principal cause of inadequate domestic investment and of underdevelopment in general in Latin America was, then, the domestic economic, political, and social structure of underdevelopment, which itself was generated and maintained by foreign trade and finance. Of the remaining potentially investible capital, the structure of underdevelopment directed a large part into mining, agricultural, transport, and commercial enterprises for *export* to the metropolis, much of the rest to luxury *import* from the metropolis, and only very little into manufacturing and consumption related to the *internal market*. Thanks to foreign trade and finance the economic and political interests of the mining, agricultural, and commercial bourgeoisie —or three legs of the economic table, as Claudio Véliz dubbed their nineteenth-century descendants—did not lie with internal economic development. (For more detailed analysis, see pp. 85-98 above.)

Until the advent of imperialism, the only exception to this pattern had been the weakening of the ties of foreign trade and finance during metropolitan wars or depressions, such as during the seventeenth century, and the initial absence of such effective ties between the metropolis and isolated non-export-oriented regions, which permitted a temporary or incipient autonomous capital accumulation and industrial development for the internal market, such as that of eighteenth-century São Paulo in Brazil, Tucumán and others in Argentina, Asunción in Paraguay, Querétaro and Puebla in Mexico, and others (Frank

1966a).

In the colonial era of capitalist development, then, foreign finance was primarily an adjunct to stimulate the pillage of resources, the exploitation of labor, and the colonial trade which initiated the development of the European metropolis and simultaneously the underdevelopment of the Latin American satellites.

2. Industrialization, Free Trade, and Underdevelopment

The economic and political ascendancy of Great Britain and the political independence of Latin America after the Napoleonic Wars left three major interest groups to decide the future of Latin America through their tripartite struggle: (1) The Latin American agricultural, mining, and commercial interests who sought to maintain the underdevelopment-generating, export-economy structure—and only wanted to dislodge their Iberian rivals from their privileged positions in it; (2) the industrial and other interest groups from the aforementioned and other interior regions, who sought to defend their budding but still weak development-generating economies from more free trade and foreign finance, which was threatening to force them out of existence; and (3) the victorious and industrializing British whose Foreign Secretary Lord Canning noted in 1824: "Spanish America is free; and if we do not mismanage our affairs sadly, she is English." The battle lines were drawn, with the traditional Latin American import-export and the metropolitan industrial-merchant bourgeoisies in natural alliance against the weak Latin American provincial and industrial nationalists. The outcome was practically predetermined by the past historical process of capitalist development, which had stacked the cards this way.

In 1824, in accord with Canning's guideline remarks, Britain began—mostly through Baring Brothers—to make massive loans to various Latin American governments who had begun life with debts incurred for the expenses of the wars of independence and even debts inherited from their colonial predecessors. The loans, of course, were granted to pave the way for trade with

Britain, and in some cases they were accompanied by investments in mining and other activities. But the time was not yet ripe.

Reviewing this episode, Rosa Luxemburg asks with Tugan-Baranowski, whom she quotes: "But from where did the South American countries take the means to buy twice as many commodities in 1825 as in 1821? The British themselves supplied these means. The loans floated on the London stock exchange served as payment for imported goods." And she comments, quoting Sismondi:

> As long as this singular commerce lasted, in which the English only asked the (Latin) Americans to be kind enough to buy English merchandise with English capital, and to consume them for their sake, the prosperity of English manufacture appeared dazzling. It was not more income but rather English capital which was used to push on consumption: the English themselves bought and paid for their own goods which they sent to (Latin) America, and thereby merely forwent the pleasure of using these goods (Luxemburg 1964: 422-424).

Under these conditions, foreign trade and finance were certainly not sufficiently profitable to the metropolis; and British foreign loans to Latin America did indeed dry up around 1830 and did not reappear for a quarter of a century. For foreign *trade* alone has never been the metropolis' principal interest, and least of all trade with countries, such as many Latin American ones of the time, whose primary-goods export capacity had been seriously damaged by wartime deterioration of mines and stimulation of subsistence farming and in which nationalist and industrial interests had begun to impose tariff protection and behind it (as in Mexico) to set up fully as modern textile factories as existed in contemporary England. (And for foreign investment alone, as we know it today, metropolitan capitalism had not yet developed enough.) This situation in Latin America had to be remedied before foreign trade and finance could play a major role in continued capitalist development. In the succeeding two decades, trade and finance did themselves contribute to the necessary changes in Latin America, but only in combination with metropolitan diplomacy, naval blockades, as well as foreign and civil wars.

During the period of the mid-twenties to the mid-forties or fifties, the nationalist interests from the interior were still able to force their governments to impose protective tariffs in many countries. Industry, national-flag shipping, and other development-generating activities showed spurts of life. At the same time, Latin Americans themselves rehabilitated old mines and opened new ones, and began to develop their agricultural and other primary-goods export sectors. To permit and promote internal economic development as well as to respond to increasing external demand for raw materials, the liberals pressed for land and other reforms as well as immigration that would increase the domestic labor force and expand the internal market.

The export-import, metropolitan-oriented Latin American bourgeoisies and their national mining and agricultural allies opposed this autonomous capitalist development because, with tariff protection, it took place at the cost of their export-import interests; and they fought and defeated the provincial and industrial nationalists, who claimed the protection of federal states' rights in the federalist-unitarist civil wars of the thirties and forties. The metropolitan powers aided their Latin American junior trade partners with arms, naval blockades, and where necessary direct military intervention and instigation of new wars, such as that of the Triple Alliance against Paraguay, which lost six out of seven members of its male population in the defense of its nationally financed railroad and genuinely independent, autonomously generated development effort.

Trade and the sword were readying Latin America for metropolitan free trade by eliminating the competition of Latin American industrial development; and, with the victory of the outward-oriented economic interest groups over the inward-oriented ones, ever more of the Latin American economy and state as well had to be subordinated to the metropolis. Only then would trade become free and would foreign finance again come into its own. A contemporary Argentinian nationalist noted, "After 1810 . . . the country's balance of trade had been consistently unfavorable, and at the same time native merchants had suffered irreparable losses. Both wholesale export trade and retail import commerce had passed into foreign hands. The conclusion seems inescapable, therefore, that the opening of the country to foreigners proved harmful on balance. Foreigners displaced natives not only in commerce but in industry and agriculture as well" '(quoted in Burgin 1946: 234). Another added:

It is not possible that Buenos Aires should have sacrificed blood and wealth solely for the purpose of becoming a consumer of the products and manufacture of foreign countries, for such is degrading and does not correspond to the great potentialities which nature has bestowed upon the country. . . . It is erroneous to assume that protection breeds monopoly. The fact is that Argentina which has been under a regime of free trade for over twenty years is now controlled by a handful of foreigners. If protection was going to dislodge foreign merchants from their positions of economic preeminence, the country would have occasion to congratulate itself on making the first step toward regaining its economic independence. . . . The nation cannot continue without restricting foreign trade, since restriction alone would make industrial expansion possible; it must no longer endure the weight of foreign monopoly which strangles every attempt at industrialization (quoted in Burgin 1946: 234).

But the country continued to endure that weight. As Burgin correctly analyzes in his study of Argentine federalism:

The economic development of post-revolutionary Argentina was characterized by a shift of the economic center of gravity from the interior towards the seacoast, brought about by the rapid expansion of the latter and the simultaneous retrogression of the former. The uneven character of economic development resulted in what was to some extent a self-perpetuating inequality. The country became divided into poor and rich provinces. The Interior provinces were forced to relinquish ever larger portions of the national income to Buenos Aires and other provinces of the East (Burgin 1946: 81).

In Brazil, Chile, Mexico, throughout Latin America, industrialists, patriots, and farsighted economists similarly denounced this same inevitable process of capitalist development. But in vain. World capitalist development and the sword had made free trade the order of the day. And with it came foreign finance.

Free trade, as the German nationalist Freidrich List aptly noted, became Great Britain's principal export good. It was not for nothing that Manchester Liberalism was born in Cottonopolis. But it was embraced with enthusiasm, as Claudio Véliz has pointed out, by the three legs of the Latin American economic and political table, which had survived since colonial times, had defeated their domestic rivals oriented to national development, captured the Latin American state, and were now naturally allied and subservient to the foreign metropolitan interests; they wanted free foreign trade to secure their and the foreigners' closed national monopoly.

Free trade between the strong metropolis and the weak Latin American countries immediately produced a balance of payments deficit for the latter. To finance the deficit, of course, the metropolis offered and the satellite governments accepted, foreign finance; and in the 1850's foreign loans again began to make their presence felt in Latin America. They did not eliminate the deficits, of course; they only financed and necessarily increased the payments deficits and underdevelopment in Latin America. It was not uncommon to devote 50 percent of export earnings to financing this foreign debt and the continued economic development of the metropolis. In Latin America, in the meantime, the foreign deficit and financing resulted in continual automatic gold standard, or forced paper-standard currency devaluation and domestic inflation. This resulted in an increased capital flow from Latin America to the metropolis, since the former thus had to pay more for the latter's manufactures and the latter less for the former's raw materials. In Latin America, devaluation and inflation further benefited the native and foreign merchants and property owners while expropriating those whose labor produced this wealth and robbing them not only of their real income but also of their small landed and other property.

More than opening Latin America to trade, the development of industrial capitalism and free trade involved the adaptation of the whole economic, political, and social structure of Latin America to the new metropolitan needs. Compensatory foreign finance was of necessity one of the metropolitan instruments for generating this development of Latin American underdevelopment.

3. Imperialist Expansion and Latin American Underdevelopment

The previous period paved the way for the emergence of imperialism and its new forms of foreign finance both in the metropolis and in Latin America, where free trade and liberal land and other reforms had concentrated land into fewer hands, thus creating a larger agricultural and unemployed labor force, and had brought forth governments dependent on the metropolis, who now opened the door not only to more metropolitan trade but to the new imperialist investment finance, which was quick to take advantage of these developments.

The new metropolitan demand for raw materials and Latin American profitability of production and export attracted both private and public Latin American capital into expanding the infrastructure necessary for raw-material export production. In Brazil, Argentina, Paraguay, Chile, Guatemala, and Mexico— probably in other countries as well—domestic or national capital built the first railroad. In Chile, it opened up the nitrate and copper mines that were to become the world's principal supplier of commercial fertilizer and red metal; in Brazil it established the coffee plantations that supplied nearly all the world's tables, and it operated similarly elsewhere. Only after this proved to be a booming business—as has happened time and again in Latin American history since—and after Britain had to find outlets for its steel, did foreign capital enter into these sectors and take over as well the ownership and management of these initially Latin American enterprises by buying out, often with

Latin American capital, the concessions of these nationals. An Argentinian, for instance, asks:

> How was development financed? . . . It was done among our-selves with national resources and not with foreign capital. . . . Between 1852 and 1890 Argentina got the majority of the elements of modern progress by itself: the rest of the railways that would make up the national network (the north-eastern of Entre Rios, the north-central from Córdoba to Tucumán, the Andean, etc.), gas lighting, the horsedrawn streetcars in the capital and the interior, the port of Buenos Aires. . . . A movement to transfer national firms to foreign companies began in 1877. The first and typical case, or the model for later transactions, was the sale of the "Compania de Consumidores de Gas de Buenos Aires" . . . [which was] sold to "the Buenos Aires Gas Company Limited," along with the contract that the former had with the municipality of the Argentinian capital, without the expenditure of one cent. Payment was made this way: the English company ordered the printing of stock certificates in English, equal to the capital of the Compania de Consumidores, plus a block of certificates for five million pounds, for business expenditures (because it was lacking even that); and these were issued when the company took possession of the factory that it bought so comfortably. . . . The only British capital invested in "The Buenos Aires Gas Company Limited" was the paper and print-ing of the stock certificates. . . . Between the last quarter of the nineteenth century and the first of the twentieth, Argentina trans-ferred in a similar way the Western Railway, that of Entre Rios, and the Andean one to British firms that in most cases did not invest more money than they needed "for promotion" of the deal. (Irazusta 1963: 71-73. For a similar but later foreign "investment" in Brazil see Frank 1964b.)

In Chile, the originally pennyless British worker and now legendary John T. North made himself the world "Nitrate King" by buying nitrate mines and railroad bonds at a rate depressed by the War of the Pacific to 10 percent of their face value; he paid with $6 million loaned to him by the Chilean Bank of Valparaiso. His real investment came later, after he had already made millions: he invested a hundred thousand in the civil war overthrow of President Balmaceda with H.M. Royal Navy assistance. Balmaceda's principal election promise had been to nationalize the nitrate mines and to use their profits for industrial and agricultural development of Chile instead of Great Britain. (See pp. 73-85.) Calculations of the "profitability of imperialism," such as that of J. Fred Rippy in his *British Investments in Latin America 1822-1949*, have since then counted the book value as the "investment" and the registered earnings as "profits" while probably earmarking the political payments and payoffs as necessary production "expense." In the same way Strachey and others have tried to show that imperialism did not or does not really pay.

Nonetheless, metropolitan loan capital did flow into Latin America. But the terms imposed on Latin America by most of the railroad and utility bonds purchased in London, Paris, Berlin, and New York were such that once repayment was begun, the capital was rapidly repaid several times over. Notoriously, however, many of these bonds were defaulted on; or payment was delayed and partial. Why, then, was this foreign finance offered and who paid for it? Fred J. Rippy supplies part of the answer:

After all the commissions, fees, discounts, and printing costs had been deducted and service funds for the first eighteen months withheld, the Latin Americans found themselves close to the short end of the deal, with cash in hand equivalent to about 60 percent of the contracted debt. For a net of some £ 12 million, they had obligated themselves to the extent of more than £ 21 million. . . . Four groups are most likely to benefit from such investments: (1) bond-selling bankers and speculators; (2) shipping companies; (3) officials and agents of the recipient countries; (4) manufacturers, managers, and other technicians from investing countries . . . by and large probably benefit most of all. . . . English bankers, brokers, and exporters and grafting Latin American bureaucrats had profited at the expense of British investors (Rippy 1959: 11, 22, 173, 32).

Latin American governments also transferred national enterprises and capital into foreign hands—for a payoff to themselves. If the existing government was unwilling or politically unable to do so, a military coup with metropolitan assistance soon installed a military government, which needed only three or four years of existence to grant, in the name of foreign finance, enough 99-year concessions to foreign monopolies so that they might operate under democratic regimes as well—a tradition which the military dictatorships of our times have modernized under the guidance of Uncle Sam. Everywhere, the "state [was] reduced to its real role, that of a political machinery for exploiting peasant economy for capitalist purposes—the real function, this, of all Oriental [and Latin American] states in the period of capitalist imperialism" (Luxemburg 1964: 445).

In a word, this foreign finance was and largely still is an instrument which permits the metropolitan and satellite bourgeoisie to develop and prosper by combining the savings or, as at present, the taxes of the people in the metropolis with the work of the people in the satellites. This accounts for the profuse bourgeois propaganda in support of this foreign finance.

The timing of foreign finance was—and is—another piece in the jigsaw puzzle of capitalist development as a whole. Rippy (1959: 11) points out that "the capital flow was very irregular. The major part of this British capital moved to Latin America in the 1880's and during the decade following 1902." That is, it did not do so in the depression decade of the nineties, particularly after the world crisis of 1893. Thus, as in the free trade period before, and afterwards in the twentieth century, the flow of foreign finance from the metropolis to Latin America quite logically increased during profitable economic upswings and decreased during downswings, a fact quite contrary to the theory of international trade and finance which would have finance be equilibrating by flowing out of the metropolis when profits are low. Imperialist foreign finance was and is disequilibrating instead and thus contributes to the disequilibrium of the whole capitalist system. Indeed, orthodox theory also maintains that the automatic function of the market makes foreign finance flow equilibratingly from the country with a balance-of-payments surplus to the deficit country—and from the rich to the poor. The fact is that they do the reverse and thus serve to increase the deficit and poverty of the Latin

American satellites while augmenting the surplus and wealth of the European and North American metropolis.

The significance and "profitability" of imperialist foreign finance lies not in the net earnings of foreign investment, however calculated, but in their place in capitalist development and underdevelopment. Imperialist finance directed a large net flow of capital from the poor underdeveloped Latin American countries to the rich developed ones of the metropolis even at the height of Lenin's "capital export" imperialism; Cairncross (1953: 180) estimates Britain's export of capital at £ 2,400 million and the income from its investments at £ 4,100 million between 1870 and 1913. Latin America supplied the metropolis with needed industrial raw materials and cheap food for their workers at terms of trade ever more favorable to the metropolis —which helped to stem the rise of metropolitan wages, and to provide foreign markets for capital equipment and consumer goods—thus helping to maintain high monopoly prices and profits in the metropolis while exerting further downward pressure on real wages.

In Latin America, this same imperialist trade and finance did more than increase the amount of production, trade, and profit by accumulating about U.S. $10,000 million of investment capital there. The imperialist metropolis used its foreign trade and finance to penetrate the Latin American economy far more completely and to use the latter's productive potential far more efficiently and exhaustively for metropolitan development than the colonial metropolis had ever been able to do. As Rosa Luxemburg noted of a similar process elsewhere, "stripped of all obscuring connecting links, these relations consist in the simple fact that European capital has largely swallowed up the Egyptian peasant economy. Enormous tracts of land, labour, and labour products without number, accruing to the state as taxes, have ultimately been converted into European capital and have been accumulated" (Luxemburg 1964: 438).

Indeed, in Latin America imperialism went further. It not only availed itself of the state to invade agriculture; it took over nearly all economic and political institutions to incorporate the entire economy into the imperialist system. The latifundia grew at a pace and to proportions unknown in all previous history, especially in Argentina, Uruguay, Brazil, Cuba, Mexico, and Central America. With the aid of the Latin American governments, foreigners came to own—usually for next to nothing—immense tracts of land. And where they did not get the land, they got its products anyway; because the metropolis also took over and monopolized the merchandising of agricultural and most other products. The metropolis took over Latin American mines and expanded their output, sometimes exhausting irreplaceable resources, such as the Chilean nitrates, in a few years. To get these raw materials out of Latin America and to get its equipment and goods in, the metropolis stimulated the construction of ports and railroads and, to service all this, public utilities. The railroad network and electric grid, far from being grid-like, was ray-like and connected the hinterland of each country and sometimes of several countries with the port of entry and exit, which was in turn connected to the metropolis. Today, four score years later, much of this export-import pattern still remains, in part because the railroad right-of-way is still laid out that way and, more important, because the metropolitan-oriented urban, economic, and political development which nineteenth-century imperialism generated in Latin America gave rise to vested interests who, with metropolitan support, managed to maintain and expand this development of Latin American underdevelopment during the twentieth century.

Implanted in the colonial epoch and deepened in the free trade era, the structure of underdevelopment was consolidated in Latin America by nineteenth-century imperialist trade and finance. Latin America was converted into a primary monoproduct export economy, with its latifundium and expropriated rural proletariat or even lumpen-proletariat exploited by a satellized bourgeoisie acting through the corrupt state of a non-country: "Barbarous Mexico" (Turner), the "Banana Republics" of Central America (which are not company stores but "company countries"), "The Inexorable Evolution of the Latifundium: Overproduction, Economic Dependence, and

Growing Poverty in Cuba" (Guerra y Sánchez), "British Argentina," and "Pathological Chile." (On Chilean economic inferiority see p. 84, where work written by historian Francisco Encino in 1912 is quoted.)

With the development of nineteenth-century imperialism, foreign finance came to play an almost equal part with foreign trade in harnessing Latin America to capitalist development and in transforming its economy, society, and polity until the structure of Latin America underdevelopment was firmly consolidated.

C. NEO-IMPERIALISM AND BEYOND

With World War I the world capitalist system began a new stage of its development. This was not so much the shift of the metropolitan center from Europe to the United States, as the associated transformation of what had been industrial and then financial capitalism into monopoly capitalism. Beginning typically in the United States but then arising also in Europe and Japan, the simple industrial firm or financial house of old was replaced by the nationally-based but world-embracing and really international giant monopoly corporation, which is a multi-industry, mass assembly-line producer of standardized products—and now of new technology as well—and is its own worldwide purchasing agent, salesman, financier, and often de facto government in many satellite countries and increasingly in many metropolitan ones as well. The corporate state was its logical extension in the thirties as the warfare state is in the sixties. Responding to the new needs of the metropolitan monopoly corporation and state, twentieth-century neo-imperialist development has brought forth new instruments of foreign investment and finance; and it has made these, more than foreign trade itself, into the principal international relationship by which monopoly capitalist development is furthered in the metropolis at the cost of the development of still deeper underdevelopment in Latin America.

1. Metropolitan Crisis and Latin American Development

In Latin America, World War I had given the satellite economies a respite from foreign trade and finance as well as other ties with the metropolis. Accordingly, as had happened before and would again, Latin Americans temporarily generated their own industrial development, mostly for the internal consumer goods market. No sooner did the war end, than did metropolitan industry, now increasingly based in the United States, expand into precisely those regions and sectors, especially consumer goods manufactured in Buenos Aires and São Paulo, which Latin Americans had just opened up industrially for themselves and shown to be profitable. Here, then, supported by their financial, technological, and political power, the giant American and British corporations displaced and even replaced —that is depatriated—Latin American industry. The balance-of-payments crises which naturally followed were met by foreign loans to cover the Latin American deficits and to extract governmental concessions for increased metropolitan penetration of the Latin American economies. The 1929 Crash sharply reduced foreign finance, along with foreign trade and prices, and hence slowed the transfer of satellite investible resources to the metropolis. The Depression of 1930 weakened economic ties with Latin America and reduced metropolitan political interference in the continent. This situation was maintained until the early 1950's by the recession of 1937, World War II, and the following reconstruction period. It created economic conditions and permitted political changes in Latin America which resulted in the beginning of its strongest nationalist policy and biggest independent industrialization drive since the post-independence 1830's and 1840's, and possibly ever. In Brazil, the Revolution of 1930 gave the industrial interests a share of state power, brought the increasingly nationalist Getulio Vargas into the Presidency, and permitted the industrialization of São Paulo. In Mexico, World War I had permitted the survival and continuation of the anti-imperialist Mexican Revolution of 1910; the Depression occasioned and permitted the Revolution's consolidation under the presidency of the nationalist General Cárdenas, who expropriated all foreign oil and distributed much domestic land and paved the way for the industrialization of the 1940's. Throughout Latin America, the crisis in the metropolis was the time of the then progressive nationalist movements of Haya de la Torre in Peru, Aguirre Cerda in Chile, Rómulo Gallegos and Rómulo Betancourt in Venezuela, and Perón in Argentina. Now, industrialization was not limited to producing consumer goods for the high income market, as the metropolis had done in Latin America; but it included the building—through public and private *domestic,* not foreign, finance—of capital-goods-producing heavy industry, such as steel, chemicals, electric power and machinery.

2. Metropolitan Expansion and Latin American Underdevelopment

With the end of the Korean War, this Latin American honeymoon was brought to a close. Neo-imperialist metropolitan expansion—now primarily through the foreign trade and finance of the international monopoly corporation—again went into full swing, fully reincorporated Latin America into the process of world capitalist development, and renewed the process of Latin American underdevelopment. The traditional metropolitan-satellite trade relations of exchanging manufactured goods for raw materials at terms of trade that are increasingly unfavorable to Latin America, the satellite balance-of-payments deficits and crises, and the associated metropolitan compensatory and permanent emergency loans regained their old importance. But now these were joined and aggravated, and Latin America's structural underdevelopment deepened, by the neo-imperialist drive of the metropolitan giant monopoly's investment finance to penetrate and take over Latin American manufacturing and service industries and to incorporate these as well into the monopoly's private empire. Meanwhile, the majority of Latin America's people grew absolutely poorer and poorer.

The first essentials of metropolitan monopoly corporate investment finance were already analyzed with insight and, as it turns out, with foresight at the end of the 1920's by J. F. Normano in his *The Struggle for South America.* (See pp. 172-173 above for excepts from Normano's analysis.)

By 1950, 300 American corporations accounted for more than 90 percent of American direct investment holdings in Latin America and since then "the degree of concentration has been consolidated still more" (United Nations 1964b: 233).

In the 1950's the international monopoly corporation went beyond this simple installation of foreign industry inside Latin American protective tariff walls, which guarantee high prices and profits. First, the foreign assembly plant and merchandising organization set up a sort of a putting-out system, in which Latin American medium and small manufacturers produce parts for local assembly by the metropolitan monopoly, who prescribes their industrial processes, determines their output, is their only buyer of the same, reduces its own capital expenditure by relying on the investment and credit of its Latin American contractors and sub-contractors, and shifts the costs and losses of cyclical and increasingly secular excess capacity on these Latin American manufacturers, while keeping the lion's share of the profit from this arrangement to itself for re-investment and expansion in Latin America or for remission to the metropolis and other parts of its world-wide operation.

In recent years, the metropolitan monoplies have carried this process of metropolitan-satellite integration a step further by associating themselves with Latin American industrial and/or financial groups or even public institutions in so-called mixed enterprises. In Latin America, this process is often defended as protective of the national interest and even stimulated as conducive to economic progress by those who benefit from it—i.e., Latin American "great bourgeois" partners or their representatives. These people are proponents of Mexican or Brazilian participation in the financing and control of these enterprises or the "Chileanization" (instead of nationalization) of copper through 25, 49, or 51 percent Chilean government shares in American copper mines.* In the United States, this process has just been consecrated in a "Letter to the American People" by the Republican Coordinating Committee headed by an ex-Ambassador to Mexico, in which this kind of "association" is recommended as the best Alliance for Progress of "truly equal opportunities," along with the military dictatorship that "can provide the necessary stability to keep the Communists from taking over in periods of political and economic transition."

In this new association with Latin American capital and government, the metropolitan monopoly gladly takes a junior partnership initially, for that requires less capital of its own. Indeed, frequently the foreign corporation arrives with little or no capital of its own and raises its share locally by banking on its international reputation and credit-worthiness. Thus, according to the United States Department of Commerce, of the total capital obtained and employed from all sources by United States operations in Brazil in 1957, 26 percent came from the United States and the remainder was raised in Brazil, including 36 percent from Brazilian sources outside the American firms (McMillan 1964: 205). That same year, of the capital in American direct investment in Canada, 26 percent came from the United States while the remainder was raised in Canada. (See Safarian 1966: 235, 241 for all data on Canada.) By 1964, however, the part of American investment in Canada that entered from the United States had declined to 5 percent, making the average American contribution to the total capital used by

---

*The American *Time-Life* affiliated Spanish language magazine, *Visión* (1965:89) observes: "In general, the large firms are more inclined to welcome foreign capital than are the small ones. Some associations of small manufacturers, especially in Mexico and Brazil, never tire of speaking out against the installation of competing firms with foreign capital. That is not the attitude of the bigger industrialists. They think that the firms with foreign capital raise employment, thus increasing the internal market for all kinds of goods and at the same time helping to dampen social pressures. At the same time, they recognize that the foreign firms bring with them new techniques. . . ."

American firms in Canada during the period 1957-1964 only 15 percent. All the remainder of the "foreign investment" was raised in Canada through retained earnings (42 percent), depreciation charges (31 percent), and funds raised by American firms on the Canadian capital market (12 percent). According to a survey of American direct investment firms operating in Canada in the period 1950-1959, 79 percent of the firms raised over 25 percent of the capital for their Canadian operations in Canada, 65 percent of the firms raised over 50 percent in Canada, and 47 percent of the American firms with investments in Canada raised all of the capital for their Canadian operations in Canada and none in the United States. There is reason to believe that this American reliance on foreign capital to finance American "foreign investment" is still greater in the poor underdeveloped countries, which are weaker and more defenseless than Canada. This, then, is the source of the flow of capital on investment account from the poor underdeveloped countries to the rich developed ones.

The metropolitan corporation's main contribution to the joint enterprises, then, is a technological package of patents, designs, industrial processes, high-salaried technicians and, last but not least, trademarks and salesmanship; most of the finance capital is Latin American as are the tax, exclusive license, and other concessions, and—perhaps most important—tariff protection. The international monopoly corporation then proceeds to take full advantage of its technological monopoly, its financial reserve, and its direct or indirect political power, to draw increasingly more profits than its Latin American partners out of their common enterprise, to reinvest these and to gain increasing control over the enterprise, sector, economy, and country of Latin America in which it operates. In the process its Latin American business partners are politically emasculated and then used to sway the Latin American governments to create a still better investment climate for "foreign" capital.

This association of the metropolitan monopoly with Latin American business and government—or more accurately this

absorption of the latter by the former—is by no means limited
to manufacturing industry. It of course includes banking and
finance (such as insurance), and extends to international and
domestic wholesale and retail trade, which become increasingly
monopolized; to agricultural production, including the financing
of inputs and the processing of output, for the world and domestic market; and to all kinds of services ranging from movies,
piped-in-music, and towel service to press, radio, television and,
last but not least, advertising (as any viewer may observe to
his pleasure or displeasure, since 95 percent of all goods adver-
tized on Mexican and other Latin American television screens
are American trademarks sold through Western, F.B.I., and
counter-spy programs of no uncertain ideological content).

The vertical and horizontal integration of a corporation which
operates in or even controls several of these sectors of the Latin
American market, not to mention the world market, of course
permits higher profits in each of the corporation's lines taken
individually and from its operations taken as a whole. Much the
same thing is true for American firms operating in Latin America
as a whole, since American banks lend Latin American deposits
to American corporations, which buy from and sell to each other
and place their ads through American advertising agencies,
who use their power over the Latin American mass media—
which far exceeds their power at home—to pressure for the
adoption of economic and political policies in favor of metropolitan and against Latin American popular interests. Integrated
monopoly capitalist finance in Latin America thus generates
external economies in several senses: external to any one economic sector, external to any one metropolitan monopoly, and
external to any Latin American economy which thereby loses
still more capital to the metropolis.

Today, capitalist development is taking a still further step.
Having already gone from export finance to investment finance to
a monopoly finance that absorbs Latin American national economies into the corporate empire, capitalist development is now
preparing to absorb the Latin American continent as a whole

into the metropolitan monopoly corporation. The United States has recently begun to sponsor and finance Latin American Economic Integration, and is trying to achieve acceptance of an Inter-American Common Market, which would include the United States and Canada. Yet even without the latter, the bulk of intra-Latin American trade in manufactures under the Montevideo Treaty is by United States corporations, such as Kaiser and General Electric, which can thus manufacture in one Latin American country for export to another. Beyond these multilateral foreign trade and finance arrangements, the American metropolis is also entering into bilateral ones, which are a kind of sub-imperialism. The United States seems to have selected Brazil in South America (since the 1964 military coup), and to a lesser extent Mexico in Central America, as economic and political fifth columns or beachheads in Latin America from which American monopoly capital and its government capture the markets and governments of the lesser countries, after American technology, foreign finance, and political influence have created the necessary expansionist conditions there. This integrationist or sub-imperialist development of course augments the economic and political disequilibrium both within these Latin American countries and among them, just as does world monopoly capitalist expansion as a whole (Marini 1964).

The principal impulse of these neo-imperialist forms of uneven world capitalist development and uneven Latin American underdevelopment are the increasing expansion and monopolization of the American-based international corporation and its new technological revolution. The consequences of this capitalist development in Latin America go far beyond benevolent foreign investment finance and the beneficent introduction of advanced foreign technology.

The metropolitan technological revolution of automation, cybernation, and monopoly unification of entire industrial processes with its consequent rapid obsolescence of machinery, underutilization of capacity, and excess of industrial equipment leads to the transfer of recently obsolete or unemployed equipment from the metropolis to Latin America—often without changing ownership (though written off for tax purposes at the home office and charged to the Latin American subsidiary at exorbitant bookkeeping prices, which increase its supposed costs, reduce its apparent profits, and help draw foreign exchange out of the recipient country).

In Latin America, the international monopoly corporation uses this technology to compete with and eliminate or absorb local rivals, who lack the funds or suppliers to buy, or cannot get import licenses for similar equipment. This is called raising the technological level of the Latin American economy and eliminating inefficiency. Everywhere—in the capitalist world, that is—American technology is becoming the new source of monopoly power and the new basis of economic colonialism and political neo-colonialism. Thus the American business magazine, U.S. *News and World Report* (July 18, 1966: 69) reports:

> The fear is suddenly very real that Europe—falling further and further behind the U.S. in technology— is going to wind up within a decade as an "underdeveloped area." . . . The result, Europeans say, is that the Continent is becoming, technologically, an "American colony." . . . Says a prominent German engineer: "The way things are going, we will be a backward area within 10 years. Then you'll find us knocking at America's door for handouts, just like any other underdeveloped country."

The international corporation which controls this technology thus increases its monopoly power over its Latin American associates in their common mixed firms, over its Latin American rivals in other firms, and over the Latin American economy in general. In the latter, as a result, the capital/labor ratio rises, excess capacity grows, and the general wage level declines. For these reasons and because this foreign investment has a largely foreign multiplier and does not increase domestic purchasing power correspondingly, periodic over-investment crises become more frequent and prolonged, while cyclical and structural unemployment increases in Latin America. When this happens, the weak Latin American firms are swallowed up by their bigger and stronger compatriots, thus increasing the degree of monopoly, and the Latin American firms are bought up at bargain-basement prices by the still bigger and stronger metropolitan monopolies, thus increasing the degree of monopoly and de-Latin-Americanization still further. During 1964, while the per capita national income went down 6 percent in Brazil, its largest steel producer was bought by Bethlehem Steel. (See pp. 181-190 and Frank 1965b.) Thus, the use of existing Latin American capital equipment, the direction of new Latin American investment, and the selection of Latin America's import mix from the metropolis are ever more determined by metropolitan needs and convenience; and they correspond less and less to the development needs of Latin America and to the social needs of its people.

This monopoly-capitalist foreign finance, beyond supplying the profits with which more and more of the Latin American economy is bought up by the metropolitan monopolies, of course generates an ever larger remission of profits by these foreign firms and flow of capital from Latin America to the United States.[*]

The conservative estimates of the United States Department of Commerce show that between 1950 and 1965 the total flow of capital on investment account from the United States to the rest of the world was $23.9 billion, while the corresponding capital inflow from profits was $37.0 billion, for a net inflow

[*]The profit rate of metropolitan monopolies in Latin America is unknown but certainly higher than the 5 percent they often claim. The following facts can afford us an idea: The average return on invested capital in United States manufacturing is over 10 percent. The 200 largest American corporations own 5 percent of corporate assets but earn 68 percent of the profits; they therefore earn more than the average profit rate. The corporations with foreign operations, which are the largest, earn two to four times as much on their capital abroad than they do at home; and they earn a still higher multiple on their Latin American operations than they do on their foreign (including European and Canadian) operations taken as a whole. (For sources see Baran and Sweezy 1966: 87, 194-199; Michaels 1966: 48-49; Mandel II, 1962: 86-87; Gerassi estimates profits for particular firms by recalculating them from their published financial statements.)

into the United States of $13.1 billion. Of these totals, $14.9 billion flowed from the United States to Europe and Canada while $11.4 billion flowed in the opposite direction, for a net outflow from the United States of $3.5 billion. Yet, between the United States and all other countries—that is mainly the poor, undeveloped ones—the situation is reversed: $9.0 billion of investment flowed to these countries while $25.6 billion in profits flowed out of them, for a net inflow from the poor to the rich of $16.6 billion. The corresponding flow between the United States and Latin America was $3.8 billion from the United States to Latin America and $11.3 billion from Latin America to the United States, for a net outflow from Latin America to the United States of $7.5 billion (Magdoff 1966: 39).

Since the international corporations evade taxes and exchange restrictions by regular overpricing the home office sales to their Latin American subsidiaries, and underpricing its purchases from them, part of their profits are hidden under the cost items; and the real remission of profits from investments in, and therewith of capital from, Latin America to the metropolis is higher than that registered by either the metropolitan · or the Latin American governments.

But foreign operations range beyond foreign investments. The foreign corporations' remission of profits on direct investments costs Latin America (except Cuba) about 14 percent of all of its current earnings of foreign exchange from the export of goods and services. But other registered and hidden capital transfers out of Latin America account for another 11 percent of its foreign exchange earnings and the service of its foreign debt an additional 15 percent, which brings Latin America's yearly capital outflow of financial payments to 40 percent of its foreign earnings. Latin America's payments for other foreign services or invisibles, such as transportation (10 percent), travel abroad (6 percent), and other services absorb another 21 percent of its earnings, for a grand total of 61 percent of Latin America's foreign exchange earnings—over $6,000 million a year, or 7 percent of its GNP and nearly half of its gross (or probably more than all its net) investment—paid to foreigners, almost entirely in the metropolis, for these invisible services rendered, which do not include one penny's worth of physical commodities shipped to Latin America. Little wonder that Latin America has a large chronic balance-of-payments deficit and inadequate investment despite the fact that it has a balance of (commodity) trade surplus and adequate resources (Frank 1965a).

Meanwhile, Latin America's terms of trade have declined, partly as a result of the monopoly-capitalist finance reviewed above, since the international monopoly corporation's pricing policy and its determination of Latin America's economic structure negatively affect the latter's terms of trade. Between 1950 and 1962, the prices of Latin America's imports rose 10 percent but the prices of its exports fell 12 percent, so that while its imports rose 42 percent its exports had to rise 53 percent to cover them (United Nations 1964a: 32). In consequence, Latin America lost 25 percent of the purchasing power it derives from its exports, or an equivalent of 3 percent of its GNP (United Nations 1964c: 33). This loss of 3 percent of Latin America's GNP on trade account—added to the 7 percent of GNP it loses on service account, or even only the 5 percent (40 percent of foreign exchange earnings) on account of financial payments to foreigners—is equivalent to 8 percent to 10 percent of its GNP, that is probably double or triple the amount of capital Latin America is now devoting to net investment. By way of comparison, total expenditures for education in Latin America, from kindergarten through university, both public and private, amount to only 2.6 percent of its GNP (Lyons 1964: 63). Adding the percentage of GNP and the multiple of net investment foregone as a result of present unemployment of labor and resources in Latin America—compared to that which would have obtained by the continuation of the industrialization drive of the 1930's, a drive aborted by the entry of metropolitan investment finance capitalism after the Korean War—the loss of Latin America's investible surplus due to neo-imperialism is still greater, perhaps doubling again. And if we could additionally estimate the misemployment of Latin America's labor and the misuse of its capital engendered by neo-imperialist absorption of Latin America's economy and its devotion to world and metropolitan monopoly-capitalist development instead of to Latin American economic development, we would get a more accurate measure of the misallocation of Latin America's resources, of its economic development foregone, and of the structural underdevelopment that neo-imperialist monopoly finance generates in Latin America today.*

*Novik and Farba have estimated the loss of Chile's potential surplus due to the following: To the metropolis on account of copper production and export alone—5 percent of national income; due to unemployment—15 percent; unused industrial capacity—8 percent; agricultural production below immediate potential—3 percent; or about 30 percent of national income sacrificed to these factors in structural underdevelopment. By far the largest loss of economic surplus (which overlaps somewhat with the former and cannot be properly added to these in its entirety) corresponds to the maldistribution of income: the income received in excess of the annual income of middle-income receivers is 3 percent of Chile's national income, and in excess of the level of low-income receivers it is 50 percent. This distribution of income in Chile and Latin America, which is getting increasingly unequal, is both a reflection and a determinant of the high and growing degree of economic and political monopoly, which is supported and generated by the metropolitan presence in Latin America. Like all monopoly, it occasions a vast misallocation of the resources of the whole economy, which is the basis of concentration of income enjoyed by the few. This misallocation of resources extends not only to the kind of goods that are produced—passenger cars instead of trucks, busses, and tractors—but to the way they are produced: three dozen foreign manufacturers now produce or assemble automobiles in Latin America for an annual market of about 500,000 cars, or an average of 12,000 units per year per manufacturer. Twelve firms set up assembly lines in Venezuela for a total national automobile market of 30,000 units for all of them put together. In Europe, the average market per manufacturer is 250,000 and in the United States, of course, about ten times that (Visión 1965: 100). The monopoly capitalism which occasions this kind of resource allocation (12 firms producing 30,000 cars) and income distribution (surplus waste equal to 50 percent of the national income) is certainly in the interest of the metropolitan super-monopolies. But, contrary to what is sometimes claimed, the maintenance and development of this monopoly-capitalist Latin American underdevelopment is evidently also the immediate basis of the economic and political survival of the largest sectors of the Latin American bourgeoisie, which are the first to defend this structure.

This neo-imperialist development of declining terms of trade, chronic deficits and recurrent crises in Latin America's balance of payments, and increased requirements of roads, power, and technically-trained personnel to service the metropolitan establishment in Latin America has led the metropolis to create a whole set of new alphabet soup financial institutions to deal with these situations and to service these needs just as it did in the nineteenth century. Some of these are United Nations organizations, like the World Bank (IBRD) and the International Monetary Fund (IMF). Others are independent, like the General Agreement on Trade and Tariffs (GATT); and several are formally or effectively U.S. dependencies, like the Export-Import Bank (Eximbank), The Bank of Inter-American Development (BID), etc. Though there is specialization of labor among them, they all serve essentially the same functions in Latin America: they support the incorporation through investment finance of the Latin American economy into the structure of metropolitan monopoly capitalism, not by paying for, but by financing the inevitably resulting deficits and the new needs for infrastructure and technical personnel, which is to be supplied, with the support of the Alliance for Progress, by social development of human capital (most metropolitan economic theorizing now marks this as the most important of all development capital); in addition, they often pay for as well as finance the investment costs in Latin America of wholly or partially metropolitan-owned corporations, who receive these loans directly, or indirectly through Latin American governments. Some authoritative observers have characterized some of these institutions. The United Nations Economic Commission for Latin America observes:

> The credit operations of the Eximbank (of the U.S. Government) and the IBRD (or World Bank of the United Nations) continue to be restricted to loans for concrete projects. It is argued that this is due to the desire of both banks to combine their technical knowledge with that of the borrowers in necessary prior research and study . . . as well as to permit a stricter control over the use of the

funds. . . . Also of long standing, is the inclination of both the Eximbank and the IBRD to finance the component of the projects which is imported. . . . In the third place, the Eximbank and the IBRD have for a long time tried to avoid making loans that might compete with private foreign capital. This resulted in a credit pattern concentrated above all in infrastructure rather than industrial uses (United Nations ECLA 1964c: 239-240).

In his *U.S. Private and Government Investment Abroad,* Raymond Mikesell (1962: 477, 482) goes on to note that "The Bank (Eximbank) is fundamentally an instrument of the policy of the United States. . . . Political considerations carry much weight in deciding on the requests for loans or even in encouraging the initial or official inquiries of the foreign borrowers." After quoting Mikesell the United Nations observes that "it is therefore evident that the Eximbank must be considered a basic instrument of the foreign policy of the United States" (United Nations ECLA 1964b: 252). However diplomatically, these qualified observers speak quite clearly of how and why these metropolitan institutions direct and sway Latin American economic and political policy. On threat of withholding this financing and creating unmanageable balance-of-payments and political crises for the Latin American governments, these foreign loan agencies of the metropolis literally blackmail the increasingly dependent Latin American governments into adopting monetary and fiscal policies and investment plans prescribed for them by the metropolis and for the benefit of the metropolis.

This is the principal activity in Latin America of the United Nations International Monetary Fund. For two decades, the IMF has been forcing tight money policies—externally devaluationist, domestically restrictionist and structurally inflationist—on dozens of Latin American governments. While the IMF relies on classical international trade and monetary theory to becloud the issue with theoretic justifications of its policy of blackmail—which it calls exacting responsibility from the Latin American governments—the principal net effects of this IMF policy in Latin America have been (1) recurrent devaluation of its currencies, which turns the terms of trade against Latin America and makes it cheaper for the metropolitan monopolies to buy up the Latin American economy through foreign investment; (2) enforced convertibility of Latin American currencies, which permits the international monopolies to convert their Latin American earnings readily into dollars and gold; (3) enforced capital loans from other metropolitan institutions, so compensatory IMF short-term loans and standby credits (which come with economic and political strings attached) can be obtained; (4) simultaneous structural unemployment and inflation in the Latin American domestic economy which, with devaluation, favor foreign and domestic property owners at the expense of Latin American wage and salary earners whose real income is forced down; and (5) the consequent decline of Latin America's terms of trade and the aggravation of balance of payments deficits, which occasions renewed and increased dependence on the IMF and on other metropolitan loan and investment instruments for more foreign finance, which is accompanied by a further dose of the IMF medicine and basic neo-imperialist policy for Latin America, in an unending vicious spiral.

This spiral is reflected in the fact that the share of its foreign exchange earnings which Latin America must devote to the service of its foreign debt rises more and more—from 5 percent in 1951-56, to 11 percent in 1956-60, to 16 percent in 1961-63. Thanks to the Alliance for Progress, Latin America's debt service is undoubtedly even higher today and will inevitably rise still more in the future. Yet, according to an Associated Press news item of April 5, 1965, "the Eximbank is taking out 100 million dollars more a year than it is lending" to Latin America already.

Where the domestic Latin American economic and political contradictions created by this neo-imperialist development can no longer be immediately resolved within the confines of the bourgeois democratic states (now occupied by their own army and police which—with American technical training, political orientation, military advisors and equipment*—repress labor, student and other demonstrations against the state's economic and political policy), or if the contradictions cannot be resolved without infringing too much on metropolitan interests, the task of resolving them is assigned to a military dictatorship. The task invariably involves lowering the income of the majority and giving still more concessions to metropolitan interests and privileges to their Latin American economic associates and political allies—and the containment of popular resistance by killing, exiling, or imprisoning the people's leaders and terrorizing the people themselves. These Latin American economic and political measures are an integral part of neo-imperialist development and policy; this is attested to by the metropolitan proponents of military aid to Latin America (which was doubled by President Kennedy in the first year of his administration) and by American government officials (such as all of President Johnson's State Department Latin America experts) who say that not all military coups are equal: some are more equal than others.

Neo-imperialist monopoly capitalism has rapidly and effectively penetrated and incorporated the Latin American economy, polity, society, and culture. Like colonial and imperialist development before it, only more so, this neo-imperialist penetration of Latin America has found old Latin American interest groups and created new ones that are allied and subservient to metropolitan interests and policy. They increasingly monopolize the Latin American economy and share among them the spoils of exploiting the people of Latin America (and to a lesser extent the people of the metropolis). But neo-imperialism has gone further.

---

*It may not be amiss to observe that U.S. equipment for Latin American police and anti-guerrilla forces, who are engaged in repressing popular movements directly, is always the most modern and efficient available. On the other hand, the armed forces are frequently equipped with obsolete and even defective weapons or planes, which the United States is taking out of use, but whose sale to Latin America still helps the U.S. balance of payments, as former Secretary of Defense McNamara is so proud of pointing out. (I owe this observation to Marta Frank.)

The metropolitan economic satellization of Latin American industry is inevitably satellizing the Latin American industrial bourgeoisie as well. The nationalist industrial or industrial nationalist policy of the 1930's and 1940's is no more; more and more Latin American industrialists already have become—or in the near future will become—associates, partners, bureaucrats, suppliers, and clients of mixed foreign-Latin American enterprises and groups, which becloud and obscure Latin American national interests and—more important—which increasingly tie the personal economic interests of the individual Latin American bourgeois industrialist tail to the metropolitan neo-imperialist dog. Thus, the so-called (or mis-called) Latin American national bourgeoisie, far from growing stronger and more independent as Latin American industry develops under metropolitan direction, gets weaker and more dependent each year.

Yet monopoly capitalist development does more than tie the Latin American bourgeoisie to the metropolis economically by satellizing its industrial, commercial, and financial establishments. Neo-imperialism, as we saw above, satellizes the Latin American economy as a whole and ingrains structural underdevelopment deeper and deeper into it. Since the metropolis pre-empts an increasing share of the most profitable Latin American business and forces the remainder into growing economic difficulties, the Latin American bourgeoisie that lives off this less profitable business is left no choice but to fight—even if vainly—for its survival by increasing the degree of wage and price exploitation of its petty bourgeoisie, workers, and peasants, in order to squeeze some additional blood out of that stone; and at times, the Latin American bourgeoisie must resort to direct military force to do so. For this reason—no doubt more than for idealistic or even ideological reasons—almost the entire Latin American bourgeoisie is thus thrown into political alliance with —that is into the arms of—the metropolitan bourgeoisie. They have more than a common long-term interest in defending the system of capitalist exploitation; even in the short run, the Latin American bourgeoisie cannot be national or defend nationalist interests by opposing foreign encroachment in alliance with Latin American workers and peasants—as the Popular Front rule book would have them do—because the same neo-imperialist encroachment is forcing the Latin American bourgeoisie to exploit its supposed worker and peasant allies ever more and is thus forcing the bourgeoisie to forego this remaining source of political support. While the Latin American bourgeoisie is pursuing wage, price, and political policies that exploit its workers and repress their legitimate demands for relief from this growing exploitation, the Latin American bourgeoisie cannot rally their support against the metropolitan bourgeoisie; meanwhile, the economic inefficiency of this exploitation interferes with domestic saving for investment and obliges the bourgeoisie to turn abroad for immediate foreign finance.*

Therefore, neo-imperialism and monopoly capitalist development in Latin America are drawing and driving the entire Latin American bourgeois class—including its comprador, bureaucratic, and national segments—into ever closer economic and political alliance with and dependence on the imperialist metropolis. The political task of reversing the development of Latin American underdevelopment therefore falls to the people themselves, and the road of national or state capitalism to economic development is already foreclosed to them by neo-imperialist development today.

*As was noted above, the Brazilian bourgeoisie has been trying to find an additional way out, first through the "independent" foreign policy of Presidents Quadros and Goulart (who sought new markets in Africa, Latin America, and the socialist countries) and, after that proved impossible in an already imperialized world, through the "interdependent" sub-imperialist foreign policy, begun by the present military government as a junior partner to the United States. Brazilian sub-imperialism also requires low wages in Brazil, so that the Brazilian bourgeoisie can enter the Latin American market on a low cost basis, which with obsolete but still modern American equipment is the only basis it has. In the sub-imperialized countries of Latin America, the Brazilian invasion also leads to depressing wages, since doing so is the local bourgeoisie's only possible defensive reaction. Thus, sub-imperialism also aggravates the contradictions between the bourgeoisie and labor in each of these countries. (For further analysis, see Marini 1964.)

D. SUMMARY AND CONCLUSIONS

The essentials of foreign investment and aid in neo-imperialist development, Latin American underdevelopment, and the necessity of their political implications as outlined above, are summarized by the authoritative statements and unmistakable actions of the highest representatives of the North and Latin American bourgeoisies. The United States Commission on Foreign Economic Policy has stated:

[Foreign investment] is a means to provide markets for American industry and agriculture; in the long run it contributes to the general growth of foreign trade and prosperity by influencing the rise in productivity and income abroad: it is a means of first importance to permit the development of the raw materials of other countries, so as to satisfy the growing civilian and military needs of the American economy; and it is a means which should be still more important by which the national income of the United States grows through the widest and most profitable investment opportunities for American capital (quoted in Cámara Textil 1957: 48 and retranslated from the Spanish by the author).

The Mexican economist, Octaviano Campos Salas, summarized the consequences of this foreign investment for the Latin American countries:

(a) Private foreign capital takes over high profit sectors permanently, expelling or not permitting the entry of domestic capital, by relying on the ample financial resources of its home office and on the political power which it sometimes exercises. (b) The permanent takeover of important sectors of economic activity impedes domestic capital formation and creates problems of balance of payments instability. (c) Private direct foreign investment interferes with anticyclical monetary and fiscal policy—it comes when there are expansions and withdraws during depression. (d) The demands by private foreign investors for concessions to form a "favorable climate" for investment in the receiving countries are unlimited and excessive. (e) It is much cheaper and more consistent with the underdeveloped countries' aspirations to economic independence to hire foreign technicians and to pay royalties for the use of patents than to accept the permanent control of their economies by powerful foreign consortia. (f) Foreign private capital does not adapt itself to development planning (quoted in Cámara Textil 1957: 48).

Arturo Frondizi was of substantially the same opinion:

It is not amiss to remember that foreign capital usually acts as an agent which perturbs the morality, the politics, and the economy of Argentina. . . . Once established, thanks to excessively liberal concessions, foreign capital obtained bank credits which permitted it to expand its operations and therefore its profits. These profits are immediately sent abroad as if all of the investment capital had been imported by the country. In this way, the domestic economy came to strengthen foreign capitalization and to weaken itself. . . . The natural tendency of foreign capital in our country has been, in the first place, to settle in areas of high profits. . . . When Argentinian effort, intelligence, and perseverance created an independent economic opportunity, foreign capital destroyed it or tried to create difficulties for it. . . . Foreign capital had and has a decisive influence in the social and political life of our country. . . . The press is usually also an active instrument of this process of submission. . . . Foreign capital has had special influence in the political life of our nation, allying itself with the conservative oligarchy . . . those who are tied to foreign capital by economic ties (directors, bureaucratic personnel, lawyers, newspapers that receive advertisements, etc.) and those who, without having economic relations, end up being dominated by the political and ideological climate created by foreign capital (Frondizi 1958: 55-76).

The full significance of these analyses of the reality of imperialist and neo-imperialist investment and its consequences for Latin America become entirely clear only if we take into account some further observations of Frondizi and note his and Campos Salas' later position and conduct with respect to imperialist investment. Frondizi went on to warn his countrymen in his above quoted electoral campaign book, *Politics and Petroleum:*

In matters of economic policy, good intentions—a subjective matter—are of no interest; what counts is the concrete results of the policy pursued—its objective aspect. . . . Foreign capital maintains a special state of conscience, which predisposes to hand-over or submission. This state of conscience invades all the corners of the country, all the social sectors that act economically and politically; it reflects itself in all aspects of national life, as if it were historical fatalism in the face of which there is no alternative but to bow down. National possibilities are renounced. What is more terrible in this process of psychological capture created by imperialism is that persons of good faith, be they intelligent or ignorant, knowingly or not serve imperialism by defending its interests and the need to respect its continued presence. In this way, men and people lose the conscience of their own personality and of the mission they should fulfill as their historical obligation (Frondizi 1958: 123, 76).

The overbearing weight of objective historical reality over subjective good intentions was strikingly confirmed by Frondizi himself when, as the President of Argentina who had been elected on the above platform, he indeed succumbed to this state of economic, political, and psychological capture created by imperialism, renounced Argentina's national possibilities, and went down in history as the man who handed all of his country's petroleum and most of the remainder of its economy over to American monopoly capital. The above-quoted Mexican economist, Octaviano Campos Salas has since become Minister of the Treasury in the present government of Mexico and now grants American monopoly capital the concessions which he once called "unlimited and excessive" and presides over what he termed the progressive metropolitan "permanent takeover of important sectors of economic activity which impedes domestic capital formation."

Wishful thinking and propaganda aside, in reality the trend in the annual growth and decline of the Gross National Product per capita (and of the national income per capita) in Latin America is as follows (United Nations ECLA 1964b: 6):

	GNP	National Income
1950-55	+2.2%	+1.9%
1955-60	+1.7%	+1.4%
1961-62	+0.8%	0.0%
1962-63	—1.0%	—0.8%

While per capita food production rose 12 percent in the whole world between 1934-1938 and 1963-64, and 45 percent in the Soviet Union and Eastern Europe (which are universally known for their agricultural failure), Latin America's per capita production of food fell 7 percent and its distribution among the people is every day more unequal. The absolute standard of living of the majority of Latin Americans is going down (Frank 1968, calculated from data supplied by the United Nations Food and Agricultural Organization—FAO.) For them, evidently, the only way out of Latin American underdevelopment is armed revolution leading to socialist development.

REFERENCES CITED

Alemparte, Julio
  1924   *La regulación económica en Chile durante la colonia.*
          Santiago, Universidad de Chile

APEC
  1962   *A economia brasileira e suas perspectivas 1962.* Rio de
          Janeiro, a Edições APEC

APEC
  1963   *A economia brasileira e suas perspectivas, maio 1963.*

Arcila Farias, Eduardo
  1957   *El Régimen de la encomienda en Venezuela.* Escuela de
          Estudios Hispano-Americanos, Sevilla

Baer, Werner
  1964   "Regional Inequality and Economic Growth in Brazil."
          Economic Development and Cultural Change (Chicago),
          XII, No. 3, April

Bagú, Sergio
  1949   *Economía de la sociedad colonial: Ensayo de la historia
          comparada de América Latina.* Buenos Aires, El Ateneo

Baran, Paul A.
  1957   *The Political Economy of Growth.* New York, Monthly
          Review Press

Baran, Paul A. and Sweezy, Paul M.
  1966   *Monopoly Capital.* New York, Monthly Review Press

Baraona, Rafael, Ximena Aranda, and others
  1960   *Valle del Putaendo: Estudio de estructura agraria.* San-
          tiago, Instituto de Geografía de la Universidad de Chile

Barbosa, Julio
  1963   "Pesquisa sôbre o sistema de posse e uso da tierra,
          Mocambeiro, M.G." in CIDA 1963 (see below)

Boeke, J. H.
  1953   *Economics and Economic Policy of Dual Societies.* New
          York, Institute of Pacific Relations

Borah, Woodrow
1951 "New Spain's Century of Depression." *Ibero-Americana* (Berkeley), No. 35

Borde, Jean, and Mario Góngora
1956 *Evolución de la propiedad rural en el Valle del Puango.* Santiago, Instituto de Geografía de la Universidad de Chile

Brasil, Jocelín
1963 *O pão, o feijão, e as fôrças ocultas.* Rio de Janeiro, Civilização Brasileira

Burgin, Miron
1946 *The Economic Aspects of Argentine Federalism 1820-1852.* Cambridge, Harvard University Press

Cairncross, A. K.
1953 *Home and Foreign Investment, 1880-1913.* Cambridge

Cámara Textil del Norte
1957 "Las Inversiones Extranjeras y el Desarrollo Económico de México" en *Problemas Agrícolas e Industriales de México.* Mexico, Vol. IX, No. 1-2

Cardoso, Fernando Henrique
1961 "Tensões sociais no campo e reforma agrária." *Revista Brasileira de Estudos Políticos,* No. 12, October

Céspedes del Castillo, Guillermo
1957 "La sociedad colonial americana en los siglos XVI y XVII." In J. Vinceno Vives, ed., *Historia económica y social de España y América, Barcelona,* Editorial Teide, Vol. III

Chevalier, François
1956 "La formación de los grandes latifundios en México." *Problemas Agrícolas y Industriales de México,* January-March, published in English as *The Growth of the Latifundium in Mexico,* Berkeley, University of California Press, 1965.

CIDA
1963 Comité Interamericano de Desarrollo Agrícola. Unpublished studies. On deposit at Centro Latinoamericano de Pesquisas em Ciências Sociais, Rio de Janeiro

Classe Operária
1963   *A Classe Operária*, No. 444

Comercio Exterior
1964   Banco Nacional de Comercio Exterior, México, S.A.

Comercio Exterior
1965   Banco Nacional de Comercio Exterior, México, S.A.

Comissão Nacional de Política Agrária
1955   *Aspectos Rurais Brasileiros*. Rio de Janeiro, Ministério
        da Agricultura

Conjuntura Económica
1962   *Conjuntura Económica*, XVI, No. 4, April

Conjuntura Económica
1964   *Conjuntura Económica*, XVII, No. 2, February

Conjuntura Económica
1965   *Conjuntura Económica*, XVIII, No. 2, February

Conselho Nacional de Economia
1963   *Exposição geral da situação económica do Brasil 1962.*
        Rio de Janeiro, Conselho Nacional de Economia

Correio da Manhã
1963   *Correio da Manhã*, June 6

Correio da Manhã
1965   *Correio da Manhã*, January 31

Costa, José Geraldo da
1963   "Garanhuns." In CIDA 1963 (see above)

Costa Pinto, L. A.
1948   "A estrutura da sociedade rural brasileira." *Sociologia*,
        (São Paulo), X, No. 2

Dávila, Carlos
1950   *Nosotros, los de las Américas*. Santiago, Editorial del
        Pacífico

Della Piazza, Paulo
1963   "Santarem." In CIDA 1963 (see above)

Desenvolvimento & Conjuntura
1957   *Desenvolvimento & Conjuntura*, No. 2, August

Desenvolvimento & Conjuntura
1958   *Desenvolvimento & Conjuntura*, No. 7, July

Desenvolvimento & Conjuntura
1959   *Desenvolvimento & Conjuntura*, No. 4, April

Economic Bulletin for Latin America
1964   "The Growth and Decline of Import Substitution in
        Brazil," United Nations Economic Commission for Latin
        America (New York and Santiago), IX, No. 1, March

Ellis Júnior, Alfredo
1937   *A evolução da economia paulista e suas causas.* São
        Paulo, Companhia Editôra Nacional

Encina, Francisco
1912   *Nuestra Inferioridad Económica: Sus Causas y Conse-
        quencias.* Santiago.

Ferrer, Aldo
1963   *La Economía Argentina.* Mexico, Fondo de Cultura
        Económica (translated as *The Argentinian Economy,*
        Berkeley, University of California Press, 1966)

Fôlha de São Paulo
1963   *Fôlha de São Paulo,* May 26

Ford, A. G.
1962   *The Gold Standard 1180–1914, Britain and Argentina.*
        Oxford, Clarendon Press

Frank, Andrew Gunder
1962   "Mexico: The Janus Faces of Twentieth-Century Bour-
        geois Revolution." *Monthly Review* (New York), Vol. 14,
        No. 7, November (Also in *Whither Latin America?*, New
        York, Monthly Review Press, 1963)

Frank, Andrew Gunder
1963a   "The Varieties of Land Reform." *Monthly Review* (New
        York), Vol. 15, No. 12, April (Also in *Whither Latin
        America?*, New York, Monthly Review Press, 1963)

Frank, Andrew Gunder
1963b   "Brazil: Exploitation or Aid?" *The Nation* (New York),
        Vol. 197, No. 16, November 16 (also in *Peace News,*
        London, Jan. 17, 1964)

Frank, Andrew Gunder
1964a   "Brazil: The Goulart Ouster." *The Nation* (New York), Vol. 198, No. 18, April 27

Frank, Andrew Gunder
1964b   "On the Mechanisms of Imperialism: The Case of Brazil." *Monthly Review* (New York), Vol. 16, No. 5, September

Frank, Andrew Gunder
1965a   "Services Rendered." *Monthly Review* (New York), Vol. 17, No. 2, June (Also "El costo de importaciones en América Latina," *Presente Económico* (Mexico), June 1965 and "¿Servicios Extranjeros o Desarrollo Nacional?" *Comercio Exterior* (México), Vol. XI, No. 2, February 1966

Frank, Andrew Gunder
1965b   "Brazil: One Year from Gorillas to Guerrillas." *The Minority of One* (Passaic, N.J.), VII, No. 7 (68), July

Frank, Andre
1965c   "¿Con que modo de producción convierte la gallina maíz en huevos de oro?" *El Gallo Ilustrado*, Suplemento de *El Día* (México), No. 175, October 31. Treated in greater detail in "Mexican Agriculture from Conquest to Revolution: An Economic Historical Analysis" (Unpublished) and "The Growth of the Latifundium in Latin America: A Comparative Analysis" (unpublished)

Frank, Andre Gunder
1966a   "The Development of Underdevelopment." *Monthly Review* (New York), Vol. 18, No. 4, September

Frank, Andrew Gunder
1966b   "La inestabilidad urbana en América Latina" *Cuadernos Americanos* (México), Year XV, No. 1, January–February (English translation: "Unstable Urban Latin America," *Comparative Studies of International Development*. St. Louis, 1966)

Frank, Andre Gunder
1968   "Hunger." Ann Arbor, Michigan, Radical Education Project

Frantz, Jacob
1963 "Os produtores de algodão." *Semanário*, May 30–June 6

Frondizi, Arturo
1958 *A Luta Antiimperialista*. São Paulo, Editora Brasiliense (translated from the Spanish *Política y Petroleo*, Buenos Aires)

Frondizi, Silvio
1956 *La realidad argentina: Ensayo de interpretación sociológica. La revolución socialista*, Buenos Aires, Praxis, Vol. II.

Fuentes, Carlos
1963 "The Argument of Latin America." In *Whither Latin America?*, New York, Monthly Review Press

Furtado, Celso
1959 *A formação económica do Brasil*. Rio de Janeiro, Fundo de Cultura (English translation: *The Economic Growth of Brazil*, Berkeley, University of California Press, 1963)

Furtado, Celso
1962 *A pré-revolução brasileira*. Rio de Janeiro, Fundo de Cultura

Furtado, Celso
1964 *Dialética do desenvolvimento*. Rio de Janeiro, Fundo de Cultura

Geiger, Pedro Pinchus, and Myriam Gõmes Coelho Mesquita
1956 *Estudos rurais da baixada fluminense*. Rio de Janeiro, Instituto Brasileiro de Geografia e Estatística

Gerassi, John
1963 *The Great Fear*. New York, Macmillan Co.

Góngora, Mario
1960 *Origen de los "inquilinos" de Chile central*. Santiago, Editorial Universitaria

González Casanova, Pablo
1965 *La democracia en México*. México, Ediciones Era

Guerra y Sánchez, Ramiro
1964 *Sugar and Society in the Caribbean—An Economic His-*

tory of Cuban Agriculture. New Haven, Yale University Press. (Translation of *Azúcar y Población en las Antillas,* Havana)

Guilherme, Wanderley
1963   *Introdução ao estudo das contradições sociais no Brasil.* Rio de Janeiro, Instituto Superior de Estudos Brasileiros

Guimarães, Alberto Passos
1963   "População e reforma agrária." *Jornal do Brasil,* May 26

Horowitz, Irving Louis
1964   *Revolution in Brazil: Politics and Society in a Developing Nation.* New York, Dutton

Hutchison, Bertram
1963   "The Migrant Population of Urban Brazil," *América Latina* (Rio de Janeiro), Vol. 6, No. 2

Ianni, Octavio
1961   "A constituição do proletariade agrícola no Brasil." *Revista Brasileira de Estudos Políticos,* No. 12, October

IBGE   *Censo agrícola do 1950.* Rio de Janeiro, Instituto Brasileiro de Geografia e Estatística

IBGE   *Censo demográfico do 1950.*

Instituto Brasileiro do Café
1962   *Programa de racionalização da cafeicultura brasileira.* São Paulo, IBC

Instituto de Economía
1963   *La economía de Chile en el período 1950–1963.* Santiago, Universidad de Chile

Instituto Nacional Indigenista
1962   *Los centros coordinadores indigenistas.* México, INI

Irazusta, Julio
1963   *Influencia económica británica en el Rio de la Plata.* Buenos Aires, EUDEBA

Jobet, Julio César
1955   *Ensayo crítico del desarrollo económico-social de Chile.* Santiago, Editorial Universitaria

Johnson, Dale
   1964   "The Structural Dynamics of the Chilean Economy."
            Mimeographed

Julião, Francisco
   1962   "Que são as Ligas Camponesas?" *Cadernos do Povo*,
            Civilização Brasileira, Rio de Janeiro

Kuusinen, O. W., Y. A. Arbatov, and others
   N.D.   *Fundamentals of Marxism-Leninism.* Moscow, Foreign
            Languages Publishing House

Lacoste, Yves
   1961   *Os países subdesenvolvidos.* São Paulo, Difusão Euro-
            péia do Livro

Lagos, Ricardo
   1962   *La concentración del poder económico en Chile.* San-
            tiago, Editorial del Pacífico

Lambert, Jacques
   N.D.   *Os dois Brasís.* Rio de Janeiro, Ministério da Educação e
            Cultura

Lima, Heitor Ferreira
   1961   *Formação industrial do Brasil: Período colonial.* Rio de
            Janeiro, Fundo de Cultura

Luxemburg, Rosa
   1964   *The Accumulation of Capital.* New York, Monthly Review
            Press

Lyons, Raymond F. (ed.)
   1964   *Problems and Strategies of Educational Planning. Lessons
            from Latin America.* Paris, International Institute for
            Educational Planning

Magdoff, Harry
   1966   "Economic Aspects of U.S. Imperialism." *Monthly Re-
            view,* New York, November. Reprinted in Harry Magdoff,
            The Age of Imperialism, New York, Monthly Review
            Press, 1969

Malpica, Carlos
   1963   *Guerra a muerte al latifundio.* Lima, Movimiento
            Izquierdista Revolucionario, Ediciones Voz Rebelde

Manchester, Allan K.
1933   *British Preeminence in Brazil: Its Rise and Fall.* Chapel Hill, University of North Carolina Press

Mandel, Ernest
1962   *Traité d'Economie Marxiste.* Paris, Rene Julliard, 2 vols. (translated as *Marxist Economic Theory,* New York, Monthly Review Press, 1969)

Mariátegui, José Carlos
1934   *Siete ensayos de interpretación de la realidad peruana.* Lima, Editorial Librería Peruana, 2a ed.

Marini, Ruy Mauro
1964   "Brazilian Interdependence and Imperialist Integration." *Monthly Review* (New York), Vol. 17, No. 7, December

Marroquín, Alejandro
1957   *La ciudad mercado (Tlaxiaco).* México, Universidad Nacional Autónoma de México, Imprenta Universitaria

Marroquín, Alejandro
1956   "Consideraciones sobre el problema económico de la región Tzeltal-Tzotzil." *América Indígena* (México), XVI, No. 3, June

Marx, Karl
N.D.   *Capital,* translated from the third German edition. Moscow, Foreign Languages Publishing House

McBride, George M.
1936   *Chile: Land and Society.* New York, American Geographical Society

McMillan, Claude Jr., Richard F. Gonzalez and Leo G. Erickson
1964   *International Enterprise in a Developing Economy. A Study of U.S. Business in Brazil.* M.S.U. Business Studies, East Lansing, Michigan State University Press

Medina, Carlos Alberto de
1963   "Jardinópolis e Sertãozinhoe." In CIDA 1963 (see above)

Michaels, David
1966   "Monopoly in the United States." *Monthly Review* (New York), Vol. 17, No. 11, April

Mikesell, Raymond F. (ed.)
1962   *U.S. Private and Government Investment Abroad.* Eugene, University of Oregon Books

Miranda, José
1947   "La función económica del encomendero en los orígenes del régimen colonial: Nueva España (1525–1531)," in *Anales,* Instituto Nacional de Antropología e Historia, Vol. 2, México, Secretaría de Educación Pública. Republished in book form by Universidad Nacional Autónoma de México, 1965

Miranda, José
1952   *El tributo indígena en la Nueva España durante el siglo XVI.* México, Colegio de México

Monbeig, Pierre
1952   *Pionniers et planteurs de São Paulo.* Paris, Armand Colin

Myrdal, Gunnar
1957   *Economic Theory and Underdeveloped Regions.* London, Duckworth (In the United States: *Rich Lands and Poor,* New York, Harper, 1957)

Newsweek
1965   *Newsweek,* March 8

Nolff, Max
1962   "Industria manufacturera," in *Geografía económica de Chile,* Vol. 3, Santiago, Corporación de Fomento de la Producción

Normano, J. F.
1931   *The Struggle for South America.* Boston, Houghton Mifflin

Normano, J. F.
1945   *Evolução econômica do Brasil.* São Paulo, Companhia Editôra Nacional. Translation from the English original, *Brazil: A Study of Economic Types,* Chapel Hill, University of North Carolina Press, 1935

Novik Macovos, Nathan, and Jorge Farba Levin
1963   *La potencialidad de crecimiento de la economía chilena.* Santiago, Universidad de Chile, Facultad de Ciencias Económicas (thesis)

Núñez Leal, Victor
1946   *Coronelismo, enxada, e voto.* Rio de Janeiro

OCEPLAN
1964   *Las bases técnicas del plan de acción del gobierno popular.* Santiago, Comando Nacional de la Candidatura Presidencial del Dr. Salvador Allende (mimeographed)

Ots Capdequi, José M.
1946   *El régimen de la tierra en la America española durante el período colonial.* Ciudad Trujillo, Editora Montalvo

Paixão, Moacir
1959   "Elementos da questão agrária." *Revista Brasiliense,* No. 44, July–August

Pinto Santa Cruz, Anibal
1962   *Chile: Un caso de desarrollo frustrado.* Santiago, Editorial Universitaria

Pinto Santa Cruz, Anibal
1964   "Diez años de economía chilena en el periodo 1950–1963." *Panorama Económico,* Santiago (Subsequently incorporated in *Chile: Una economía difícil,* México, Fondo de Cultura Económica, 1965)

Plano Trienal
1962   "Estratificación social y estructura de clase." *Revista de 1963–1965.* Brasília, Presidência da República

Prado Júnior, Caio
1960   "Contribuição para a análise da questão agrária no Brasil." *Revista Brasiliense,* No. 28, March–April

Prado Júnior, Caio
1962   *História econômica do Brasil.* 7th edition, São Paulo, Editôra Brasiliense (Spanish translation: *Historia económica del Brasil,* Buenos Aires, Editora Futuro, 1960)

Prensa Latina
1965   *Prensa Latina,* March 26. México, Agencia Informativa Latinoamericana

Quintanilla Paulet, Antonio
N.D.   "La reforma agraria y las comunidades de indígenas." In *La reforma agraria en el Perú,* Lima, Comisión para la Reforma Agraria y la Vivienda

Ramírez Necochea, Hernán
1958   *Balmaceda y la contrarevolución de 1891.* Santiago, Editorial Universitaria

Ramírez Necochea, Hernán
1959   *Antecendentes económicos de la independencia de Chile.* Santiago, Editorial Universitaria

Ramírez Necochea, Hernán
1960   *Historia del imperialismo en Chile.* Santiago, Austral

Rangel, Ignacio
1961   *Questão agrária brasileira.* Rio de Janeiro & Brasília, Presidência da República, Conselho do Desenvolvimento (mimeographed)

Redfield, Robert
1941   *The Folk Culture of Yucatan.* Chicago, University of Chicago Press

Redfield, Robert
1960   *The Little Community and Peasant Society and Culture.* Chicago, University of Chicago Press

Rippy, J. Fred
1959   *British Investments in Latin America 1822-1949.* Minneapolis, University of Minnesota Press

Safarian, A. E.
1966   *Foreign Ownership of Canadian Industry.* Toronto, McGraw-Hill Company of Canada, pp. 235-241

Santos Martínez, Pedro
1961   *Historia económica de Mendoza durante el virreinato, 1776–1810.* Madrid, Universidad Nacional de Cuyo, Instituto González Fernández Oviedo

Schattan, Salomão
1959   "Estrutura económica da lavoura paulista." *Revista Brasiliense,* September-October

Schattan, Salomão
1961   "Estrutura económica da agricultura paulista." *Revista Brasileira de Estudos Políticos,* No. 12, October

Sée, Henri
1961   Orígenes del capitalismo moderno. México, Fondo de
        Cultura Económica

Sepúlveda, Sergio
1959   El trigo chileno en el mercado mundial. Santiago Edi-
        torial Universitaria

Simonsen, Roberto C.
1939   Brazil's Industrial Evolution. São Paulo, Escuela Livre
        de Sociologia e Política

Simonsen, Roberto C.
1962   Historia económica do Brasil (1500-1820), 4th edition.
        São Paulo, Companhia Editôra Nacional

Singer, Paul
1961   "Agricultura e desenvolvimento económico." Revista
        Brasileira de Estudos Políticos, October

Singer, Paul
1963   "A agricultura na região da Bacia do Paraná-Uruguai."
        Revista de Estudos Sócio-Econômicos, (São Paulo) May

Sodré, Nelson Werneck
N.D.   Formação histórica do Brasil. São Paulo, Editôra
        Brasiliense

Stavenhagen, Rodolfo
1962   "Estratificación social y estructura de clase." Revista de
        Ciencias Políticas y Sociales (México), No. 27, January-
        March

Stavenhagen, Rodolfo
1963   "Clases, colonialismo y aculturación: Ensayo sobre un
        sistema de relaciones interétnicas en Mesoamérica."
        América Latina (Rio de Janeiro), Vol. 6, No. 4, October-
        December

Toynbee, Arnold
1962   The Economy of the Western Hemisphere. London and
        New York, Oxford University Press

Turner, John Kenneth
   1964   *México Bárbaro.* Mexico, Ediciones del Instituto Na-
           cional de la Juventud Mexicana (originally published in
           English as *Barbarous Mexico* in 1908)

United Nations
   1963   United Nations Economic Commission for Latin
           America, *The Social Development of Latin America in
           the Postwar Years.* New York-Santiago, E/CN. 12/660/
           May 11

United Nations
   1964a   Conference on World Trade and Development. *Review
           of the Trends in World Trade.* New York (E/CONF.
           46/12. Feb. 26, 1964)

United Nations
   1964b   Economic Commission for Latin America. *Estudio
           Económico de América Latina, 1963.* New York (C/CN.
           12/696/Rev. 1, Noviembre)

United Nations
   1964c   Economic Commission for Latin America. *El Financia-
           miento Externo de América Latina.* New York (E/CN.
           12/649/Rev. 1, Diciembre)

U.S. News and World Report
   1966   July 18

Véliz, Claudio
   1963   "La mesa de tres patas." *Desarrollo Económico* (Buenos
           Aires), Vol. 3, No. 1-2, April-September

Vera Valenzuela, Mario
   1961   *La política económica del cobre en Chile.* Santiago,
           Universidad de Chile

Vinhas, Moisés
   1962   "As classes e camadas do campo no estado de São Paulo."
           Estudos Sociais, No. 13, June .

Vinhas de Queiróz, Maurício
   1962   *Os grupos econômicos no Brasil.* Rio de Janeiro, Uni-
           versidade do Brasil, Instituto de Ciências Sociais (mimeo-
           graphed)

Vistazo
 1964   Vistazo. Santiago, July 27

Visión
 1965   *Progreso 64/65—Revista del Desarrollo Latinoamericano.*
 New York

Wagley, Charles, and Marvin Harris
 1955   "A Typology of Latin American Subcultures." *American Anthropologist,* Vol. 57, No. 3, June

Williams, Eric
 1944   *Capitalism and Slavery.* Chapel Hill, University of North Carolina Press. Reprinted by Russell & Russell, New York, 1964

Wolf, Eric R.
 1955   "Types of Latin American Peasantry." *American Anthropologist,* Vol. 57, No. 3, June

Wolf, Eric R.
 1959   *Sons of the Shaking Earth.* Chicago, University of Chicago Press

Zavala, Silvio
 1943   *New Viewpoints on the Spanish Colonization of America.* Philadelphia, University of Pennsylvania Press

INDEX